King Solomon's

Books of Wisdom

King Solomon's Books of Wisdom

A Direct Translation

by

Daniel A. Elias

Tzeruf Co

Author: *Daniel A. Elias, J.D.*

Publisher: Tzeruf Co
235 S. Lyon Ave # 39
Hemet, CA 92543 USA
mail@tzeruf.com

SAN Number 853-0203

© 2013 by Tzeruf Co.
Printed in USA

All rights reserved. No part of this publication may be reproduced or transmitted in any form or by any means, electronic or mechanical, including photocopying, recording, or by any information storage an d retrieval system, without permission in writing from Tzeruf Co.

Publisher's Cataloging-in-Publication data

Elias, Daniel A.

   King Solomon's Books of Wisdom

English Paperback   ISBN 978-0-9792826-6-9

Dedication:

I dedicate this book to

King Solomon......

the wisest man who every lived

Table of Contents

Preface xi
King Solomon's Bio ks-1
Bible verses re: King Solomon ks-11

Ecclesiastes (Kohelet) e-25
    Chapter 1 .... e-27
    Chapter 2 .... e-30
    Chapter 3 .... e-35
    Chapter 4 .... e-39
    Chapter 5 .... e-42
    Chapter 6 .... e-46
    Chapter 7 .... e-48
    Chapter 8 .... e-52
    Chapter 9 .... e-56
    Chapter 10 .... e-60
    Chapter 11 .... e-63
    Chapter 12 .... e-65

Proverbs p-69

CHAPTER 1	p-71
CHAPTER 2	p-75
CHAPTER 3	p-77
CHAPTER 4	p-81
CHAPTER 5	p-84
CHAPTER 6	p-87
CHAPTER 7	p-91
CHAPTER 8	p-94
CHAPTER 9	p-98
CHAPTER 10	p-100
CHAPTER 11	p-103
CHAPTER 12	p-106
CHAPTER 13	p-109
CHAPTER 14	p-112
CHAPTER 15	p-116
CHAPTER 16	p-120
CHAPTER 17	p-123
CHAPTER 18	p-127
CHAPTER 19	p-130
CHAPTER 20	p-133
CHAPTER 21	p-136
CHAPTER 22	p-139
CHAPTER 23	p-142
CHAPTER 24	p-146
CHAPTER 25	p-150
CHAPTER 26	p-153
CHAPTER 27	p-156
CHAPTER 28	p-159
CHAPTER 29	p-162
CHAPTER 30	p-165
CHAPTER 31	p-169

SONG OF SONGS	s-172
CHAPTER 1	s-174
CHAPTER 2	s-177
CHAPTER 3	s-180
CHAPTER 4	s-182
CHAPTER 5	s-185
CHAPTER 6	s-188
CHAPTER 7	s-190
CHAPTER 8	s-192

Preface

TRANSLATIONS

The objective of the translated Hebrew in this book is;
1) to help to be fluent in the reading of Hebrew,
2) to learn Hebrew vocabulary by seeing the translation directly below the Hebrew word one is reading.
3) to memorize parts of the verses of the sacred scriptures
4) to easily increase kavanah or thought in the Psalms and Prayers
5) to feed the soul the effects of bible code while reading the biblical verses

One translated Hebrew word of a verse contains so much subtle information. There is the root, the prefix, the affix, dropped weak letters, gutturals, dagesh lene, dagesh forte, it's sentence grammatical name, etc. Much of the english grammar has been left out by necessity; ie. the translation "the" was put in only when there was a specific prefix letter Heh, not where a prefix has a patach.

Every expression in the [ongoing] present tense can variably be expressed in the future tense as well as in the past tense because anything that is ongoing in the present tense has already happened and will continue to happen.

I would have preferred to translate the tenses of the verbs as they actually appear instead of looking to the sentence meaning to infer the past, present or future. This best reflects the Hebrew language thought. However in order to make the text as simple to understand for the majority of people who do not understand this concept I have kept the verb tenses simple.

The vast majority of the Hebrew words in the Bible are very easy to translate. Generally everyone agrees on their meanings and these words are used in everyday life in Israel. but hard hebrew words

The Eskimos have 20 words for snow. This same principle applies to the Hebrew words found in the Torah. There may be 20 Hebrew words that have been translated with the same English word, but each of these similar Hebrew words have an extensive detailed specific and differing explanation.

When I was translating verses I listed hard to translate words and made notes on what other translators have put for a meaning and what possible roots the word could be derived from. In the end on those words it's a best estimate as to their meanings.

King Solomon's Bio

Almost all of what we know of king Solomon is gleaned from the biblical books Chronicles 2 and Kings 1. His name comes from the Hebrew word meaning "peace." The city of King Solomon in Jerusalem is thought to be on the slope leading down from what is now the Al Aqsa mosque. Israeli archaeologists have been excavating the site for many decades yet no evidence of the existence of King Solomon has been found. No mention of his name has been found on any tablet, inscription, tax record or pot decoration.

Born

He was the second son of King David and Bathsheba (II Sam. xii. 23-25), the tenth son of King David. He was born in 848 BCE (Jewish calendar 2912). He was known by 7 different names: Shlomo, Yedidya, Bin, Itiel, Yakeh, Agur, and Kohelet.

King David appointed Solomon king of Israel when he was only 12 years old. The same blessing that king David gave to Solomon when he appointed him king is the same blessing given to a young boy today on the day of their bar mitzvah. He had to struggle in order to gain control of the kingdom, but afterwards he enjoyed a peaceful reign.

He is known for being the greatest king that ever ruled Israel. His reign started approximately 967 BC. It was the greatest and most powerful kingdom the Hebrews would ever see. It was called the "golden era". The magnificence and splendor of the kingdom was unrivaled anywhere. Trade was carried on overland with Tyre, Egypt and Arabia, and by sea with Spain, India and along the coasts of Africa. Solomon accumulated vast wealth from many nations. His kingdom had 12 districts. His kingdom ranged from Egypt to the Euphrates river. He ruled for 40 years. The first four years he reigned from outside of Jerusalem. The next 36 years he reigned from inside Jerusalem. David, his father: also reigned forty years.

Succession of King David

Solomon became king after the death of his father David. According to the biblical book Kings 1, when David was " old and advanced in years" "he could not get warm." "So they sought for a beautiful young woman throughout all the territory of Israel, and found Abishag the Shunammite, and brought her to the king."

David's fourth son, Adonijah, appeared heir-apparent to the throne after the death of his elder brothers Amnon and Absalom. While David was in this state, Adonijah acted to have himself declared king.

But Bathsheba, a wife of David and Solomon's mother, along with the prophet Nathan induced David to proclaim Solomon king.

Adonijah fled and took refuge at the altar, and received pardon for his conduct from Solomon on the condition that he show himself "a worthy man." (1 Kings 1:5-53)

Adonijah asked to marry Abishag the Shunammite, but King Solomon denied authorization for such an engagement, even though Bathsheba pleaded on Adonijah's behalf. Just as was Absalom's rebellion against Solomon, to possess the royal harem, this was in that society at that time, tantamount to claiming the throne. Abishag was then seized and put to death (1 Kings 2:13-25).

David's general Joab was killed, in accord with David's deathbed request to King Solomon, because he had killed generals Abner and Amasa during a peace (2 Samuel 20:8-13; 1 Kings 2:5). David's priest Abiathar was exiled by Solomon because he had sided with rival Adonijah. Abiathar is a descendent of Eli, which has important prophetic significance. (1 Kings 2:27) Shimei was confined to Jerusalem and killed three years later, when he went to Gath to retrieve some runaway servants, in part because he had cursed David when Absalom, David's son, rebelled against David. (1 Kings 2:1-46)

The First Temple

One of his crowning achievements that he is credited with is building the first great holy temple. The 4th year of his reign he started to build the temple. It took 7 years to complete. It was overlaid throughout with gold. The Bible's description of Solomon's Temple suggests that the inside ceiling was 180 feet long, 90 feet wide, and 50 feet high. The highest point on the Temple that King Solomon built was actually 120 cubits tall (about 20 stories or about 207 feet)

His Building

Solomon was also renowned for his other building projects in which he used slave labor from the Hittites, Amorites, Perizzites, Hivites and Jebusites. He spent 13 years building his own palace, and also built a city wall, a citadel called the Millo, a palace for the daughter of Pharaoh (who was one of his wives) and facilities for foreign traders. He erected cities for chariots and horsemen and created storage cities. He extended Jerusalem to the north and fortified cities with chariots and horsemen near the mountains of Judah and Jerusalem.

His Writings

He wrote 3 books of the bible, Ecclesiastes, Song of Solomon, and Proverbs. He has composed over 3,000 proverbs and 1,005 songs.

According to the Talmud, Solomon is one of the 48 prophets.

His wisdom

Dignitaries from many nations came to him to hear his wisdom.

Solomon is considered as one of the Prophets, in whom the Holy Spirit dwelt.

He is said to have understood the languages of the beasts and the birds and to have had no need of relying on witnesses in delivering a judgment, inasmuch as by simply looking at the contending parties he knew which was right and which was wrong.

His wisdom is stated to have excelled that of the Egyptians (I Kings v. 10), which assertion is the basis of the following legend: "When Solomon was about to build the Temple he applied to Pharaoh, King of Egypt, for builders and architects. Pharaoh ordered his astrologers to choose all the men who would die in the current year; and these he sent to Solomon. The latter, however, by simply looking at them, knew what their fate was to be; consequently he provided them with coffins and shrouds and sent them back to Egypt. Moreover, he gave them a letter for Pharaoh informing him that if he was in want of articles required for the dead, it was not necessary for him to send men, but that he might apply direct for the materials he needed."

One of the qualities most ascribed to Solomon is his wisdom. Solomon prayed:

"Give Thy servant an understanding heart to judge Thy people and to know good and evil."1 Kings 3:9

"So God said to him, 'Since you have asked for this and not for long life or wealth for yourself, nor have asked for the death of your enemies but for discernment in administering justice, I will do what you have asked...'" (1 Kings 3:11-12)[9] The Hebrew Bible also states that: "The whole world sought audience with Solomon to hear the wisdom God had put in his heart." (1 Kings 10:24)

Solomon was one of those men to whom names were given by God before their birth, being thus placed in the category of the just.

Besides his three principal names, Jedidiah (II Sam. xii. 25), Kohelet (Eccl.), and Solomon, various others are assigned to him by the Rabbis, namely, Agur, Bin, Jakeh, Lemuel, Ithiel, and Ucal, the interpretations of which, according to the earlier school, are as follows: "He who gathered the words of the Torah, who understood them, who later enunciated them, who said to God in his heart, 'I have the power; consequently, I may transgress the prescriptions of the Torah.' " The later school, on the other hand, adopts the following explanations: Agur = "he who girt his loins"; Bin = "he who built the Temple"; Jakeh = "he who reigned over the whole world"; Ithiel = "he who understood the signs of God"; and Ucal = "he who could withstand them." Solomon was also one of those who were styled "bachurim" (="chosen"), "yedidim" (="friends"), and "ahubim" (="beloved ones"). Solomon's instructor in the Torah was Shimei, whose death marked Solomon's first lapse into sin (Ber. 8a).

Solomon passed forty days of fasting so that God might bestow upon him the spirit of wisdom (Pesi. R. 14 [ed. Friedmann, p. 59a, b]; Num. R. xix. 3; Eccl. R. vii. 23; Midr. Mishle i. 1, xv. 29).

Trade

With the Phoenicians he united with in maritime commerce, sending out a fleet once in three years from Ezion-geber, at the head of the

Gulf of Akaba, to Ophir, presumably on the eastern coast of the Arabian peninsula. From this distant port, and others along the route, he derived huge amounts of gold and tropical products.

Gold

Solomon hoarded gold and silver. "The king made silver and gold as common in Jerusalem as stones." (2 Chron. 1:16 & 1 Kings 10:27) Certainly, King Solomon's reign was the golden era of Israel, and the World.

King Solomon Inherited his Father's Gold

A "talent" is a weight measure. And there is the "long" or "royal" talent which was about double the "short" or "ordinary" talent.

a) 1 Chron. 22:14- Gold stockpiled by David was 4,000 tons (4,000,000 kilos = 8,800,000 ounces)

b) 1 Chron.22:14 -King David's silver was 40,000 tons (40,000,000 kilos = 88,000,000 ounces)

c) 1 Chron.29:4 -Finest gold from David was 115 tons = 115,000 kilos = 583,000 ounces.

d) 1 Chron. 29:4 -Pure silver from King David was 265 tons = 265,000 kilos = 418,000 ounces.

e) 1 Chron.29:7-Gold from officials was 190 tons or 190,000 kilos or 418 ounces.

f) 1 Chron.29:7- Silver from officers was 380 tons or 380,000 kilos or 836,000 ounces.

Book of Kings & Gold

g) 1 Kings 10:22- Gold and silver every three year voyage of commercial ships. Solomon ruled forty years so that allows about 12 voyages. If the gold-silver volume is approximately that of 1 Kings 9:28 of 16 tons x 12 = 192 tons or 192,000 kilos or 422,400 ounces.

h) 1 Kings 9:11, Gold was 5 tons or 5,000 kilos = 11,000 ounces.

i) 1 Kings 9:28 Gold was 16 tons or 16,000 kilos=35,200 ounces.

j) 1 Kings 10:10- Gold was 5 tones or 5,000 kilos or 11,000 ounces.

k) 1 Kings 10:14- Gold was 25 tons yearly for 40 years = 1000 tons = 1,000,000 kilos or 220,000,000 ounces.

l) 1 Kings 10:15- Granting that 25 tons of gold come from other sources annually x 40 year reign = 1000 tons = 1,000,000 kilos or 20,000,000 ounces.

m) 1 Kings 10:22- Granting that we have 16 tons as in 1 Kings 9:28 from this source, this is 16,000 kilos or 35,200 ounces.

Political Districts

Among Solomon's main achievements as an administrator was to divide the country into 12 administrative districts run by governors, in addition to Judah. It is important to note that the districts were not bordered according to the 12 tribes.

Following the custom of the day, he secured for himself a wife from each of the neighboring royal houses, thus binding the nations to him by domestic ties. These various alliances introduced to the Israelitish court a princess from Egypt (for whom the king erected a special residence), and others from the Moabite, Ammonite, Edomite, Zidonian, and Hittite courts, who brought with them certain alien customs and religions, and, best of all, a kind of guaranty of peace.

Queen Sheba

The Queen of Sheba traveled with a train of attendants, carrying much wealth, from southwestern Arabia, about 1,500 miles distant, to test the wisdom of Israel's ruler.

His Wives

His wives are described as foreign princesses, including Pharaoh's daughter and women of Moab, Ammon, Sidon and of the Hittites. These wives are depicted as leading Solomon astray. The only wife that is mentioned by name is Naamah, who is described as the Ammonite. She was the mother of Solomon's successor, Rehoboam.

His downfall was that he had many foreign wives. In Kings 1 it states that he had 700 wives and 300 concubines. He allowed these wives to worship foreign gods. He constructed images of these gods for them to worship these other gods. Moses warns that the king should not have too many horses or too many wives (Deut. 17:17). The great Torah commentator Rashi tells us that this means no more than 18, and that King David had only six. The Middle East in Solomon's time is made up of many city-states and all the kings of these city-states wanted to send their daughters to marry King Solomon and in this way form an alliance with him.

According to Rashi in Kings 1-10:13, the words "all her desires" refers to the following ... "He had relations with her, and from her was born Nebuchadnezzar. And he destroyed the temple which stood for 410 years in the portion of the 12 tribes." (This quote is from Rabbi Yitzchak Luria [the 'Ari'], the famed 16th century Kabbalist in Sefat.)

The King's Throne

Solomon's throne is described at length in Targum Sheni, which is compiled from three different sources, and in two later Midrash. According to these, there were on the steps of the throne twelve golden lions, each facing a golden eagle. There were six steps to the throne, on which animals, all of gold, were arranged in the following order: on the first step a lion opposite an ox; on the second, a wolf opposite a sheep; on the third, a tiger opposite a camel; on the fourth, an eagle opposite a peacock, on the fifth, a cat opposite a cock; on the sixth, a sparrow-hawk opposite a dove. On the top of the throne was a dove holding a sparrow-hawk in its claws, symbolizing the dominion of Israel over the Gentiles. The first midrash claims that six steps were constructed because Solomon foresaw that six kings would sit on the throne, namely, Solomon, Rehoboam, Hezekiah, Manasseh, Amon, and Josiah. There was also on the top of the throne a golden candelabrum, on the seven branches of the one side of which were engraved the names of the seven patriarchs Adam, Noah, Shem, Abraham, Isaac, Jacob, and Job, and on the seven of the other the names of Levi, Kohath, Amram, Moses, Aaron, Eldad, Medad, and, in addition, Hur (another version has Haggai). Above the candelabrum was a golden jar filled with olive-oil and beneath it a golden basin which supplied the jar with oil and on which the names of Nadab, Abihu, and Eli and his two sons were engraved. Over the throne, twenty-four vines were fixed to cast a shadow on the king's head.

By a mechanical contrivance the throne followed Solomon wherever he wished to go. Supposedly, due to another mechanical trick, when the king reached the first step, the ox stretched forth its leg, on which Solomon leaned, a similar action taking place in the case of the animals on each of the six steps. From the sixth step the eagles raised the king and placed him in his seat, near which a golden serpent lay coiled. When the king was seated the large eagle placed the crown on his head, the serpent uncoiled itself, and the lions and eagles moved upward to form a shade over him. The dove then descended, took the scroll of the Law from the Ark, and placed it on Solomon's knees. When the king sat, surrounded by the Sanhedrin, to judge the people, the wheels began to turn, and the beasts and fowls began to utter their respective cries, which frightened those who had intended to bear false testimony. Moreover, while Solomon was ascending the throne, the lions scattered all kinds of fragrant spices. After Solomon's death, Pharaoh Shishak, when taking away the treasures of the Temple (I Kings xiv. 26), carried off the throne, which remained in Egypt till Sennacherib conquered that country. After Sennacherib's fall Hezekiah gained possession of it, but when Josiah was slain by Pharaoh Necho, the latter took it away. However, according to rabbinical accounts, Necho did not know how the mechanism worked and so accidentally struck himself with one of the lions causing him to become lame; Nebuchadnezzar, into whose possession the throne subsequently came, shared a similar fate. The throne then passed to the Persians, who their king Darius was the first to sit successfully on Solomon's throne since his death, and after that the throne passed into the possession of the Greeks and Ahasuerus.

Horses

Kings I states that he owned 12,000 horses with horsemen and 1,400 chariots. Remains of stalls for 450 horses have in fact been found in Megiddo.

The Myths

Early adherents of the Kabbalah portray Solomon as having sailed through the air on a throne of light placed on an eagle, which brought him near the heavenly gates as well as to the dark mountains behind which the fallen angels Uzza and Azzael were chained; the eagle would rest on the chains, and Solomon, using the magic ring, would compel the two angels to reveal every mystery he desired to know.

The King's Downfall

Solomon's downfall came in his old age. He had taken many foreign wives, whom he allowed to worship other gods. He even built shrines for the sacrifices of his foreign wives. Within Solomon's kingdom, he placed heavy taxation on the people, who became bitter. He also had the people work as soldiers, chief officers and commanders of his chariots and cavalry. He granted special privileges to the tribes of Judah and this alienated the northern tribes. The prophet Ahijah of Shiloh prophesied that Jeroboam son of Nebat would become king over ten of the 12 tribes, instead of one of Solomon's sons.

The King Sins

According to 1 Kings 11:9-13, it was because of these sins that "the Lord punishes Solomon by tearing the kingdom in two";

And the Lord was angry with Solomon, because his heart had turned away from the Lord, the God of Israel, who had appeared to him twice and had commanded him concerning this thing, that he should not go after other gods. But he did not keep what the LORD commanded. Therefore the Lord said to Solomon, "Since this has been your practice and you have not kept my covenant and my statutes that I have commanded you, I will surely tear the kingdom from you and will give it to your servant. Yet for the sake of David your father I will not do it in your days, but I will tear it out of the hand of your son. However, I will not tear away all the kingdom, but I will give one tribe to your son, for the sake of David my servant and for the sake of Jerusalem that I have chosen.

His Death

According to the Hebrew Bible and historical research, Solomon died of natural causes at around 80 years of age.

His son, Rehoboam succeeded him as king. The ten northern tribes revolted and formed their own kingdom, Israel. From then on the Hebrews had two kingdoms, Israel and Judah.

After his death Nebuchadnezzar conquered the land.

The Succession of King Solomon

Upon Solomon's death, his son, Rehoboam, succeeded him as king. However, ten of the Tribes of Israel refused to accept him as king. This caused the Kingdom that was united, to split and formed two nations. The northern Kingdom called Israel was ruled by Jeroboam. The southern Kingdom was called Judah, and Rehoboam continued to reign there.

The Warring Kingdoms

Outside Solomon's kingdom, Hadad, of the royal family of Edom, rose up as an adversary of Israel. Rezon son of Eliada, ruler of Aram also fought Solomon, and created tension between the two kingdoms that was to last even after Solomon's reign ended.

BIBLE VERSES RE: KING SOLOMON

CORONATION OF KING SOLOMON

Kings 1 Chapter 1

1 Now king David was old and stricken in years; and they covered him with clothes, but he gat no heat.

2 Wherefore his servants said unto him, Let there be sought for my lord the king a young virgin: and let her stand before the king, and let her cherish him, and let her lie in thy bosom, that my lord the king may get heat.

3 So they sought for a fair damsel throughout all the coasts of Israel, and found Abishag a Shunammite, and brought her to the king.

4 And the damsel was very fair, and cherished the king, and ministered to him: but the king knew her not.

5 Then Adonijah the son of Haggith exalted himself, saying, I will be king: and he prepared him chariots and horsemen, and fifty men to run before him.

6 And his father had not displeased him at any time in saying, Why hast thou done so? and he also was a very goodly man; and his mother bare him after Absalom.

7 And he conferred with Joab the son of Zeruiah, and with Abiathar the priest: and they following Adonijah helped him.

8 But Zadok the priest, and Benaiah the son of Jehoiada, and Nathan the prophet, and Shimei, and Rei, and the mighty men which belonged to David, were not with Adonijah.

9 And Adonijah slew sheep and oxen and fat cattle by the stone of Zoheleth, which is by En-rogel, and called all his brethren the king's sons, and all the men of Judah the king's servants:

10 But Nathan the prophet, and Benaiah, and the mighty men, and SOLOMON his brother, he called not.

11 Wherefore Nathan spake unto Bath-sheba the mother of SOLOMON, saying, Hast thou not heard that Adonijah the son of Haggith doth reign, and David our lord knoweth it not?

12 Now therefore come, let me, I pray thee, give thee counsel, that thou mayest save thine own life, and the life of thy son SOLOMON.

13 Go and get thee in unto king David, and say unto him, Didst not thou, my lord, O king, swear unto thine handmaid, saying, Assuredly SOLOMON thy son shall reign after me, and he shall sit upon my throne? why then doth Adonijah reign?

14 Behold, while thou yet talkest there with the king, I also will come in after thee, and confirm thy words.

15 And Bath-sheba went in unto the king into the chamber: and the king was very old; and Abishag the Shunammite ministered unto the king.

16 And Bath-sheba bowed, and did obeisance unto the king. And the king said, What wouldest thou?

17 And she said unto him, My lord, thou swarest by the LORD thy God unto thine handmaid, saying, Assuredly SOLOMON thy son shall reign after me, and he shall sit upon my throne.

18 And now, behold, Adonijah reigneth; and now, my lord the king, thou knowest it not:

19 And he hath slain oxen and fat cattle and sheep in abundance, and hath called all the sons of the king, and Abiathar the priest, and Joab the

captain of the host: but SOLOMON thy servant hath he not called.

20 And thou, my lord, O king, the eyes of all Israel areupon thee, that thou shouldest tell them who shall sit on the throne of my lord the king after him.

21 Otherwise it shall come to pass, when my lord the king shall sleep with his fathers, that I and my son SOLOMON shall be counted offenders.

22 And, lo, while she yet talked with the king, Nathan the prophet also came in.

23 And they told the king, saying, Behold Nathan the prophet. And when he was come in before the king, he bowed himself before the king with his face to the ground.

24 And Nathan said, My lord, O king, hast thou said, Adonijah shall reign after me, and he shall sit upon my throne?

25 For he is gone down this day, and hath slain oxen and fat cattle and sheep in abundance, and hath called all the king's sons, and the captains of the host, and Abiathar the priest; and, behold, they eat and drink before him, and say, God save king Adonijah.

26 But me, even me thy servant, and Zadok the priest, and Benaiah the son of Jehoiada, and thy servant SOLOMON, hath he not called.

27 Is this thing done by my lord the king, and thou hast not shewed it unto thy servant, who should sit on the throne of my lord the king after him?

28 Then king David answered and said, Call me Bath-sheba. And she came into the king's presence, and stood before the king.

29 And the king sware, and said, As the LORD liveth, that hath redeemed my soul out of all distress,

30 Even as I sware unto thee by the LORD God of Israel, saying, Assuredly SOLOMON thy son shall reign after me, and he shall sit upon my throne in my stead; even so will I certainly do this day.

31 Then Bath-sheba bowed with her face to the earth, and did reverence to the king, and said, Let my lord king David live for ever.

32 And king David said, Call me Zadok the priest, and Nathan the prophet, and Benaiah the son of Jehoiada. And they came before the king.

33 The king also said unto them, Take with you the servants of your lord, and cause SOLOMON my son to ride upon mine own mule, and bring him down to Gihon:

34 And let Zadok the priest and Nathan the prophet anoint him there king over Israel: and blow ye with the trumpet, and say, God save king SOLOMON.

35 Then ye shall come up after him, that he may come and sit upon my throne; for he shall be king in my stead: and I have appointed him to be ruler over Israel and over Judah.

36 And Benaiah the son of Jehoiada answered the king, and said, Amen: the LORD God of my lord the king say so too.

37 As the LORD hath been with my lord the king, even so be he with SOLOMON, and make his throne greater than the throne of my lord king David.

38 So Zadok the priest, and Nathan the prophet, and Benaiah the son of Jehoiada, and the Cherethites, and the Pelethites, went down, and caused SOLOMON to ride upon king David's mule, and brought him to Gihon.

39 And Zadok the priest took an horn of oil out of the tabernacle, and anointed SOLOMON. And they blew the trumpet; and all the people

said, God save king SOLOMON.

40 And all the people came up after him, and the people piped with pipes, and rejoiced with great joy, so that the earth rent with the sound of them.

41 And Adonijah and all the guests that were with him heard it as they had made an end of eating. And when Joab heard the sound of the trumpet, he said, Wherefore is this noise of the city being in an uproar?

42 And while he yet spake, behold, Jonathan the son of Abiathar the priest came: and Adonijah said unto him, Come in; for thou art a valiant man, and bringest good tidings.

43 And Jonathan answered and said to Adonijah, Verily our lord king David hath made SOLOMON king.

44 And the king hath sent with him Zadok the priest, and Nathan the prophet, and Benaiah the son of Jehoiada, and the Cherethites, and the Pelethites, and they have caused him to ride upon the king's mule:

45 And Zadok the priest and Nathan the prophet have anointed him king in Gihon: and they are come up from thence rejoicing, so that the city rang again. This is the noise that ye have heard.

46 And also SOLOMON sitteth on the throne of the kingdom.

47 And moreover the king's servants came to bless our lord king David, saying, God make the name of SOLOMON better than thy name, and make his throne greater than thy throne. And the king bowed himself upon the bed.

48 And also thus said the king, Blessed be the LORD God of Israel, which hath given one to sit on my throne this day, mine eyes even seeing it.

49 And all the guests that were with Adonijah were afraid, and rose up,

and went every man his way.

50 And Adonijah feared because of SOLOMON, and arose, and went, and caught hold on the horns of the altar.

51 And it was told SOLOMON, saying, Behold, Adonijah feareth king SOLOMON: for, lo, he hath caught hold on the horns of the altar, saying, Let king SOLOMON swear unto me today that he will not slay his servant with the sword.

52 And SOLOMON said, If he will shew himself a worthy man, there shall not an hair of him fall to the earth: but if wickedness shall be found in him, he shall die.

53 So king SOLOMON sent, and they brought him down from the altar. And he came and bowed himself to king SOLOMON: and SOLOMON said unto him, Go to thine house.

King Solomon's Kingdom

Kings 1 Chapter 2

12 Then sat SOLOMON upon the throne of David his father; and his kingdom was established greatly.

13 And Adonijah the son of Haggith came to Bath-sheba the mother of SOLOMON. And she said, Comest thou peaceably? And he said, Peaceably.

14 He said moreover, I have somewhat to say unto thee. And she said, Say on.

15 And he said, Thou knowest that the kingdom was mine, and that all Israel set their faces on me, that I should reign: howbeit the kingdom is turned about, and is become my brother's: for it was his from the LORD.

16 And now I ask one petition of thee, deny me not. And she said unto

him, Say on.

17 And he said, Speak, I pray thee, unto SOLOMON the king, (for he will not say thee nay,) that he give me Abishag the Shunammite to wife.

18 And Bath-sheba said, Well; I will speak for thee unto the king.

19 Bath-sheba therefore went unto king SOLOMON, to speak unto him for Adonijah. And the king rose up to meet her, and bowed himself unto her, and sat down on his throne, and caused a seat to be set for the king's mother; and she sat on his right hand.

20 Then she said, I desire one small petition of thee; I pray thee, say me not nay. And the king said unto her, Ask on, my mother: for I will not say thee nay.

21 And she said, Let Abishag the Shunammite be given to Adonijah thy brother to wife.

22 And king SOLOMON answered and said unto his mother, And why dost thou ask Abishag the Shunammite for Adonijah? ask for him the kingdom also; for he is mine elder brother; even for him, and for Abiathar the priest, and for Joab the son of Zeruiah.

23 Then king SOLOMON sware by the LORD, saying, God do so to me, and more also, if Adonijah have not spoken this word against his own life.

24 Now therefore, as the LORD liveth, which hath established me, and set me on the throne of David my father, and who hath made me an house, as he promised, Adonijah shall be put to death this day.

25 And king SOLOMON sent by the hand of Benaiah the son of Jehoiada; and he fell upon him that he died.

26 And unto Abiathar the priest said the king, Get thee to Anathoth, unto thine own fields; for thou art worthy of death: but I will not at this

time put thee to death, because thou barest the ark of the Lord GOD before David my father, and because thou hast been afflicted in all wherein my father was afflicted.

27 So SOLOMON thrust out Abiathar from being priest unto the LORD; that he might fulfil the word of the LORD, which he spake concerning the house of Eli in Shiloh.

28 Then tidings came to Joab: for Joab had turned after Adonijah, though he turned not after Absalom. And Joab fled unto the tabernacle of the LORD, and caught hold on the horns of the altar.

29 And it was told king SOLOMON that Joab was fled unto the tabernacle of the LORD; and, behold, he is by the altar. Then SOLOMON sent Benaiah the son of Jehoiada, saying, Go, fall upon him.

30 And Benaiah came to the tabernacle of the LORD, and said unto him, Thus saith the king, Come forth. And he said, Nay; but I will die here. And Benaiah brought the king word again, saying, Thus said Joab, and thus he answered me.

31 And the king said unto him, Do as he hath said, and fall upon him, and bury him; that thou mayest take away the innocent blood, which Joab shed, from me, and from the house of my father.

32 And the LORD shall return his blood upon his own head, who fell upon two men more righteous and better than he, and slew them with the sword, my father David not knowing thereof, to wit, Abner the son of Ner, captain of the host of Israel, and Amasa the son of Jether, captain of the host of Judah.

33 Their blood shall therefore return upon the head of Joab, and upon the head of his seed for ever: but upon David, and upon his seed, and upon his house, and upon his throne, shall there be peace for ever from the LORD.

34 So Benaiah the son of Jehoiada went up, and fell upon him, and slew

him: and he was buried in his own house in the wilderness.

35 And the king put Benaiah the son of Jehoiada in his room over the host: and Zadok the priest did the king put in the room of Abiathar.

36 And the king sent and called for Shimei, and said unto him, Build thee an house in Jerusalem, and dwell there, and go not forth thence any whither.

37 For it shall be, that on the day thou goest out, and passest over the brook Kidron, thou shalt know for certain that thou shalt surely die: thy blood shall be upon thine own head.

38 And Shimei said unto the king, The saying is good: as my lord the king hath said, so will thy servant do. And Shimei dwelt in Jerusalem many days.

39 And it came to pass at the end of three years, that two of the servants of Shimei ran away unto Achish son of Maachah king of Gath. And they told Shimei, saying, Behold, thy servants be in Gath.

40 And Shimei arose, and saddled his ass, and went to Gath to Achish to seek his servants: and Shimei went, and brought his servants from Gath.

41 And it was told SOLOMON that Shimei had gone from Jerusalem to Gath, and was come again.

42 And the king sent and called for Shimei, and said unto him, Did I not make thee to swear by the LORD, and protested unto thee, saying, Know for a certain, on the day thou goest out, and walkest abroad any whither, that thou shalt surely die? and thou saidst unto me, The word that I have heard is good.

43 Why then hast thou not kept the oath of the LORD, and the commandment that I have charged thee with?

44 The king said moreover to Shimei, Thou knowest all the wickedness

which thine heart is privy to, that thou didst to David my father: therefore the LORD shall return thy wickedness upon thine own head;

45 And king SOLOMON shall be blessed, and the throne of David shall be established before the LORD for ever.

46 So the king commanded Benaiah the son of Jehoiada; which went out, and fell upon him, that he died. And the kingdom was established in the hand of SOLOMON.

SOLOMON'S DAILY PROVISIONS

Kings 1 Chapter 4

22 And SOLOMON's provision for one day was thirty measures of fine flour, and threescore measures of meal,

23 Ten fat oxen, and twenty oxen out of the pastures, and an hundred sheep, beside harts, and roebucks, and fallowdeer, and fatted fowl.

TYPICAL JUDGMENT OF KING SOLOMON

Kings 1 Chapter 3

16 Then came there two women, that were harlots, unto the king, and stood before him.

17 And the one woman said, O my lord, I and this woman dwell in one house; and I was delivered of a child with her in the house.

18 And it came to pass the third day after that I was delivered, that this woman was delivered also: and we were together; there was no stranger with us in the house, save we two in the house.

19 And this woman's child died in the night; because she overlaid it.

20 And she arose at midnight, and took my son from beside me, while thine handmaid slept, and laid it in her bosom, and laid her dead child in my bosom.

21 And when I rose in the morning to give my child suck, behold, it was dead: but when I had considered it in the morning, behold, it was not my son, which I did bear.

22 And the other woman said, Nay; but the living is my son, and the dead is thy son. And this said, No; but the dead is thy son, and the living is my son. Thus they spake before the king.

23 Then said the king, The one saith, This is my son that liveth, and thy son is the dead: and the other saith, Nay; but thy son is the dead, and my son is the living.

24 And the king said, Bring me a sword. And they brought a sword before the king.

25 And the king said, Divide the living child in two, and give half to the one, and half to the other.

26 Then spake the woman whose the living child was unto the king, for her bowels yearned upon her son, and she said, O my lord, give her the living child, and in no wise slay it. But the other said, Let it be neither mine nor thine, but divide it.

27 Then the king answered and said, Give her the living child, and in no wise slay it: she is the mother thereof.

28 And all Israel heard of the judgment which the king had judged; and they feared the king: for they saw that the wisdom of God was in him, to do judgment.

Queen of Sheba

Kings 1 Chapter 10

1 And when the queen of Sheba heard of the fame of SOLOMON concerning the name of the LORD, she came to prove him with hard questions.

2 And she came to Jerusalem with a very great train, with camels that bare spices, and very much gold, and precious stones: and when she was come to SOLOMON, she communed with him of all that was in her heart.

3 And SOLOMON told her all her questions: there was not any thing hid from the king, which he told her not.

4 And when the queen of Sheba had seen all SOLOMON's wisdom, and the house that he had built,

5 And the meat of his table, and the sitting of his servants, and the attendance of his ministers, and their apparel, and his cupbearers, and his ascent by which he went up unto the house of the LORD; there was no more spirit in her.

6 And she said to the king, It was a true report that I heard in mine own land of thy acts and of thy wisdom.

7 Howbeit I believed not the words, until I came, and mine eyes had seen it: and, behold, the half was not told me: thy wisdom and prosperity exceedeth the fame which I heard.

8 Happy are thy men, happy arethese thy servants, which stand continually before thee, and that hear thy wisdom.

9 Blessed be the LORD thy God, which delighted in thee, to set thee on the throne of Israel: because the LORD loved Israel for ever, therefore made he thee king, to do judgment and justice.

10 And she gave the king an hundred and twenty talents of gold, and of spices very great store, and precious stones: there came no more such abundance of spices as these which the queen of Sheba gave to king SOLOMON.

11 And the navy also of Hiram, that brought gold from Ophir, brought in from Ophir great plenty of almug trees, and precious stones.

12 And the king made of the almug trees pillars for the house of the LORD, and for the king's house, harps also and psalteries for singers: there came no such almug trees, nor were seen unto this day.

13 And king SOLOMON gave unto the queen of Sheba all her desire, whatsoever she asked, beside that which SOLOMON gave her of his royal bounty. So she turned and went to her own country, she and her servants.
Samuel Chapter 12

24 And David comforted Bath-sheba his wife, and went in unto her, and lay with her: and she bare a son, and he called his name Solomon: and the LORD loved him.

25 And he sent by the hand of Nathan the prophet; and he called his name Jedidiah, because of the LORD.

WIVES

Kings 1 Chapter 11

1 But king SOLOMON loved many strange women, together with the daughter of Pharaoh, women of the Moabites, Ammonites, Edomites, Zidonians, and Hittites;

2 Of the nations concerning which the LORD said unto the children of Israel, Ye shall not go in to them, neither shall they come in unto you: for surely they will turn away your heart after their gods: SOLOMON clave

unto these in love.

3 And he had seven hundred wives, princesses, and three hundred concubines: and his wives turned away his heart.

Ecclesiastes (Kohelet)

Chapter 1

מגילת קהלת פרק א.

דִּבְרֵי קֹהֶלֶת בֶּן־דָּוִד מֶלֶךְ בִּירוּשָׁלָם:
_{speakings Kohelet son – David king in Jerusalem}

1 The words of the Preacher, the son of David, king in Jerusalem.

הֲבֵל הֲבָלִים אָמַר קֹהֶלֶת הֲבֵל הֲבָלִים הַכֹּל הָבֶל:
_{vanity the all vanities vanity Kohelet said vanities vanity}

2 Vanity of vanities, saith the Preacher, vanity of vanities; all is vanity.

מַה־יִּתְרוֹן לָאָדָם בְּכָל־עֲמָלוֹ שֶׁיַּעֲמֹל תַּחַת הַשָּׁמֶשׁ:
_{the sun under that he labors his labor - in all to Adam profit - what}

3 What profit hath a man of all his labour which he taketh under the sun?

דּוֹר הֹלֵךְ וְדוֹר בָּא וְהָאָרֶץ לְעוֹלָם עֹמָדֶת:
_{stands to forever and the earth comes and generation goes generation}

4 One generation passeth away, and another generation cometh: but the earth abideth for ever.

וְזָרַח הַשֶּׁמֶשׁ וּבָא הַשָּׁמֶשׁ וְאֶל־מְקוֹמוֹ שׁוֹאֵף זוֹרֵחַ הוּא שָׁם:
_{there it radiant gasping his place - and unto the sun and comes the sun and radiant}

5 The sun also ariseth, and the sun goeth down, and hasteth to his place where he arose.

הוֹלֵךְ אֶל־דָּרוֹם וְסוֹבֵב אֶל־צָפוֹן סוֹבֵב הֹלֵךְ הָרוּחַ
_{the wind goes encircles north – unto and encircles south – unto goes}

וְעַל־סְבִיבֹתָיו שָׁב הָרוּחַ:
_{the wind returns it's circuits - and upon}

6 The wind goeth toward the south, and turneth about unto the north; it whirleth about continually, and the wind returneth again according to his circuits.

כָּל־הַנְּחָלִים הֹלְכִים אֶל־הַיָּם וְהַיָּם אֵינֶנּוּ מָלֵא
_{full isn't and the sea the sea – unto going ones the rivers – all}

אֶל־מְקוֹם שֶׁהַנְּחָלִים הֹלְכִים שָׁם הֵם שָׁבִים לָלָכֶת:
_{to go returning ones them there going ones that the rivers place – unto}

7 All the rivers run into the sea; yet the sea is not full; unto the place from whence the rivers come, thither they return again.

כָּל־הַדְּבָרִים יְגֵעִים לֹא־יוּכַל אִישׁ לְדַבֵּר
_{to speak man able - not weary ones the speakings – all}

לֹא־תִשְׂבַּע עַיִן לִרְאוֹת וְלֹא־תִמָּלֵא אֹזֶן מִשְּׁמֹעַ:
_{from hearing ear it full - and not to see eye it satisfied – not}

8 All things are full of labour; man cannot utter it: the eye is not satisfied with seeing, nor the ear filled with hearing.

מַה־שֶּׁהָיָה הוּא שֶׁיִּהְיֶה וּמַה־שֶּׁנַּעֲשָׂה הוּא שֶׁיֵּעָשֶׂה
that it will be done   it   that has been done - and what   that will be   it   that has been – what

וְאֵין כָּל־חָדָשׁ תַּחַת הַשָּׁמֶשׁ:
the sun   under   new – all   and isn't

9 The thing that hath been, it is that which shall be; and that which is done is that which shall be done: and there is no new thing under the sun.

יֵשׁ דָּבָר שֶׁיֹּאמַר רְאֵה־זֶה חָדָשׁ הוּא
it   new   this - that - see   that he says   matter   there is

כְּבָר הָיָה לְעֹלָמִים אֲשֶׁר הָיָה מִלְּפָנֵנוּ:
from before us   was   which   to forevers   it was   already

10 Is there any thing whereof it may be said, See, this is new? it hath been already of old time, which was before us.

אֵין זִכְרוֹן לָרִאשֹׁנִים וְגַם לָאַחֲרֹנִים שֶׁיִּהְיוּ
that they will be   to followings   and also   to beginnings   remembrance   isn't

לֹא־יִהְיֶה לָהֶם זִכָּרוֹן עִם שֶׁיִּהְיוּ לָאַחֲרֹנָה:
to come after   that they will be   with   remembrance   to them   it will be – not

11 There is no remembrance of former things; neither shall there be any remembrance of things that are to come with those that shall come after.

אֲנִי קֹהֶלֶת הָיִיתִי מֶלֶךְ עַל־יִשְׂרָאֵל בִּירוּשָׁלָםִ:
in Jerusalem   Israel – upon   king   I was   Kohelet   I

12 I the Preacher was king over Israel in Jerusalem.

וְנָתַתִּי אֶת־לִבִּי לִדְרוֹשׁ וְלָתוּר בַּחָכְמָה
in wisdom   and to survey   to inquire   my heart – that   and I gave

עַל כָּל־אֲשֶׁר נַעֲשָׂה תַּחַת הַשָּׁמָיִם
the heavens   under   done   which – all   upon

הוּא עִנְיַן רָע נָתַן אֱלֹהִים לִבְנֵי הָאָדָם לַעֲנוֹת בּוֹ:
in it   to be humbled   the Adam   to sons   Elohim   gave   bad   experience   it

13 And I gave my heart to seek and search out by wisdom concerning all things that are done under heaven: this sore travail hath God given to the sons of man to be exercised therewith.

רָאִיתִי אֶת־כָּל־הַמַּעֲשִׂים שֶׁנַּעֲשׂוּ תַּחַת הַשָּׁמֶשׁ
the sun   under   that it done   the works – all – that   I have seen

וְהִנֵּה הַכֹּל הֶבֶל וּרְעוּת רוּחַ:
soul   and vexation   vanity   the all   and here

14 I have seen all the works that are done under the sun; and, behold, all is vanity and vexation of spirit.

מְעֻוָּת לֹא־יוּכַל לִתְקֹן וְחֶסְרוֹן לֹא־יוּכַל לְהִמָּנוֹת:
to be accounted   able – not   and lacking   to set order   it will be able – not   from distorted

15 That which is crooked cannot be made straight: and that which is wanting cannot be numbered.

דִּבַּ֨רְתִּי אֲנִ֤י עִם־לִבִּי֙ לֵאמֹ֔ר אֲנִ֗י הִנֵּ֤ה הִגְדַּ֙לְתִּי֙
   I have been great   here   I   to say   heart – with   I   I spoke

וְהוֹסַ֣פְתִּי חָכְמָ֔ה עַ֛ל כָּל־אֲשֶׁר־הָיָ֥ה לְפָנַ֖י עַל־יְרוּשָׁלָ֑͏ִם
Jerusalem - upon   before   was - which – all   upon   wisdom   and I acquired

וְלִבִּ֛י רָאָ֥ה הַרְבֵּ֖ה חָכְמָ֥ה וָדָֽעַת׃
   and knowledge   wisdom   the much   saw   and my heart

16 I communed with mine own heart, saying, Lo, I am come to great estate, and have gotten more wisdom than all they that have been before me in Jerusalem: yea, my heart had great experience of wisdom and knowledge.

וָאֶתְּנָ֤ה לִבִּי֙ לָדַ֣עַת חָכְמָ֔ה וְדַ֥עַת הוֹלֵל֖וֹת וְשִׂכְל֑וּת
and follies   madnesses   and know   wisdom   to know   my heart   and I gave

יָדַ֕עְתִּי שֶׁגַּם־זֶ֥ה ה֖וּא רַעְי֥וֹן רֽוּחַ׃
   soul   vexation   it   this - that also   I knew

17 And I gave my heart to know wisdom, and to know madness and folly: I perceived that this also is vexation of spirit.

כִּ֛י בְּרֹ֥ב חָכְמָ֖ה רָב־כָּ֑עַס
   vexation – much   wisdom   in much   like

וְיוֹסִ֥יף דַּ֖עַת יוֹסִ֥יף מַכְאֽוֹב׃
pain   he will add   knowledge   and he will add

18 For in much wisdom is much grief: and he that increaseth knowledge increaseth sorrow.

Chapter 2

מגילת קהלת פרק ב

אָמַרְתִּי אֲנִי בְּלִבִּי לְכָה־נָּא אֲנַסְּכָה בְשִׂמְחָה וּרְאֵה בְטוֹב

וְהִנֵּה גַם־הוּא הָבֶל:

1. I said from my heart, Come now, I will test happiness, and see from good; and, here, also it is vanity.

לִשְׂחוֹק אָמַרְתִּי מְהוֹלָל וּלְשִׂמְחָה מַה־זֹּה עֹשָׂה:

2. Laughter I said, it's foolishness; and happiness what does it do?

תַּרְתִּי בְלִבִּי לִמְשׁוֹךְ בַּיַּיִן אֶת־בְּשָׂרִי וְלִבִּי נֹהֵג בַּחָכְמָה

וְלֶאֱחֹז בְּסִכְלוּת עַד אֲשֶׁר־אֶרְאֶה אֵי־זֶה טוֹב

לִבְנֵי הָאָדָם אֲשֶׁר יַעֲשׂוּ תַּחַת הַשָּׁמַיִם מִסְפַּר יְמֵי חַיֵּיהֶם:

3. I sought in my heart to give myself to wine, yet guiding my heart with wisdom; and to lay hold on folly, till I might see what was good for the sons of men, which they should do under the heaven all the days of their life.

הִגְדַּלְתִּי מַעֲשָׂי בָּנִיתִי לִי בָּתִּים נָטַעְתִּי לִי כְּרָמִים:

4. I made great works for myself; I built houses; I planted vineyards;

עָשִׂיתִי לִי גַּנּוֹת וּפַרְדֵּסִים וְנָטַעְתִּי בָהֶם עֵץ כָּל־פֶּרִי:

5. I made gardens and orchards, and I planted trees in them of all kinds of fruits;

עָשִׂיתִי לִי בְּרֵכוֹת מָיִם לְהַשְׁקוֹת מֵהֶם יַעַר צוֹמֵחַ עֵצִים:

6. I made pools of water, to water with it a forest of growing trees.

קָנִיתִי עֲבָדִים וּשְׁפָחוֹת וּבְנֵי־בַיִת הָיָה לִי גַּם מִקְנֶה בָקָר

וָצֹאן הַרְבֵּה הָיָה לִי מִכֹּל שֶׁהָיוּ לְפָנַי בִּירוּשָׁלָ͏ִם:

7. I acquired servants and maidens, and had servants born in my house; also I had great possessions of herds and flocks, more than all who were in Jerusalem before me;

כָּנַסְתִּי לִי גַּם־כֶּסֶף וְזָהָב וּסְגֻלַּת מְלָכִים וְהַמְּדִינוֹת

ECCLESIASTES - CHAPTER 2

עָשִׂיתִי לִי שָׁרִים וְשָׁרוֹת
and women singers   men singers   to me   I made

וְתַעֲנוּגוֹת בְּנֵי הָאָדָם שִׁדָּה וְשִׁדּוֹת:
and concubines   concubine   the Adam   sons   and delights

8. I gathered also silver and gold, and the treasure of kings and of the provinces; I acquired men singers and women singers, and, the delight of men, many women.

וְגָדַלְתִּי וְהוֹסַפְתִּי מִכֹּל שֶׁהָיָה לְפָנַי בִּירוּשָׁלָ͏ִם
in Jerusalem   before   that was   from all   and I increased   and I was great

אַף חָכְמָתִי עָמְדָה לִּי:
to me   it stood   my wisdom   then

9. And I was great, and increased more than all that were before me in Jerusalem; also my wisdom remained with me.

וְכֹל אֲשֶׁר שָׁאֲלוּ עֵינַי לֹא אָצַלְתִּי מֵהֶם
from them   I withheld   not   my eyes   I asked it   which   and all

לֹא־מָנַעְתִּי אֶת־לִבִּי מִכָּל־שִׂמְחָה כִּי־לִבִּי שָׂמֵחַ מִכָּל־עֲמָלִי
my labor - from all   happy   my heart - like   happiness - from all   my heart - that   restrain - not

וְזֶה־הָיָה חֶלְקִי מִכָּל־עֲמָלִי:
my labor - from all   my portion   was - and this

10. And whatever my eyes desired I kept not from them, I did not restrain my heart from any joy; for my heart rejoiced in all my labor; and this was my portion of all my labor.

וּפָנִיתִי אֲנִי בְּכָל־מַעֲשַׂי שֶׁעָשׂוּ יָדַי וּבֶעָמָל שֶׁעָמַלְתִּי לַעֲשׂוֹת
to doings   that I labored   and in labor   my hand   that it did   my works - in all   I   and I faced

וְהִנֵּה הַכֹּל הֶבֶל וּרְעוּת רוּחַ וְאֵין יִתְרוֹן תַּחַת הַשָּׁמֶשׁ:
the sun   under   profit   and isn't   soul   and vexing   vanity   the all   and here

11. Then I looked at all the works that my hands had done, and at the labor that I had labored to do; and, behold, all was vanity and a striving after wind, and there was nothing to be gained under the sun.

וּפָנִיתִי אֲנִי לִרְאוֹת חָכְמָה וְהוֹלֵלוֹת וְסִכְלוּת
and follies   and madness   wisdom   to see   I   and I faced

כִּי מֶה הָאָדָם שֶׁיָּבוֹא אַחֲרֵי הַמֶּלֶךְ אֵת אֲשֶׁר־כְּבָר עָשׂוּהוּ:
done it   already - which   that   the king   after   that he comes   the Adam   what   like

12. And I turned myself to behold wisdom, and madness, and folly; for what can the man do who comes after the king? even that which has been already done.

וְרָאִיתִי אָנִי שֶׁיֵּשׁ יִתְרוֹן לַחָכְמָה מִן־הַסִּכְלוּת
the follies - from   to wisdom   profit   that there is   I   and I saw

כִּיתְרוֹן הָאוֹר מִן־הַחֹשֶׁךְ:
the darkness - from   the light   like profits

13. Then I saw that wisdom excels folly, as far as light excels darkness.

הֶחָכָם עֵינָיו בְּרֹאשׁוֹ וְהַכְּסִיל בַּחֹשֶׁךְ הוֹלֵךְ

he goes   in darkness   and the folly one   in his head   his eyes   the wise

וְיָדַעְתִּי גַם־אָנִי שֶׁמִּקְרֶה אֶחָד יִקְרֶה אֶת־כֻּלָּם:

all – that   it meets   one   that event   I – also   and I knew

14. The wise man's eyes are in his head; but the fool walks in darkness; and I myself perceived also that one event happens to them all.

וְאָמַרְתִּי אֲנִי בְּלִבִּי כְּמִקְרֵה הַכְּסִיל גַּם־אֲנִי יִקְרֵנִי

it meets me   I – also   the fool   like event   in my heart   I   and I said

וְלָמָּה חָכַמְתִּי אֲנִי אָז יוֹתֵר וְדִבַּרְתִּי בְלִבִּי שֶׁגַּם־זֶה הָבֶל:

vanity   this – that also   in my heart   and I said   other   than   I   I wise   and why

15. Then said I in my heart, As it happens to the fool, so it happens even to me; and why was I then more wise? Then I said in my heart, that this also is vanity.

כִּי אֵין זִכְרוֹן לֶחָכָם עִם־הַכְּסִיל לְעוֹלָם

to forever   the fool – with   to wise   remembrance   isn't   like

בְּשֶׁכְּבָר הַיָּמִים הַבָּאִים הַכֹּל נִשְׁכָּח

will be forgotten   the all   the coming ones   the days   in that already

וְאֵיךְ יָמוּת הֶחָכָם עִם־הַכְּסִיל:

the fool – with   the wise   he dies   and how

16. For there is no remembrance of the wise more than of the fool for ever; seeing that which now is in the days to come shall all be forgotten. And how dies the wise man? just like the fool.

וְשָׂנֵאתִי אֶת־הַחַיִּים

the life – that   and I hated

כִּי רַע עָלַי הַמַּעֲשֶׂה שֶׁנַּעֲשָׂה תַּחַת הַשָּׁמֶשׁ

the sun   under   that done   the work   upon me   bad   like

כִּי־הַכֹּל הֶבֶל וּרְעוּת רוּחַ:

soul   and vexing   vanity   the all – like

17. Therefore I hated life; because the work that is done under the sun was grievous to me; for all is vanity and striving after wind.

וְשָׂנֵאתִי אֲנִי אֶת־כָּל־עֲמָלִי שֶׁאֲנִי עָמֵל תַּחַת הַשָּׁמֶשׁ

the sun   under   labor   that I   my labor – all – that   I   and I hated

שֶׁאַנִּיחֶנּוּ לָאָדָם שֶׁיִּהְיֶה אַחֲרָי:

my after   that will be   to Adam   that I leave

18. And I hated all my labor which I had taken under the sun; because I should leave it to the man that shall be after me.

Ecclesiastes - Chapter 2

וּמִי יוֹדֵעַ הֶחָכָם יִהְיֶה אוֹ סָכָל
and who   knows   the wise   he will be   or   fool

וְיִשְׁלַט בְּכָל־עֲמָלִי שֶׁעָמַלְתִּי
and he will rule   my labor - in all   that I labored

וְשֶׁחָכַמְתִּי תַּחַת הַשֶּׁמֶשׁ גַּם־זֶה הָבֶל׃
and that I was wise   under   the sun   this - also   vanity

19. And who knows whether he shall be a wise man or a fool? yet he shall have rule over all my labor in which I have labored, and in which I have showed myself wise under the sun. This also is vanity.

וְסַבּוֹתִי אֲנִי לְיַאֵשׁ אֶת־לִבִּי
and I encircled   I   to despair   my heart - that

עַל כָּל־הֶעָמָל שֶׁעָמַלְתִּי תַּחַת הַשָּׁמֶשׁ׃
upon   the labor - all   that I labored   under   the sun

20. Therefore I went about to cause my heart to despair of all the labor which I took under the sun.

כִּי־יֵשׁ אָדָם שֶׁעֲמָלוֹ בְּחָכְמָה וּבְדַעַת וּבְכִשְׁרוֹן
like - there is   Adam   that his labor   in wisdom   and knowledge   and in skill

וּלְאָדָם שֶׁלֹּא עָמַל־בּוֹ יִתְּנֶנּוּ חֶלְקוֹ
and to Adam   that not   he labor - in it   he will give it   his portion

גַּם־זֶה הֶבֶל וְרָעָה רַבָּה׃
this - also   vanity   and evil   much

21. For there is a man whose labor is with wisdom, and with knowledge, and with skill; yet to a man that has not labored in it shall he leave it for his portion. This also is vanity and a great evil.

כִּי מֶה־הֹוֶה לָאָדָם בְּכָל־עֲמָלוֹ
like   what - has   to Adam   his labor - in all

וּבְרַעְיוֹן לִבּוֹ שֶׁהוּא עָמֵל תַּחַת הַשָּׁמֶשׁ׃
and in striving   his heart   that he   labors   under   the sun

22. For what has man of all his labor, and of the striving of his heart, in which he has labored under the sun?

כִּי כָל־יָמָיו מַכְאֹבִים וָכַעַס עִנְיָנוֹ
like   all   his days   pains   and vexation   his experience

גַּם־בַּלַּיְלָה לֹא־שָׁכַב לִבּוֹ גַּם־זֶה הֶבֶל הוּא׃
in night - also   rests - not   his heart   this - also   vanity   it

23. For all his days are sorrows, and his labor grief; even in the night his heart does not rest. This also is vanity.

אֵין־טוֹב בָּאָדָם שֶׁיֹּאכַל וְשָׁתָה
isn't - good   in Adam   that he eats   and drinks

וְהֶרְאָה אֶת־נַפְשׁוֹ טוֹב בַּעֲמָלוֹ

in his labor   good   his soul – that   and the seeing

גַּם־זֹה רָאִיתִי אָנִי כִּי מִיַּד הָאֱלֹהִים הִיא:

it   the Elohim   from hand   like   I   I saw   this - also

24. There is nothing better for a man, than that he should eat and drink, and that he should make his soul enjoy good in his labor. This also I saw, that it was from the hand of God.

כִּי מִי יֹאכַל וּמִי יָחוּשׁ חוּץ מִמֶּנִּי:

from me   outside   enjoys   and who   he eats   who   like

25. For who can eat, or who can enjoy pleasure more than I?

כִּי לְאָדָם שֶׁטּוֹב לְפָנָיו נָתַן חָכְמָה וְדַעַת וְשִׂמְחָה

and happiness   and knowledge   wisdom   gives   before him   that good   to Adam   like

וְלַחוֹטֶא נָתַן עִנְיָן לֶאֱסוֹף וְלִכְנוֹס לָתֵת לְטוֹב לִפְנֵי הָאֱלֹהִים

the Elohim   before   to good   to give   and to collect   to gather   experience   gives   and to sinner

גַּם־זֶה הֶבֶל וּרְעוּת רוּחַ:

wind   and grazing   vanity   this - also

26. For God gives to a man who is good in his sight; wisdom, and knowledge, and joy; but to the sinner he gives the task of gathering and heaping up, that he may give it to one who is good before God. This also is vanity and striving after wind.

Chapter 3

מגילת קהלת פרק ג

לְכֹ֖ל זְמָ֑ן וְעֵ֥ת לְכָל־חֵ֖פֶץ תַּ֥חַת הַשָּׁמָֽיִם׃
to all   time   and season   purpose - to all   under   the heaven

1. To every thing there is a season, and a time to every purpose under the heaven;

עֵ֥ת לָלֶ֖דֶת וְעֵ֥ת לָמֽוּת
season   to be born   and time   to die

עֵ֥ת לָטַ֖עַת וְעֵ֥ת לַעֲק֥וֹר נָטֽוּעַ׃
season   to plant   and time   to uproot   planted

2. A time to be born, and a time to die; a time to plant, and a time to pluck up that which is planted;

עֵ֥ת לַהֲר֖וֹג וְעֵ֥ת לִרְפּ֑וֹא
season   to kill   and time   to heal

עֵ֥ת לִפְר֖וֹץ וְעֵ֥ת לִבְנֽוֹת׃
season   to break down   and time   to buildings

3. A time to kill, and a time to heal; a time to break down, and a time to build up;

עֵ֥ת לִבְכּ֖וֹת וְעֵ֣ת לִשְׂח֑וֹק
season   to weep   and time   to laugh

עֵ֥ת סְפ֖וֹד וְעֵ֥ת רְקֽוֹד׃
season   wail   and time   skip happily

4. A time to weep, and a time to laugh; a time to mourn, and a time to dance;

עֵ֚ת לְהַשְׁלִ֣יךְ אֲבָנִ֔ים וְעֵ֖ת כְּנ֣וֹס אֲבָנִ֑ים
season   to throw away   stones   and time   gather   stones

עֵ֣ת לַחֲב֔וֹק וְעֵ֖ת לִרְחֹ֥ק מֵחַבֵּֽק׃
season   to embrace   and time   to be far   from embracing

5. A time to cast away stones, and a time to gather stones together; a time to embrace, and a time to refrain from embracing;

עֵ֥ת לְבַקֵּ֖שׁ וְעֵ֣ת לְאַבֵּ֑ד
season   to seek   and time   to lose

עֵ֥ת לִשְׁמ֖וֹר וְעֵ֥ת לְהַשְׁלִֽיךְ׃
season   to heed   and time   to the cast away

6. A time to seek, and a time to lose; a time to keep, and a time to cast away;

עֵ֥ת לִקְר֖וֹעַ וְעֵ֣ת לִתְפּ֑וֹר
season   to tear   and time   to sew together

עֵ֥ת לַחֲשׁ֖וֹת וְעֵ֥ת לְדַבֵּֽר׃
season   to be silent   and time   to speak

7. A time to rend, and a time to sew; a time to keep silence, and a time to speak;

עֵת לֶאֱהֹב וְעֵת לִשְׂנֹא
season to love and time to hate

עֵת מִלְחָמָה וְעֵת שָׁלוֹם׃
season war and time peace

8. A time to love, and a time to hate; a time of war, and a time of peace.

מַה־יִּתְרוֹן הָעוֹשֶׂה בַּאֲשֶׁר הוּא עָמֵל׃
profit - what the doing in which he labors

9. What gains has he who works in that in which he labors?

רָאִיתִי אֶת־הָעִנְיָן אֲשֶׁר נָתַן אֱלֹהִים
I saw the experience – that which given Elohim

לִבְנֵי הָאָדָם לַעֲנוֹת בּוֹ׃
to sons the Adam to humbled in it

10. I have seen the tasks, which God has given to the sons of men to be exercised in it.

אֶת־הַכֹּל עָשָׂה יָפֶה בְעִתּוֹ גַּם אֶת־הָעֹלָם נָתַן בְּלִבָּם
the all - that he did beautiful in his time also that – the forever he gave in their hearts

מִבְּלִי אֲשֶׁר לֹא־יִמְצָא הָאָדָם אֶת־הַמַּעֲשֶׂה
from without which not – he finds the Adam that – the works

אֲשֶׁר־עָשָׂה הָאֱלֹהִים מֵרֹאשׁ וְעַד־סוֹף׃
which - does the Elohim from beginning till - and end

11. He has made every thing beautiful in his time; also he has set the mystery of the world in their heart, so that no man can find out the work which God has made from the beginning to the end.

יָדַעְתִּי כִּי אֵין טוֹב בָּם
I know like isn't good in them

כִּי אִם־לִשְׂמוֹחַ וְלַעֲשׂוֹת טוֹב בְּחַיָּיו׃
like with - to rejoice and to doing good in his life

12. I know that there is nothing better for them, than to rejoice, and to do good in his life.

וְגַם כָּל־הָאָדָם שֶׁיֹּאכַל וְשָׁתָה
and also all – the Adam that he eat and drink

וְרָאָה טוֹב בְּכָל־עֲמָלוֹ מַתַּת אֱלֹהִים הִיא׃
and see good in all - his labor gift Elohim it

13. And also that it is the gift of God that every man should eat and drink, and enjoy the good of all his labor.

יָדַעְתִּי כִּי כָּל־אֲשֶׁר יַעֲשֶׂה הָאֱלֹהִים הוּא יִהְיֶה לְעוֹלָם
I know like all – that he does the Elohim it will be to forever

עָלָיו אֵין לְהוֹסִיף
upon him isn't to add to

וּמִמֶּנּוּ אֵין לִגְרֹעַ
and from it nothing to take away

וְהָאֱלֹהִים עָשָׂה שֶׁיִּרְאוּ מִלְּפָנָיו׃
and the Elohim does that they will fear from before him

14. I know that, whatever God does, it shall be for ever; nothing can be added to it, nor any thing taken from it; and God does it, that men should fear before him.

מַה־שֶּׁהָיָה כְּבָר הוּא וַאֲשֶׁר לִהְיוֹת כְּבָר הָיָה
what - that has been already it and which to will be already was

וְהָאֱלֹהִים יְבַקֵּשׁ אֶת־נִרְדָּף׃
and the Elohim he seeks that - driven away

15. That which is, already has been; and that which is to be has already been; and God seeks what has been driven away.

וְעוֹד רָאִיתִי תַּחַת הַשָּׁמֶשׁ מְקוֹם הַמִּשְׁפָּט שָׁמָּה הָרֶשַׁע
and again I saw under the sun place the judgment there that the wickedness

וּמְקוֹם הַצֶּדֶק שָׁמָּה הָרָשַׁע׃
and place the righteous there the wicked

16. And moreover I saw under the sun that in the place of judgment wickedness was there; and that in the place of righteousness, iniquity was there.

אָמַרְתִּי אֲנִי בְּלִבִּי אֶת־הַצַּדִּיק וְאֶת־הָרָשָׁע יִשְׁפֹּט הָאֱלֹהִים
I said I in my heart that - the righteous and that - the wicked he will judge the Elohim

כִּי־עֵת לְכָל־חֵפֶץ וְעַל כָּל־הַמַּעֲשֶׂה שָׁם׃
like - season to all - purpose and upon all - the works there

17. I said in my heart, God shall judge the righteous and the wicked; for there is a time there for every purpose and for every work.

אָמַרְתִּי אֲנִי בְּלִבִּי עַל־דִּבְרַת בְּנֵי הָאָדָם לְבָרָם הָאֱלֹהִים
I said I in my heart upon - matters sons the Adam to purify them the Elohim

וְלִרְאוֹת שְׁהֶם־בְּהֵמָה הֵמָּה לָהֶם׃
and to see that them - beast they are to them

18. I said in my heart concerning the sons of men, that God is testing them, that they might see that they are but beasts.

כִּי מִקְרֶה בְנֵי־הָאָדָם וּמִקְרֶה הַבְּהֵמָה
like event sons - the Adam and event the beast

וּמִקְרֶה אֶחָד לָהֶם כְּמוֹת זֶה כֵּן מוֹת זֶה
and event one to them like death this thus death this

וְרוּחַ אֶחָד לַכֹּל וּמוֹתַר הָאָדָם מִן־הַבְּהֵמָה אָיִן
  isn't   the beast – from   the Adam and preeminence to all   one   and soul

כִּי הַכֹּל הָבֶל:
  vanity the all like

19. For that which befalls the sons of men befalls beasts; one thing befalls them both; as the one dies, so dies the other; They have all one breath; so that a man has no preeminence above a beast; for all is vanity.

הַכֹּל הוֹלֵךְ אֶל־מָקוֹם אֶחָד הַכֹּל הָיָה מִן־הֶעָפָר
  the dust - from was the all one place – unto goes the all

וְהַכֹּל שָׁב אֶל־הֶעָפָר:
  the dust – unto returns and the all

20. All go to one place; all are from the dust, and all turn to dust again.

מִי יוֹדֵעַ רוּחַ בְּנֵי הָאָדָם הָעֹלָה הִיא לְמָעְלָה
  to upward it the ascending the Adam sons soul knows who

וְרוּחַ הַבְּהֵמָה הַיֹּרֶדֶת הִיא לְמַטָּה לָאָרֶץ:
  to earth to beneath it the descending the beast and soul

21. Who knows whether the spirit of man goes upward, and the spirit of the beast goes downward to the earth?

וְרָאִיתִי כִּי אֵין טוֹב מֵאֲשֶׁר יִשְׂמַח הָאָדָם בְּמַעֲשָׂיו
  in his works the Adam he be happy from which good isn't like and I saw

כִּי־הוּא חֶלְקוֹ כִּי מִי יְבִיאֶנּוּ לִרְאוֹת בְּמֶה שֶׁיִּהְיֶה אַחֲרָיו:
  after him that will be in what to see he brings it who like his portion it - like

22. So I saw that there is nothing better, than that a man should rejoice in his work; for that is his portion; who can bring him to see what shall be after him?

Chapter 4

מגילת קהלת פרק ד

וְשַׁבְתִּי אֲנִי
I   and I returned

וָאֶרְאֶה אֶת־כָּל־הָעֲשֻׁקִים אֲשֶׁר נַעֲשִׂים תַּחַת הַשָּׁמֶשׁ
the sun under doing ones which the oppressions -all – that and I saw

וְהִנֵּה דִּמְעַת הָעֲשֻׁקִים וְאֵין לָהֶם מְנַחֵם
comforter to them and isn't the oppressed ones tears and here

וּמִיַּד עֹשְׁקֵיהֶם כֹּחַ וְאֵין לָהֶם מְנַחֵם׃
comforter to them and isn't power oppressing them and from hand

1. So I returned, and considered all the oppressions that are done under the sun; and behold the tears of such as were oppressed, and they had no comforter; and on the side of their oppressors there was power; but they had no comforter.

וְשַׁבֵּחַ אֲנִי אֶת־הַמֵּתִים שֶׁכְּבָר מֵתוּ
they died that already the dead ones - that I and commended

מִן־הַחַיִּים אֲשֶׁר הֵמָּה חַיִּים עֲדֶנָה׃
still living ones they are which the living - between

2. So I praised the dead who are already dead more than the living who are still alive.

וְטוֹב מִשְּׁנֵיהֶם אֵת אֲשֶׁר־עֲדֶן לֹא הָיָה
was not still - which that from both them and good

אֲשֶׁר לֹא־רָאָה אֶת־הַמַּעֲשֶׂה הָרָע אֲשֶׁר נַעֲשָׂה תַּחַת הַשָּׁמֶשׁ׃
the sun under done which the bad the work – that he sees – not which

3. And better than both of them is he who has not yet been, who has not seen the evil work that is done under the sun.

וְרָאִיתִי אֲנִי אֶת־כָּל־עָמָל וְאֵת כָּל־כִּשְׁרוֹן הַמַּעֲשֶׂה
the work skill - all and that labor - all - that I and I saw

כִּי הִיא קִנְאַת־אִישׁ מֵרֵעֵהוּ גַּם־זֶה הֶבֶל וּרְעוּת רוּחַ׃
spirit/wind and striving vanity this – also from his neighbors man – jealousy it like

4. And I saw that all labor, and every skill in work, come from a man's envy of his neighbor. This also is vanity and striving after wind.

הַכְּסִיל חֹבֵק אֶת־יָדָיו וְאֹכֵל אֶת־בְּשָׂרוֹ׃
his flesh - that and eats his hands – that folds the fool

5. The fool folds his hands together, and eats his own flesh.

טוֹב מְלֹא כַף נָחַת מִמְּלֹא חָפְנַיִם עָמָל וּרְעוּת רוּחַ׃
spirit/wind and striving labor palms from full quiet rest palm full good

6. Better is a handful with quietness, than both hands full of labor and striving after wind.

וְשַׁבְתִּי אֲנִי וָאֶרְאֶה הֶבֶל תַּחַת הַשָּׁמֶשׁ׃
the sun   under   vanity   and I saw   I   and I returned

7. Then I returned, and I saw vanity under the sun.

יֵשׁ אֶחָד וְאֵין שֵׁנִי גַּם בֵּן וָאָח אֵין־לוֹ
to him - isn't   and brother   son   also   two   and isn't   one   there is

וְאֵין קֵץ לְכָל־עֲמָלוֹ גַּם־עֵינָיו [עֵינוֹ] לֹא־תִשְׂבַּע עֹשֶׁר
riches   it satisfied – not   his eye – also   his labor - to all   ending   and isn't

וּלְמִי אֲנִי עָמֵל וּמְחַסֵּר אֶת־נַפְשִׁי מִטּוֹבָה
from goodness   my soul – that   and making lack   labor   I   and to who

גַּם־זֶה הֶבֶל וְעִנְיַן רָע הוּא׃
it   bad   and experience   vanity   this – also

8. (K) There is a man alone, without a companion; he neither has son nor brother; yet there is no end of all his labor; nor is his eye satisfied with riches. He may say, For whom do I labor, and bereave my soul of good? This also is vanity, indeed it is a bad business.

טוֹבִים הַשְּׁנַיִם מִן־הָאֶחָד אֲשֶׁר יֵשׁ־לָהֶם שָׂכָר טוֹב בַּעֲמָלָם׃
in their labor   good   reward   to them - it is   which   the one – from   the two   good ones

9. Two are better than one; because they have a good reward for their labor.

כִּי אִם־יִפֹּלוּ הָאֶחָד יָקִים אֶת־חֲבֵרוֹ
his friend - that   he rises   the one   they fall - if   like

וְאִילוֹ הָאֶחָד שֶׁיִּפּוֹל וְאֵין שֵׁנִי לַהֲקִימוֹ׃
to the his rising   second   and isn't   that he falls   the one   and his slack

10. For if they fall, the one will lift up his fellow; but woe to him that is alone when he falls; for he has not another to help him up.

גַּם אִם־יִשְׁכְּבוּ שְׁנַיִם וְחַם לָהֶם וּלְאֶחָד אֵיךְ יֵחָם׃
he warm   how   and to one   to them   and warm   both   they lye down – if   also

11. Again, if two lie together, then they have warmth; but how can one be warm alone?

וְאִם־יִתְקְפוֹ הָאֶחָד הַשְּׁנַיִם יַעַמְדוּ נֶגְדּוֹ
in his side   they will stand   the both   the one   he overpower him - and if

וְהַחוּט הַמְשֻׁלָּשׁ לֹא בִמְהֵרָה יִנָּתֵק׃
it tear apart   in quickly   not   the "from three"   and the thread

12. And if one prevail against him, two shall withstand him; a threefold cord is not quickly broken.

טוֹב יֶלֶד מִסְכֵּן וְחָכָם מִמֶּלֶךְ זָקֵן וּכְסִיל
and foolish   old   from king   and wise   from poor   born   good

אֲשֶׁר לֹא־יָדַע לְהִזָּהֵר עוֹד׃
again   to warned   know - not   which

13. Better is a poor and wise child than an old and foolish king, who no longer knows

how to take care of himself.

כִּי־מִבֵּית הָסוּרִים יָצָא לִמְלֹךְ כִּי גַּם בְּמַלְכוּתוֹ נוֹלַד רָשׁ׃
poor he born in his kingdom also like to reign he comes out the bound ones from house - like

14. For out of prison he comes to reign; or in his own kingdom had become poor.

רָאִיתִי אֶת־כָּל־הַחַיִּים הַמְהַלְּכִים תַּחַת הַשָּׁמֶשׁ
the sun under the strolling ones the living - all - that I saw

עִם הַיֶּלֶד הַשֵּׁנִי אֲשֶׁר יַעֲמֹד תַּחְתָּיו׃
in stead of him he will stand which the second the child with

15. I saw all the living who walk under the sun, with the second child that shall stand up in his stead.

אֵין־קֵץ לְכָל־הָעָם לְכֹל אֲשֶׁר־הָיָה לִפְנֵיהֶם
before them was - which to all the people - to all ending - isn't

גַּם הָאַחֲרוֹנִים לֹא יִשְׂמְחוּ־בוֹ כִּי־גַם־זֶה הֶבֶל וְרַעְיוֹן רוּחַ׃
soul and striving vanity this - also – like in it - they will be happy not the after ones also

16. There is no end of all the people, even of all who have been before them; yet they who come after shall not rejoice in him. This also is vanity and striving after wind.

שְׁמֹר רַגְלֶיךָ [רַגְלְךָ] כַּאֲשֶׁר תֵּלֵךְ אֶל־בֵּית הָאֱלֹהִים
the Elohim house - unto you go when your feet heed

וְקָרוֹב לִשְׁמֹעַ מִתֵּת הַכְּסִילִים זָבַח
sacrifice offering the fool ones from giving to listen and be near

כִּי־אֵינָם יוֹדְעִים לַעֲשׂוֹת רָע׃
bad to doings knowing ones they aren't – like

17. (K) Guard your foot when you go to the house of God; to get near to listen is better than to give the sacrifice of fools; for they consider not that they do evil.

Chapter 5

מגילת קהלת פרק ה

אַל־תְּבַהֵל עַל־פִּיךָ
_{your mouth – upon   you be rash - don't}

וְלִבְּךָ אַל־יְמַהֵר לְהוֹצִיא דָבָר לִפְנֵי הָאֱלֹהִים
_{the Elohim   before   speak   to go out   it hurry - don't   and your heart}

כִּי הָאֱלֹהִים בַּשָּׁמַיִם וְאַתָּה עַל־הָאָרֶץ
_{the earth - upon   and you   in heaven   the Elohim   like}

עַל־כֵּן יִהְיוּ דְבָרֶיךָ מְעַטִּים׃
_{little ones   your speakings   they will be   thus - upon}

1. Be not rash with your mouth, and let not your heart be hasty to utter any thing before God; for God is in heaven, and you are on earth; therefore let your words be few.

כִּי בָּא הַחֲלוֹם בְּרֹב עִנְיָן וְקוֹל כְּסִיל בְּרֹב דְּבָרִים׃
_{speakings   in much   fool   and voice   experience   in much   the dream   comes   like}

2. For a dream comes through a multitude of business; and a fool's voice is known by a multitude of words.

כַּאֲשֶׁר תִּדֹּר נֶדֶר לֵאלֹהִים אַל־תְּאַחֵר לְשַׁלְּמוֹ
_{to his pay   you delay - don't   to Elohim   vow   you vow   when}

כִּי אֵין חֵפֶץ בַּכְּסִילִים אֵת אֲשֶׁר־תִּדֹּר שַׁלֵּם׃
_{pay   you vowed – which   that   in fool ones   purpose   isn't   like}

3. When you vow a vow to God, defer not to pay it; for he has no pleasure in fools; pay what you have vowed.

טוֹב אֲשֶׁר לֹא־תִדֹּר מִשֶּׁתִּדּוֹר וְלֹא תְשַׁלֵּם׃
_{you pay   and not   from that you vow   you vow – not   which   good}

4. It is better that you should not vow, than that you should vow and not pay.

אַל־תִּתֵּן אֶת־פִּיךָ לַחֲטִיא אֶת־בְּשָׂרֶךָ
_{your flesh - that   to sin   your mouth - that   you give - don't}

וְאַל־תֹּאמַר לִפְנֵי הַמַּלְאָךְ כִּי שְׁגָגָה הִיא
_{it   error   like   the angel   before   you say - and don't}

לָמָּה יִקְצֹף הָאֱלֹהִים עַל־קוֹלֶךָ
_{your voice – upon   the Elohim   he wroth   why}

וְחִבֵּל אֶת־מַעֲשֵׂה יָדֶיךָ׃
_{your hands   works - that   and harms}

5. Do not allow your mouth to cause your flesh to sin; and do not say, before the angel, that it was an error; why should God be angry at your voice, and destroy the work of your hands?

Ecclesiastes - Chapter 5

כִּי בְרֹב חֲלֹמוֹת וַהֲבָלִים וּדְבָרִים הַרְבֵּה
like in many dreams and vanities and speakings the many

כִּי אֶת־הָאֱלֹהִים יְרָא:
like that - the Elohim fear

6. For in the multitude of dreams and many words there are also many vanities; but you, fear God.

אִם־עֹשֶׁק רָשׁ וְגֵזֶל מִשְׁפָּט וָצֶדֶק תִּרְאֶה בַּמְּדִינָה
if - oppression poor and plundering judgment and [the] righteous you see in province

אַל־תִּתְמַהּ עַל־הַחֵפֶץ
don't - what you give upon - the purpose

כִּי גָבֹהַּ מֵעַל גָּבֹהַּ שֹׁמֵר וּגְבֹהִים עֲלֵיהֶם:
like high one from above high one he heeds and high ones above them

7. If you see the oppression of the poor, and the violent perverting of judgment and justice in a province, do not be amazed by it; for he who is higher than the highest watches; and there are yet higher ones over them.

וְיִתְרוֹן אֶרֶץ בַּכֹּל הִיא [הוּא] מֶלֶךְ לְשָׂדֶה נֶעֱבָד:
and profit earth in all [she] [he] king to field he serves

8. (K) And the land has an advantage for everyone; he who works the field is a king.

אֹהֵב כֶּסֶף לֹא־יִשְׂבַּע כֶּסֶף
love silver not - he will be satisfied silver

וּמִי־אֹהֵב בֶּהָמוֹן לֹא תְבוּאָה גַּם־זֶה הָבֶל:
and who - loves in abundance not gain also - this vanity

9. He who loves silver shall not be satisfied with silver; nor he who loves abundance with gain; this also is vanity.

בִּרְבוֹת הַטּוֹבָה רַבּוּ אוֹכְלֶיהָ וּמַה־כִּשְׁרוֹן לִבְעָלֶיהָ
in increase the goodness they multiply he eats and what - skill to master

כִּי אִם־רְאִית [רְאוּת] עֵינָיו:
like with - seeing [seeing] his eyes

10. (K) When goods increase, they who eat them are increased; and what good is there to its owners, saving the beholding of them with their eyes?

מְתוּקָה שְׁנַת הָעֹבֵד אִם־מְעַט וְאִם־הַרְבֵּה יֹאכֵל
sweet sleep the servant if - little and if - the much he eats

וְהַשָּׂבָע לֶעָשִׁיר אֵינֶנּוּ מַנִּיחַ לוֹ לִישׁוֹן:
and the abundance to rich they aren't allow to him sleep

11. The sleep of a laboring man is sweet, whether he eats little or much; but the abundance of the rich will not let him sleep.

יֵשׁ רָעָה חוֹלָה רָאִיתִי תַּחַת הַשָּׁמֶשׁ
there is bad sickness I saw under the sun

עֹשֶׁר שָׁמוּר לִבְעָלָיו לְרָעָתוֹ:
to his bad   to his master   heeded   wealth

12. There is a grievous evil which I have seen under the sun; riches kept for their owner to his hurt.

וְאָבַד הָעֹשֶׁר הַהוּא בְּעִנְיַן רָע
bad   in experience   the it   the wealth   and perish

וְהוֹלִיד בֵּן וְאֵין בְּיָדוֹ מְאוּמָה:
from speck   in his hand   and isn't   son   and he begets

13. But those riches perish by bad venture; and he fathers a son, and there is nothing in his hand.

כַּאֲשֶׁר יָצָא מִבֶּטֶן אִמּוֹ עָרוֹם יָשׁוּב לָלֶכֶת כְּשֶׁבָּא
like that he came   to go   he will return   naked   his mother   from belly   he came out   when

וּמְאוּמָה לֹא־יִשָּׂא בַעֲמָלוֹ שֶׁיֹּלֵךְ בְּיָדוֹ:
in his hand   that he goes   in his labor   he lifts – not   and from speck

14. As he came forth from his mother's womb, naked shall he return to go as he came, and shall take nothing for his labor, which he may carry away in his hand.

וְגַם־זֹה רָעָה חוֹלָה כָּל־עֻמַּת שֶׁבָּא כֵּן יֵלֵךְ
he will go   thus   that comes   points – all   travailing   bad   this – and also

וּמַה־יִּתְרוֹן לוֹ שֶׁיַּעֲמֹל לָרוּחַ:
to soul   that he will labor   to him   profits – and what

15. And this also is a grievous evil, that in all points as he came, so shall he go; and what gains has he who has labored for the wind?

גַּם כָּל־יָמָיו בַּחֹשֶׁךְ יֹאכֵל וְכָעַס הַרְבֵּה וְחָלְיוֹ וָקָצֶף:
and wrathfulness   and his sickness   the many   and sorrow   he eats   in darkness   his days – all   also

16. All his days also he eats in darkness, and he has much sorrow and sickness and wrath.

הִנֵּה אֲשֶׁר־רָאִיתִי אָנִי טוֹב אֲשֶׁר־יָפֶה לֶאֱכוֹל־וְלִשְׁתּוֹת
and to drink – to eat   beautiful – which   good   I   I saw – which   here

וְלִרְאוֹת טוֹבָה בְּכָל־עֲמָלוֹ שֶׁיַּעֲמֹל תַּחַת־הַשֶּׁמֶשׁ
the sun – under   that he will labor   his labor – in all   goodness   and to see

מִסְפַּר יְמֵי־חַיָּו [חַיָּיו] אֲשֶׁר־נָתַן־לוֹ הָאֱלֹהִים כִּי־הוּא חֶלְקוֹ:
his portion   it – like   the Elohim   to you – he gives – which   his life – days   number

17. Behold that which I have seen; it is good and comely for one to eat and to drink, and to enjoy the good of all his labor in which he toils under the sun during the number of the days, which God gave him, because that is his portion.

גַּם כָּל־הָאָדָם אֲשֶׁר נָתַן־לוֹ הָאֱלֹהִים עֹשֶׁר וּנְכָסִים
and substances   wealth   the Elohim   to him – he gives   which   the Adam – all   also

וְהִשְׁלִיטוֹ לֶאֱכֹל מִמֶּנּוּ וְלָשֵׂאת אֶת־חֶלְקוֹ
and his power   to eat   from it   and carry away   his portion – that

וְלִשְׂמֹחַ בַּעֲמָלוֹ זֹה מַתַּת אֱלֹהִים הִיא:
and to be happy   in his labor   this   gift   Elohim   it

18. Every man also to whom God has given riches and wealth, and has given him power to eat of it, and to take his portion, and to rejoice in his labor; this is the gift of God.

כִּי לֹא הַרְבֵּה יִזְכֹּר אֶת־יְמֵי חַיָּיו
like   not   the many   he remembers   that – days   his life

כִּי הָאֱלֹהִים מַעֲנֶה בְּשִׂמְחַת לִבּוֹ:
like   the Elohim   humbling   in happiness   his heart

19. For he shall not much remember the days of his life, in which God provides him with the joy of his heart.

Chapter 6

מגילת קהלת פרק ו

יֵשׁ רָעָה אֲשֶׁר רָאִיתִי תַּחַת הַשָּׁמֶשׁ
there is   bad   which   I saw   under   the sun

וְרַבָּה הִיא עַל־הָאָדָם:
and much   it   upon – the Adam

1. There is an evil which I have seen under the sun, and it lies heavy upon men;

אִישׁ אֲשֶׁר יִתֶּן־לוֹ הָאֱלֹהִים עֹשֶׁר וּנְכָסִים וְכָבוֹד
man   which   he gives - to him   the Elohim   riches   and substances   and honor

וְאֵינֶנּוּ חָסֵר לְנַפְשׁוֹ מִכֹּל אֲשֶׁר־יִתְאַוֶּה
and they aren't   lacking   to his soul   from all   which - he desires

וְלֹא־יַשְׁלִיטֶנּוּ הָאֱלֹהִים לֶאֱכֹל מִמֶּנּוּ
and not - they give dominion   the Elohim   to eat   from it

כִּי אִישׁ נָכְרִי יֹאכֲלֶנּוּ זֶה הֶבֶל וָחֳלִי רָע הוּא:
like   man   stranger   they eat it   this   vanity   and disease   bad   it

2. A man to whom God has given riches, wealth, and honor, so that he lacks nothing for his soul of all that he desires, yet God does not give him power to eat of it, but a stranger eats it; this is vanity, and it is an evil disease.

אִם־יוֹלִיד אִישׁ מֵאָה וְשָׁנִים רַבּוֹת יִחְיֶה
if - he begets   man   one hundred   and years   many ones   he lives

וְרַב שֶׁיִּהְיוּ יְמֵי־שָׁנָיו וְנַפְשׁוֹ לֹא־תִשְׂבַּע מִן־הַטּוֹבָה
and many   that they will be   days - his years   and his soul   not - full it   from - the goodness

וְגַם־קְבוּרָה לֹא־הָיְתָה לּוֹ אָמַרְתִּי טוֹב מִמֶּנּוּ הַנָּפֶל:
and also - burial   not - it was   to him   I say   good   from it   the fall

3. If a man fathers one hundred children, and lives many years, so that the days of his years are many, and his soul is not content with the good, and he also has no burial; I say, that an untimely birth is better than he.

כִּי־בַהֶבֶל בָּא וּבַחֹשֶׁךְ יֵלֵךְ וּבַחֹשֶׁךְ שְׁמוֹ יְכֻסֶּה:
like - in vanity   comes   and in darkness   he goes   and in darkness   his name   it covers

4. For it comes in vanity, and departs in darkness, and his name shall be covered with darkness.

גַּם־שֶׁמֶשׁ לֹא־רָאָה וְלֹא יָדָע נַחַת לָזֶה מִזֶּה:
also - sun   not - he has seen   and not   he knows   rest   to this   from this

5. Moreover he has not seen the sun, nor known anything; this has more rest than the other.

וְאִלּוּ חָיָה אֶלֶף שָׁנִים פַּעֲמַיִם
and although   he lives   thousand   years   twice

ECCLESIASTES - CHAPTER 6

וְטוֹבָה לֹא רָאָה הֲלֹא אֶל־מָקוֹם אֶחָד הַכֹּל הוֹלֵךְ:
goes   the all   one   place - unto   the not?   he seen   not   and good

6. And though he live one thousand years twice told, yet has he seen no good; do not all go to one place?

כָּל־עֲמַל הָאָדָם לְפִיהוּ וְגַם־הַנֶּפֶשׁ לֹא תִמָּלֵא:
it filled   not   the soul - and also   to his mouth   the Adam   labor - all

7. All the labor of man is for his mouth, and yet the appetite is not filled.

כִּי מַה־יּוֹתֵר לֶחָכָם מִן־הַכְּסִיל
the fool – from   to wise   more – what   like

מַה־לֶּעָנִי יוֹדֵעַ לַהֲלֹךְ נֶגֶד הַחַיִּים:
the living ones   among   to walk   he knows   to humbled one - what

8. For what advantage has the wise man over the fool? What has the poor man who knows how to walk among the living?

טוֹב מַרְאֵה עֵינַיִם מֵהֲלָךְ־נָפֶשׁ גַּם־זֶה הֶבֶל וּרְעוּת רוּחַ:
spirit/wind   and striving   vanity   this – also   soul - from walking   eyes   from seeing   good

9. Better is the sight of the eyes than the wandering of the desire; this also is vanity and striving after wind.

מַה־שֶּׁהָיָה כְּבָר נִקְרָא שְׁמוֹ וְנוֹדָע אֲשֶׁר־הוּא אָדָם
Adam   he – which   and it known   his name   called   already   that has been - what

וְלֹא־יוּכַל לָדִין עִם שֶׁהִתַּקִּיף [שֶׁתַּקִּיף] מִמֶּנּוּ:
from he   that the mightier   if   to justice   can - and not

10. (K) That which has been was named already, and it is known what man is; nor may he contend with one who is mightier than he.

כִּי יֵשׁ־דְּבָרִים הַרְבֵּה מַרְבִּים הָבֶל מַה־יֹּתֵר לָאָדָם:
to Adam   more - what   vanity   from many ones   the many   speakings - there is   like

11. Seeing there are many things that increase vanity, what is man the better?

כִּי מִי־יוֹדֵעַ מַה־טּוֹב לָאָדָם בַּחַיִּים מִסְפַּר יְמֵי־חַיֵּי הֶבְלוֹ
his vanity   life – days   number   in lives   to Adam   good – what   knows – who   like

וְיַעֲשֵׂם כַּצֵּל אֲשֶׁר מִי־יַגִּיד לָאָדָם
to Adam   he tells - who   which   like shadow   and he does them

מַה־יִּהְיֶה אַחֲרָיו תַּחַת הַשָּׁמֶשׁ:
the sun   under   after him   will be – what

12. For who knows what is good for man in this life, all the days of his vain life which he spends like a shadow? for who can tell a man what shall be after him under the sun?

Chapter 7

מגילת קהלת פרק ז

טוֹב שֵׁם מִשֶּׁמֶן טוֹב וְיוֹם הַמָּוֶת מִיּוֹם הִוָּלְדוֹ:
good   name   from oil   good   and day   the death   from day   his birth

1. A good name is better than precious ointment; and the day of death than the day of one's birth.

טוֹב לָלֶכֶת אֶל־בֵּית־אֵבֶל מִלֶּכֶת אֶל־בֵּית מִשְׁתֶּה
good   to go   unto - mourning house   from going   unto - house   feasting

בַּאֲשֶׁר הוּא סוֹף כָּל־הָאָדָם וְהַחַי יִתֵּן אֶל־לִבּוֹ:
in which   it   end   all - the Adam   and the life   it gives   unto - his heart

2. It is better to go to the house of mourning, than to go to the house of feasting; for that is the end of all men; and the living will lay it to his heart.

טוֹב כַּעַס מִשְּׂחוֹק כִּי־בְרֹעַ פָּנִים יִיטַב לֵב:
good   vexation   from laughter   like - in badness   faces   it betters   heart

3. Sorrow is better than laughter; for by the sadness of the countenance the heart is made better.

לֵב חֲכָמִים בְּבֵית אֵבֶל וְלֵב כְּסִילִים בְּבֵית שִׂמְחָה:
heart   wise ones   in house   mourning   and heart   fool ones   in house   happiness

4. The heart of the wise is in the house of mourning; but the heart of fools is in the house of mirth.

טוֹב לִשְׁמֹעַ גַּעֲרַת חָכָם מֵאִישׁ שֹׁמֵעַ שִׁיר כְּסִילִים:
good   to hear   rebuke   wise   from man   hears   song   fool ones

5. It is better to hear the rebuke of the wise, than for a man to hear the song of fools.

כִּי כְקוֹל הַסִּירִים תַּחַת הַסִּיר כֵּן שְׂחֹק הַכְּסִיל וְגַם־זֶה הָבֶל:
like   like sound   the thorns   under   the pot   thus   laughter   the fool   and also - this   vanity

6. For as the crackling of thorns under a pot, so is the laughter of the fool; this also is vanity.

כִּי הָעֹשֶׁק יְהוֹלֵל חָכָם וִיאַבֵּד אֶת־לֵב מַתָּנָה:
like   the oppression   it boasts   wise   and it destroys   that - heart   gift

7. Surely oppression makes a wise man mad; and a bribe destroys the heart.

טוֹב אַחֲרִית דָּבָר מֵרֵאשִׁיתוֹ טוֹב אֶרֶךְ־רוּחַ מִגְּבַהּ־רוּחַ:
good   after   matter   from his beginning   good   long - spirit   from proud - spirit

8. Better is the end of a thing than its beginning; and the patient in spirit is better than the proud in spirit.

אַל־תְּבַהֵל בְּרוּחֲךָ לִכְעוֹס כִּי כַעַס בְּחֵיק כְּסִילִים יָנוּחַ:
don't - hasty   in your spirit   to be angry   like   anger   in bosom   fool ones   it rests

9. Be not hasty in your spirit to be angry; for anger rests in the bosom of fools.

אַל־תֹּאמַר מֶה הָיָה שֶׁהַיָּמִים הָרִאשֹׁנִים הָיוּ טוֹבִים מֵאֵלֶּה
from these   good ones   they were   the beginning ones   that the days   has been   what   you say - don't

כִּי לֹא מֵחָכְמָה שָׁאַלְתָּ עַל־זֶה:
this - upon   you ask   from wisdom   not   like

10. Do not say, Why were the former days better than these? because you are not asking this from wisdom.

טוֹבָה חָכְמָה עִם־נַחֲלָה וְיֹתֵר לְרֹאֵי הַשָּׁמֶשׁ:
the sun   to see   and gains   inheritance – with   wisdom   better

11. Wisdom is good with an inheritance; and by it there are gains to those who see the sun.

כִּי בְּצֵל הַחָכְמָה בְּצֵל הַכָּסֶף
the silver   in shade   the wisdom   in shade   like

וְיִתְרוֹן דַּעַת הַחָכְמָה תְּחַיֶּה בְעָלֶיהָ:
in its elevation   you live   the wisdom   knowledge   and profits

12. For wisdom is a defense, and money is a defense; and the advantage of knowledge is that wisdom gives life to those who have it.

רְאֵה אֶת־מַעֲשֵׂה הָאֱלֹהִים
the Elohim   work – that   see

כִּי מִי יוּכַל לְתַקֵּן אֵת אֲשֶׁר עִוְּתוֹ:
his bent   which   that   to straighten   he able   who   like

13. Consider the work of God; for who can make that straight, what he has made crooked?

בְּיוֹם טוֹבָה הֱיֵה בְטוֹב וּבְיוֹם רָעָה רְאֵה
see   bad   and in day   in good   it be   better   in day

גַּם אֶת־זֶה לְעֻמַּת־זֶה עָשָׂה הָאֱלֹהִים
the Elohim   made   this - to corresponding   this – that   also

עַל־דִּבְרַת שֶׁלֹּא יִמְצָא הָאָדָם אַחֲרָיו מְאוּמָה:
from speck   his after   the Adam   he finds   that not   matters – upon

14. In the day of prosperity be joyful, but in the day of adversity consider; God has made the one as well as the other, to the end that man should find nothing after him.

אֶת־הַכֹּל רָאִיתִי בִּימֵי הֶבְלִי יֵשׁ צַדִּיק אֹבֵד בְּצִדְקוֹ
in his righteousness   perishes   righteous   there is   my vanities   in days   I saw   the all - that

וְיֵשׁ רָשָׁע מַאֲרִיךְ בְּרָעָתוֹ:
in his badness   prolongs   wicked   and there is

15. All things have I seen in the days of my vanity; there is a just man who perishes in his righteousness, and there is a wicked man who prolongs his life in his wickedness.

אַל־תְּהִי צַדִּיק הַרְבֵּה וְאַל־תִּתְחַכַּם יוֹתֵר לָמָּה תִּשּׁוֹמֵם:
you be desolate yourself   why   more   you be wise - and don't   the much   righteous   you be - don't

16. Do not be too righteous; nor make yourself too wise; why should you destroy yourself?

אַל־תִּרְשַׁע הַרְבֵּה וְאַל־תְּהִי סָכָל לָמָּה תָמוּת בְּלֹא עִתֶּךָ:
your season in not you die why foolish you be - and don't the much you be wicked - don't

17. Do not be too wicked, nor be foolish; why should you die before your time?

טוֹב אֲשֶׁר תֶּאֱחֹז בָּזֶה וְגַם־מִזֶּה אַל־תַּנַּח אֶת־יָדֶךָ
your hand – that you let stop - don't from this - and also in this you seize which good

כִּי־יְרֵא אֱלֹהִים יֵצֵא אֶת־כֻּלָּם:
them all – that he comes out Elohim fear - like

18. It is good that you should take hold of this; but do not withdraw your hand from that either; for he who fears God shall come forth from them all.

הַחָכְמָה תָּעֹז לֶחָכָם מֵעֲשָׂרָה שַׁלִּיטִים אֲשֶׁר הָיוּ בָּעִיר:
in city they are which ruler ones from ten to wise it strengthens the wisdom

19. Wisdom strengthens the wise more than ten rulers who are in the city.

כִּי אָדָם אֵין צַדִּיק בָּאָרֶץ אֲשֶׁר יַעֲשֶׂה־טּוֹב וְלֹא יֶחֱטָא:
he sins and not good – he does which in earth righteous isn't Adam like

20. For there is not a just man upon earth, that does good, and does not sin.

גַּם לְכָל־הַדְּבָרִים אֲשֶׁר יְדַבֵּרוּ אַל־תִּתֵּן לִבֶּךָ
your heart give - don't they speak which the speakings - to all also

אֲשֶׁר לֹא־תִשְׁמַע אֶת־עַבְדְּךָ מְקַלְלֶךָ:
from curse you your servant - that you hear – not which

21. Also take no heed to all words that are spoken; lest you hear your servant curse you;

כִּי גַּם־פְּעָמִים רַבּוֹת יָדַע לִבֶּךָ
your heart it knows many ones several times – also like

אֲשֶׁר גַּם־אַתְּ [אַתָּה] קִלַּלְתָּ אֲחֵרִים:
other ones you cursed you – also which

22. For many times has your heart known that you yourself have cursed others.

כָּל־זֹה נִסִּיתִי בַחָכְמָה אָמַרְתִּי אֶחְכָּמָה וְהִיא רְחוֹקָה מִמֶּנִּי:
from me to far and it I will be wise I said in wisdom I proved this – all

23. All this have I proved by wisdom; I said, I will be wise; but it was far from me.

רָחוֹק מַה־שֶּׁהָיָה וְעָמֹק עָמֹק מִי יִמְצָאֶנּוּ:
he finds it who deep and deep that was – what far

24. That which is far off, and very deep, who can find it out.

סַבּוֹתִי אֲנִי וְלִבִּי לָדַעַת וְלָתוּר וּבַקֵּשׁ חָכְמָה וְחֶשְׁבּוֹן
and accounting wisdom and seek and to search out to knowledge and my heart I I surrounded

וְלָדַעַת רֶשַׁע כֶּסֶל וְהַסִּכְלוּת הוֹלֵלוֹת:
madnesses and the foolishnesses fool wicked and to know

25. I applied my heart to know, and to search, and to seek out wisdom, and the reason of things, and to know the wickedness of folly and foolishness which is madness;

וּמוֹצֶ֨א אֲנִ֜י מַ֣ר מִמָּ֗וֶת אֶת־הָֽאִשָּׁ֞ה
and find   I   bitter   from death   the woman – that

אֲשֶׁר־הִ֨יא מְצוֹדִ֧ים וַחֲרָמִ֛ים לִבָּ֖הּ אֲסוּרִ֣ים יָדֶ֑יהָ
she – which   snares   and nets   her heart   bindings   her hand

ט֞וֹב לִפְנֵ֤י הָאֱלֹהִים֙ יִמָּלֵ֣ט מִמֶּ֔נָּה
good   before   the Elohim   he will escape   from her

וְחוֹטֵ֖א יִלָּ֥כֶד בָּֽהּ׃
and sinner   he will be caught   in her

26. And I find more bitter than death the woman, whose heart is snares and nets, and her hands are fetters; whoever pleases God shall escape from her; but the sinner shall be caught by her.

רְאֵה֙ זֶ֣ה מָצָ֔אתִי אָמְרָ֖ה קֹהֶ֑לֶת אַחַ֥ת לְאַחַ֖ת לִמְצֹ֥א חֶשְׁבּֽוֹן׃
see   this   I found   I say   Kohelet   one   to one   to find   accounting

27. Behold, this have I found, said Kohelet, counting one thing to another to find out the sum;

אֲשֶׁ֛ר עוֹד־בִּקְשָׁ֥ה נַפְשִׁ֖י
which   seek – again   my soul

וְלֹ֣א מָצָ֑אתִי אָדָ֞ם אֶחָ֤ד מֵאֶ֙לֶף֙ מָצָ֔אתִי
and not   I found   Adam   one   from thousand   I found

וְאִשָּׁ֥ה בְכָל־אֵ֖לֶּה לֹ֥א מָצָֽאתִי׃
and woman   these – in all   not   I found

28. Which yet my soul seeks, but I find not; one man among a thousand have I found; but a woman among all those have I not found.

לְבַד֙ רְאֵה־זֶ֣ה מָצָ֔אתִי אֲשֶׁ֨ר עָשָׂ֧ה הָאֱלֹהִ֛ים אֶת־הָאָדָ֖ם יָשָׁ֑ר
alone   this – see   I found   which   made   the Elohim   the Adam – that   upright

וְהֵ֥מָּה בִקְשׁ֖וּ חִשְּׁבֹנ֥וֹת רַבִּֽים׃
and they   they sought   accounting ones   many

29. Behold, only this have I found, that God has made man upright; but they have sought out many schemes.

Chapter 8

מגילת קהלת פרק ח

מִי־כְּהֶחָכָם וּמִי יוֹדֵעַ פֵּשֶׁר דָּבָר
like the wise - who   and who   knows   interpretation   matter

חָכְמַת אָדָם תָּאִיר פָּנָיו וְעֹז פָּנָיו יְשֻׁנֶּא:
wisdom   Adam   it lights up   his face   and strength   his face   changed

1. Who is like the wise man? and who knows the meaning of a matter? A man's wisdom makes his face shine, and the boldness of his face is changed.

אֲנִי פִּי־מֶלֶךְ שְׁמוֹר וְעַל דִּבְרַת שְׁבוּעַת אֱלֹהִים:
I   king – mouth   heed   and upon   matters   oaths   Elohim

2. I keep the king's commandment, and in the manner of an oath of God.

אַל־תִּבָּהֵל מִפָּנָיו תֵּלֵךְ אַל־תַּעֲמֹד בְּדָבָר רָע
don't - be hasty   from facing him   you walk   don't - you stand   in matter   bad

כִּי כָּל־אֲשֶׁר יַחְפֹּץ יַעֲשֶׂה:
like   all – which   he purposes   he does

3. Do not be hasty to leave his presence; stand not in an evil thing; for he does whatever pleases him.

בַּאֲשֶׁר דְּבַר־מֶלֶךְ שִׁלְטוֹן וּמִי יֹאמַר־לוֹ מַה־תַּעֲשֶׂה:
in which   speech – king   authority   and who   he says – to him   what - you do

4. For in the word of a king there is authority; and who may say to him, What do you do?

שׁוֹמֵר מִצְוָה לֹא יֵדַע דָּבָר רָע
heed   commandment   not   know   matter   bad

וְעֵת וּמִשְׁפָּט יֵדַע לֵב חָכָם:
and time   and judgment   knows   heart   wise

5. Whoever keeps the commandment shall feel no evil thing; and a wise man's heart discerns both time and judgment.

כִּי לְכָל־חֵפֶץ יֵשׁ עֵת וּמִשְׁפָּט
like   to all - purpose   there is   time   and judgment

כִּי־רָעַת הָאָדָם רַבָּה עָלָיו:
like - bad ones   the Adam   much   upon him

6. Because to every purpose there is time and judgment, though the misery of man is great upon him.

כִּי־אֵינֶנּוּ יֹדֵעַ מַה־שֶּׁיִּהְיֶה
like - isn't you   he knows   what – that will be

כִּי כַּאֲשֶׁר יִהְיֶה מִי יַגִּיד לוֹ:
like   when   will be   who   he tells   to him

7. For he knows not that which shall be; for who can tell him when it shall be?

אֵין אָדָם שַׁלִּיט בָּרוּחַ לִכְלוֹא אֶת־הָרוּחַ
the wind - that   to retain   in wind   governor   Adam   isn't

וְאֵין שִׁלְטוֹן בְּיוֹם הַמָּוֶת וְאֵין מִשְׁלַחַת בַּמִּלְחָמָה
in war   dismissal   and isn't   the death   in day   authority   and isn't

וְלֹא־יְמַלֵּט רֶשַׁע אֶת־בְּעָלָיו:
his master – that   wickedness   he escapes - and not

8. There is no man who has power over the wind to retain the wind; nor has he authority over the day of death; and there is no discharge in that war; nor shall wickedness deliver those who are given to it.

אֶת־כָּל־זֶה רָאִיתִי וְנָתוֹן אֶת־לִבִּי לְכָל־מַעֲשֶׂה
works - to all   my heart – that   and giver   I saw   this - all - that

אֲשֶׁר נַעֲשָׂה תַּחַת הַשָּׁמֶשׁ
the sun   under   done   which

עֵת אֲשֶׁר שָׁלַט הָאָדָם בְּאָדָם לְרַע לוֹ:
to him   to bad   in Adam   the Adam   rule   which   time

9. All this have I seen, and gave my heart to every work that is done under the sun; there is a time when one man rules over another to his own hurt.

וּבְכֵן רָאִיתִי רְשָׁעִים קְבֻרִים וָבָאוּ וּמִמְּקוֹם קָדוֹשׁ יְהַלֵּכוּ
they went   holy   and from place   and they came   buried ones   wicked ones   I saw   and in thus

וְיִשְׁתַּכְּחוּ בָעִיר אֲשֶׁר כֵּן־עָשׂוּ גַּם־זֶה הָבֶל:
vanity   this-also   they did – thus   which   in city   and they forgot

10. And so I saw the wicked buried, who had come and gone from the holy place, and they were forgotten in the city where they had so done; this also is vanity.

אֲשֶׁר אֵין־נַעֲשָׂה פִתְגָם מַעֲשֵׂה הָרָעָה מְהֵרָה
quickly   the bad   works   decree   done - isn't   which

עַל־כֵּן מָלֵא לֵב בְּנֵי־הָאָדָם בָּהֶם לַעֲשׂוֹת רָע:
bad   to doings   in them   the Adam - sons   heart   full   thus - upon

11. Because sentence against an evil work is not executed speedily, the heart of the sons of men is fully set in them to do evil.

אֲשֶׁר חֹטֶא עֹשֶׂה רָע מְאַת וּמַאֲרִיךְ לוֹ
to him   and prolonged   one hundred   bad   doer   sinner   which

כִּי גַּם־יוֹדֵעַ אָנִי אֲשֶׁר יִהְיֶה־טּוֹב לְיִרְאֵי הָאֱלֹהִים
the Elohim   to fearing   good – it will be   which   I   know – also   like

אֲשֶׁר יִירְאוּ מִלְּפָנָיו:
from before him   they will fear   which

12. Though a sinner does evil one hundred times, and his days are prolonged, yet surely

I know that it shall be well with those who fear God, who fear before him;

וְטוֹב לֹא־יִהְיֶה לָרָשָׁע וְלֹא־יַאֲרִיךְ יָמִים כַּצֵּל
like shade — days — he will prolong - and not — to wicked — will be – not — and good

אֲשֶׁר אֵינֶנּוּ יָרֵא מִלִּפְנֵי אֱלֹהִים׃
Elohim — from before — fear — he isn't — which

13. But it shall not be well with the wicked, nor shall he prolong his days, which are like a shadow; because he does not fear before God.

יֶשׁ־הֶבֶל אֲשֶׁר נַעֲשָׂה עַל־הָאָרֶץ
the earth - upon — done — which — vanity - there is

אֲשֶׁר יֵשׁ צַדִּיקִים אֲשֶׁר מַגִּיעַ אֲלֵהֶם כְּמַעֲשֵׂה הָרְשָׁעִים
the wicked ones — like deeds — onto them — occurs — which — righteous ones — there is — which

וְיֵשׁ רְשָׁעִים שֶׁמַּגִּיעַ אֲלֵהֶם כְּמַעֲשֵׂה הַצַּדִּיקִים
the righteous ones — like deeds — onto them — that touches — wicked ones — and there is

אָמַרְתִּי שֶׁגַּם־זֶה הָבֶל׃
vanity — this - that also — I said

14. There is a vanity which is done upon the earth; that there are just men, to whom it happens according to the deeds of the wicked; again, there are wicked men, to whom it happens according to the deeds of the righteous; I said that this also is vanity.

וְשִׁבַּחְתִּי אֲנִי אֶת־הַשִּׂמְחָה
the happiness – that — I — and commended

אֲשֶׁר אֵין־טוֹב לָאָדָם תַּחַת הַשֶּׁמֶשׁ
the sun — under — to Adam — good - isn't — which

כִּי אִם־לֶאֱכֹל וְלִשְׁתּוֹת וְלִשְׂמוֹחַ
and to be happy — and to drink — to eat – with — like

וְהוּא יִלְוֶנּוּ בַעֲמָלוֹ יְמֵי חַיָּיו
his life — days — in his labor — they will join — and he

אֲשֶׁר־נָתַן־לוֹ הָאֱלֹהִים תַּחַת הַשָּׁמֶשׁ׃
the sun — under — the Elohim — to him - gives – which

15. And I commended mirth, because a man has no better thing under the sun, than to eat, and to drink, and to be merry; for this will go with him in his labor during the days of his life, which God gives him under the sun.

כַּאֲשֶׁר נָתַתִּי אֶת־לִבִּי לָדַעַת חָכְמָה
wisdom — to know — my heart – that — I gave — when

וְלִרְאוֹת אֶת־הָעִנְיָן אֲשֶׁר נַעֲשָׂה עַל־הָאָרֶץ
the earth - upon — done — which — the experience – that — and to see

כִּי גַם בַּיּוֹם וּבַלַּיְלָה שֵׁנָה בְּעֵינָיו אֵינֶנּוּ רֹאֶה׃
like   also   in day   and in night   sleep   in his eyes   they aren't   seeing

16. When I gave my heart to know wisdom, and to see the business that is done upon the earth; for neither by day nor by night one's eyes see sleep,

וְרָאִיתִי אֶת־כָּל־מַעֲשֵׂה הָאֱלֹהִים כִּי לֹא יוּכַל הָאָדָם לִמְצוֹא
and I saw   that – all - works   the Elohim   like   not   able   the Adam   to find

אֶת־הַמַּעֲשֶׂה אֲשֶׁר נַעֲשָׂה תַחַת־הַשֶּׁמֶשׁ
that - the works   which   done   under – the sun

בְּשֶׁל אֲשֶׁר יַעֲמֹל הָאָדָם לְבַקֵּשׁ וְלֹא יִמְצָא
in that of   which   he labors   the Adam   to seek   and not   he will find

וְגַם אִם־יֹאמַר הֶחָכָם לָדַעַת לֹא יוּכַל לִמְצֹא׃
and also   if - he says   the wise   to know   not   able   to find

17. And I saw all the work of God, for a man cannot find out the work that is done under the sun; because though a man would labor to seek it out, yet he shall not find it; , and also if a wise man claims to know it, yet shall he not be able to find it.

Chapter 9

מגילת קהלת פרק ט

כִּי אֶת־כָּל־זֶה נָתַתִּי אֶל־לִבִּי וְלָבוּר אֶת־כָּל־זֶה
  this – all – that and to clarify my heart – unto I gave this – all – that like

אֲשֶׁר הַצַּדִּיקִים וְהַחֲכָמִים וַעֲבָדֵיהֶם בְּיַד מִן הָאֱלֹהִים
the Elohim from in hand and their service and the wise ones the righteous ones which

גַּם־אַהֲבָה גַם־שִׂנְאָה אֵין יוֹדֵעַ הָאָדָם הַכֹּל לִפְנֵיהֶם:
before them the all the Adam know isn't hate – also love - also

1. For all this I laid to my heart, and sought to clarify all this, that the righteous, and the wise, and their deeds, are in the hand of God; no man knows whether it is love or hatred; all is before them.

הַכֹּל כַּאֲשֶׁר לַכֹּל מִקְרֶה אֶחָד
one event to all when the all

לַצַּדִּיק וְלָרָשָׁע לַטּוֹב וְלַטָּהוֹר וְלַטָּמֵא
and to defiled and to clean to good and to wicked to righteous

וְלַזֹּבֵחַ וְלַאֲשֶׁר אֵינֶנּוּ זֹבֵחַ כַּטּוֹב כַּחֹטֶא
like sinner like good offering sacrifice isn't them and to which and to offering sacrifice

הַנִּשְׁבָּע כַּאֲשֶׁר שְׁבוּעָה יָרֵא:
fear oath when the swearer

2. All things come alike to all; there is one event to the righteous, and to the wicked; to the good and to the pure, and to the impure; to him who sacrifices, and to him who does not sacrifices; as is the good man, so is the sinner; and he who swears as he who shuns an oath.

זֶה רָע בְּכֹל אֲשֶׁר־נַעֲשָׂה תַּחַת הַשֶּׁמֶשׁ כִּי־מִקְרֶה אֶחָד לַכֹּל
to all one event – like the sun under done – which in all bad this

וְגַם לֵב בְּנֵי־הָאָדָם מָלֵא־רָע וְהוֹלֵלוֹת בִּלְבָבָם בְּחַיֵּיהֶם
in their life in their hearts and madness bad – full the Adam – sons heart and also

וְאַחֲרָיו אֶל־הַמֵּתִים:
the dead ones – unto and his after

3. This is an evil among all things that are done under the sun, that there is one event to all; also the heart of the sons of men is full of evil, and madness is in their heart while they live, and after that they go to the dead.

כִּי־מִי אֲשֶׁר יְבֻחַר [יְחֻבַּר] אֶל כָּל־הַחַיִּים יֵשׁ בִּטָּחוֹן
in trust there is the live ones - all unto he be joined which who - like

כִּי־לְכֶלֶב חַי הוּא טוֹב מִן־הָאַרְיֵה הַמֵּת
the dead the lion – from good it life to dog - like

4. (K) For to him who is joined to all the living there is hope; for a living dog is better

than a dead lion.

כִּי הַחַיִּים יוֹדְעִים שֶׁיָּמֻתוּ
that they will die · knowing ones · the living ones · like

וְהַמֵּתִים אֵינָם יוֹדְעִים מְאוּמָה
from speck · knowing ones · they aren't · and the dead ones

וְאֵין־עוֹד לָהֶם שָׂכָר כִּי נִשְׁכַּח זִכְרָם׃
their memory · forgotten · like · reward · to them · again - and isn't

5. For the living know that they shall die; but the dead know nothing, nor do they have a reward any more; for the memory of them is forgotten.

גַּם אַהֲבָתָם גַּם־שִׂנְאָתָם גַּם־קִנְאָתָם כְּבָר אָבָדָה
perished · already · their jealousy – also · their hatred – also · their love · also

וְחֵלֶק אֵין־לָהֶם עוֹד לְעוֹלָם בְּכֹל אֲשֶׁר־נַעֲשָׂה תַּחַת הַשָּׁמֶשׁ׃
the sun · under · done – which · in all · to forever · again · to them - isn't · and portion

6. Also their love, and their hatred, and their envy, is now perished; nor have they any more a portion for ever in any thing that is done under the sun.

לֵךְ אֱכֹל בְּשִׂמְחָה לַחְמֶךָ וּשְׁתֵה בְלֶב־טוֹב יֵינֶךָ
your wine · good - in heart · and drink · your bread · in happiness · eat · go

כִּי כְבָר רָצָה הָאֱלֹהִים אֶת־מַעֲשֶׂיךָ׃
your works – that · the Elohim · pleased · already · like

7. Go your way, eat your bread with joy, and drink your wine with a merry heart; for God has already accepted your works.

בְּכָל־עֵת יִהְיוּ בְגָדֶיךָ לְבָנִים וְשֶׁמֶן עַל־רֹאשְׁךָ אַל־יֶחְסָר׃
it lack - don't · your head – upon · and oil · white ones · your clothing · they be · season – in all

8. Let your garments be always white; and let your head lack no ointment.

רְאֵה חַיִּים עִם־אִשָּׁה אֲשֶׁר־אָהַבְתָּ כָּל־יְמֵי חַיֵּי הֶבְלֶךָ
your vanity · life · days - all · you love – which · wife – with · life · see

אֲשֶׁר נָתַן־לְךָ תַּחַת הַשֶּׁמֶשׁ כֹּל יְמֵי הֶבְלֶךָ
your vanity · days · all · the sun · under · to you – given · which

כִּי הוּא חֶלְקְךָ בַּחַיִּים
in life · your portion · it · like

וּבַעֲמָלְךָ אֲשֶׁר־אַתָּה עָמֵל תַּחַת הַשָּׁמֶשׁ׃
the sun · under · labor · you – which · and in your labor

9. Live joyfully with the wife whom you love all the days of the life of your vanity, which he has given you under the sun, all the days of your vanity; for that is your portion in life, and in your labor in which you labor under the sun.

כֹּל אֲשֶׁר תִּמְצָא יָדְךָ לַעֲשׂוֹת בְּכֹחֲךָ עֲשֵׂה
כִּי אֵין מַעֲשֶׂה וְחֶשְׁבּוֹן וְדַעַת וְחָכְמָה
בִּשְׁאוֹל אֲשֶׁר אַתָּה הֹלֵךְ שָׁמָּה:

10. Whatever your hand finds to do, do it with your strength; for there is no work, nor scheme, nor knowledge, nor wisdom, in Sheol, to which you are going.

שַׁבְתִּי וְרָאֹה תַחַת־הַשֶּׁמֶשׁ כִּי לֹא לַקַּלִּים הַמֵּרוֹץ
וְלֹא לַגִּבּוֹרִים הַמִּלְחָמָה וְגַם לֹא לַחֲכָמִים לֶחֶם
וְגַם לֹא לַנְּבֹנִים עֹשֶׁר וְגַם לֹא לַיֹּדְעִים חֵן
כִּי־עֵת וָפֶגַע יִקְרֶה אֶת־כֻּלָּם:

11. I returned, and saw under the sun, that the race is not to the swift, nor the battle to the strong, nor yet bread to the wise, nor yet riches to men of understanding, nor yet favor to men of skill; but time and chance happens to them all.

כִּי גַּם לֹא־יֵדַע הָאָדָם אֶת־עִתּוֹ
כַּדָּגִים שֶׁנֶּאֱחָזִים בִּמְצוֹדָה רָעָה
וְכַצִּפֳּרִים הָאֲחֻזוֹת בַּפָּח כָּהֵם יוּקָשִׁים
בְּנֵי הָאָדָם לְעֵת רָעָה כְּשֶׁתִּפּוֹל עֲלֵיהֶם פִּתְאֹם:

12. For man also does not know his time; like the fishes that are taken in an evil net, and like the birds that are caught in the trap; so are the sons of men snared in an evil time, when it falls suddenly upon them.

גַּם־זֹה רָאִיתִי חָכְמָה תַּחַת הַשָּׁמֶשׁ וּגְדוֹלָה הִיא אֵלָי:

13. This wisdom have I seen also under the sun, and it seemed great unto me;

עִיר קְטַנָּה וַאֲנָשִׁים בָּהּ מְעָט וּבָא־אֵלֶיהָ מֶלֶךְ גָּדוֹל
וְסָבַב אֹתָהּ וּבָנָה עָלֶיהָ מְצוֹדִים גְּדֹלִים:

14. There was a little city, and few men in it; and there came a great king against it, and besieged it, and built great siege works against it;

וּמָצָא בָהּ אִישׁ מִסְכֵּן חָכָם וּמִלַּט־הוּא אֶת־הָעִיר בְּחָכְמָתוֹ
in his wisdom / the city - that / he – and escaped / wise / frugal / man / in it / and found

וְאָדָם לֹא זָכַר אֶת־הָאִישׁ הַמִּסְכֵּן הַהוּא׃
the he / the frugal / the man - that / remembered / not / and Adam

15. And a poor wise man was found in it, and he by his wisdom delivered the city; yet no man remembered that poor man.

וְאָמַרְתִּי אָנִי טוֹבָה חָכְמָה מִגְּבוּרָה וְחָכְמַת הַמִּסְכֵּן בְּזוּיָה
despised / the poor / and wisdom / from might / wise / better / I / and said

וּדְבָרָיו אֵינָם נִשְׁמָעִים׃
heard ones / they aren't / and his speaking

16. And said I, Wisdom is better than might; but the poor man's wisdom is despised, and his words are not heard.

דִּבְרֵי חֲכָמִים בְּנַחַת נִשְׁמָעִים מִזַּעֲקַת מוֹשֵׁל בַּכְּסִילִים׃
in foolish ones / ruler / from outcry / heard ones / in resting / wise ones / speech

17. The words of wise men are heard in quiet more than the shouting of him who rules among fools.

טוֹבָה חָכְמָה מִכְּלֵי קְרָב וְחוֹטֶא אֶחָד יְאַבֵּד טוֹבָה הַרְבֵּה׃
the much / good / he perishes / one / and sinner / attack / from instruments / wisdom / better

18. Wisdom is better than weapons of war; but one sinner destroys much good.

Chapter 10

מגילת קהלת פרק י

זְבוּבֵי מָוֶת יַבְאִישׁ יַבִּיעַ שֶׁמֶן רוֹקֵחַ יָקָר
valuable   perfume   oil   it emits   it stinks   dead   flys

מֵחָכְמָה מִכָּבוֹד סִכְלוּת מְעָט:
little   foolish ones   from honor   from wisdom

1. Dead flies cause the ointment of the perfumer to send forth a foul smell; so does a little folly outweigh wisdom and honor.

לֵב חָכָם לִימִינוֹ וְלֵב כְּסִיל לִשְׂמֹאלוֹ:
to his left   fool   and heart   to his right   wise   heart

2. A wise man's heart inclines him to his right hand; but a fool's heart to his left.

וְגַם־בַּדֶּרֶךְ כְּשֶׁהַסָּכָל [כְּשֶׁסָּכָל] הֹלֵךְ לִבּוֹ חָסֵר
lacking   his heart   he walks   like that the fool   in way - and also

וְאָמַר לַכֹּל סָכָל הוּא:
he   fool   to all   and he says

3. (K) And also, on the road, when a fool walks by, his understanding fails him, and he says to every one that he is a fool.

אִם־רוּחַ הַמּוֹשֵׁל תַּעֲלֶה עָלֶיךָ מְקוֹמְךָ אַל־תַּנַּח
leave - don't   your place   upon you   it rises up   the ruler   spirit – if

כִּי מַרְפֵּא יַנִּיחַ חֲטָאִים גְּדוֹלִים:
large ones   sins   it rests   healing   like

4. If the spirit of the ruler rises against you, leave not your place; for deference pacifies great offenses.

יֵשׁ רָעָה רָאִיתִי תַּחַת הַשָּׁמֶשׁ
the sun   under   I saw   bad   there is

כִּשְׁגָגָה שֶׁיֹּצָא מִלִּפְנֵי הַשַּׁלִּיט:
the ruler   from before   that goes forth   like error

5. There is an evil which I have seen under the sun, as an error which proceeds from the ruler;

נִתַּן הַסֶּכֶל בַּמְּרוֹמִים רַבִּים וַעֲשִׁירִים בַּשֵּׁפֶל יֵשֵׁבוּ:
they sit   in low rank   and rich ones   many   in high places   the foolish   he gives

6. Folly is set in great dignity, and the rich sit in low place.

רָאִיתִי עֲבָדִים עַל־סוּסִים
horses – upon   servant ones   I have seen

וְשָׂרִים הֹלְכִים כַּעֲבָדִים עַל־הָאָרֶץ:
the earth - upon   like servant ones   them walking   and princes

7. I have seen servants upon horses, and princes walking as servants upon the earth.

ECCLESIASTES - CHAPTER 10

חֹפֵר גּוּמָץ בּוֹ יִפּוֹל וּפֹרֵץ גָּדֵר יִשְּׁכֶנּוּ נָחָשׁ:

8. He who digs a pit shall fall into it; and whoever breaks a hedge, a serpent shall bite him.

מַסִּיעַ אֲבָנִים יֵעָצֵב בָּהֶם בּוֹקֵעַ עֵצִים יִסָּכֶן בָּם:

9. He who removes stones shall be hurt by them; and he who chops wood shall be endangered by that.

אִם־קֵהָה הַבַּרְזֶל וְהוּא לֹא־פָנִים קִלְקַל וַחֲיָלִים יְגַבֵּר וְיִתְרוֹן הַכְשֵׁיר חָכְמָה:

10. If the iron is blunt, and one does not whet the edge, he must apply more strength; but wisdom increases skill.

אִם־יִשֹּׁךְ הַנָּחָשׁ בְּלוֹא־לָחַשׁ וְאֵין יִתְרוֹן לְבַעַל הַלָּשׁוֹן:

11. If the serpent bites before it is charmed, there is no advantage in a charmer.

דִּבְרֵי פִי־חָכָם חֵן וְשִׂפְתוֹת כְּסִיל תְּבַלְּעֶנּוּ:

12. The words of a wise man's mouth are gracious; but the lips of a fool will swallow up himself.

תְּחִלַּת דִּבְרֵי־פִיהוּ סִכְלוּת וְאַחֲרִית פִּיהוּ הוֹלֵלוּת רָעָה:

13. The beginning of the words of his mouth is foolishness; and the end of his talk is evil madness.

וְהַסָּכָל יַרְבֶּה דְבָרִים לֹא־יֵדַע הָאָדָם מַה־שֶּׁיִּהְיֶה וַאֲשֶׁר יִהְיֶה מֵאַחֲרָיו מִי יַגִּיד לוֹ:

14. A fool is full of words; a man cannot tell what shall be; and what shall be after him, who can tell him?

עֲמַל הַכְּסִילִים תְּיַגְּעֶנּוּ אֲשֶׁר לֹא־יָדַע לָלֶכֶת אֶל־עִיר:

15. The labor of fools wearies him, for he does not know how to go to the city.

אִי־לָךְ אֶרֶץ שֶׁמַּלְכֵּךְ נָעַר וְשָׂרַיִךְ בַּבֹּקֶר יֹאכֵלוּ:

16. Woe to you, O land, when your king is a child, and your princes dine in the morning!

אַשְׁרֵיךְ אֶרֶץ שֶׁמַּלְכֵּךְ בֶּן־חוֹרִים

וְשָׂרַיִךְ   בָּעֵת   יֹאכֵלוּ בִּגְבוּרָה וְלֹא בַשְּׁתִי׃
and your princes in season they eat   in might   and not in drunkenness

17. Happy are you, O land, when your king is the son of free men, and your princes eat in due season, for strength, and not for drunkenness!

בַּעֲצַלְתַּיִם יִמַּךְ הַמְּקָרֶה וּבְשִׁפְלוּת יָדַיִם יִדְלֹף הַבָּיִת׃
in great sluggish ones collapse the beams and in idleness' hands it drips the house

18. By slothfulness the beams collapse; and through idleness of the hands the house leaks.

לִשְׂחוֹק עֹשִׂים לֶחֶם וְיַיִן יְשַׂמַּח חַיִּים
to laughter makings bread and wine it happys life

וְהַכֶּסֶף יַעֲנֶה אֶת־הַכֹּל׃
and the silver answers that – the all

19. For laughter bread is made, and wine gladdens life, and money answers all things.

גַּם   בְּמַדָּעֲךָ   מֶלֶךְ אַל־תְּקַלֵּל
also in your thoughts king don't - you curse

וּבְחַדְרֵי מִשְׁכָּבְךָ אַל־תְּקַלֵּל עָשִׁיר
and in your rooms your bed don't - you curse rich

כִּי עוֹף הַשָּׁמַיִם יוֹלִיךְ אֶת־הַקּוֹל
like bird the heavens will carry that - the voice

וּבַעַל הַכְּנָפַיִם [כְּנָפַיִם] יַגִּיד דָּבָר׃
and master the wings it will tell matter

20. (K) Curse not the king, no even in your thought; and curse not the rich in your bed chamber; for a bird of the sky shall carry the voice, and that which has wings shall tell the matter.

Chapter 11

מגילת קהלת פרק יא

שַׁלַּח לַחְמְךָ עַל־פְּנֵי הַמָּיִם כִּי־בְרֹב הַיָּמִים תִּמְצָאֶנּוּ:

you will find it   the days   in much – like   the water   face – upon   your bread   cast

1. Cast your bread upon the waters, for you shall find it after many days.

תֶּן־חֵלֶק לְשִׁבְעָה וְגַם לִשְׁמוֹנָה

to eight   and also   to seven   portion – give

כִּי לֹא תֵדַע מַה־יִּהְיֶה רָעָה עַל־הָאָרֶץ:

the earth - upon   bad   will be - what   you know   not   like

2. Give a portion to seven, and also to eight; for you know not what evil shall be upon the earth.

אִם־יִמָּלְאוּ הֶעָבִים גֶּשֶׁם עַל־הָאָרֶץ יָרִיקוּ

they pour out   the earth - upon   rain   the clouds   they be full - if

וְאִם־יִפּוֹל עֵץ בַּדָּרוֹם וְאִם בַּצָּפוֹן

in north   and if   in south   tree   it falls - and if

מְקוֹם שֶׁיִּפּוֹל הָעֵץ שָׁם יְהוּא:

it will be   there   the tree   that it falls   place

3. If the clouds are full of rain, they empty themselves upon the earth; and if the tree falls to the south, or to the north, in the place where the tree falls, there it shall lie.

שֹׁמֵר רוּחַ לֹא יִזְרָע וְרֹאֶה בֶעָבִים לֹא יִקְצוֹר:

he will reap   not   in clouds   and seer   he will sow   not   wind   heeder

4. He who observes the wind shall not sow; and he who regards the clouds shall not reap.

כַּאֲשֶׁר אֵינְךָ יוֹדֵעַ מַה־דֶּרֶךְ הָרוּחַ כַּעֲצָמִים בְּבֶטֶן הַמְּלֵאָה

the full one   in belly   like bones   the wind   way – what   know   isn't you   when

כָּכָה לֹא תֵדַע אֶת־מַעֲשֵׂה הָאֱלֹהִים אֲשֶׁר יַעֲשֶׂה אֶת־הַכֹּל:

the all – that   he makes   which   the Elohim   works - that   you know   not   like that

5. As you do not know what is the way of the wind, nor how the bones grow in the womb of her who is with child; even so you do not know the works of God who makes all.

בַּבֹּקֶר זְרַע אֶת־זַרְעֶךָ וְלָעֶרֶב אַל־תַּנַּח יָדֶךָ

your hand   withhold - don't   and to evening   your seed - that   sow   in morning

כִּי אֵינְךָ יוֹדֵעַ אֵי זֶה יִכְשָׁר הֲזֶה אוֹ־זֶה

this - or   the this   it will prosper   this   how   know   isn't you   like

וְאִם־שְׁנֵיהֶם כְּאֶחָד טוֹבִים:

good ones   like together   two them - and if

6. In the morning sow your seed, and in the evening do not withhold your hand; for you do not know which shall prosper, either this or that, or whether they both alike shall be good.

וּמָתוֹק הָאוֹר וְטוֹב לַעֵינַיִם לִרְאוֹת אֶת־הַשָּׁמֶשׁ:
and sweet the light and good to eyes to see the sun – that

7. And the light is sweet, and pleasant for the eyes to behold the sun.

כִּי אִם־שָׁנִים הַרְבֵּה יִחְיֶה הָאָדָם בְּכֻלָּם יִשְׂמָח
like years – if the many he will live the Adam in all them he happy

וְיִזְכֹּר אֶת־יְמֵי הַחֹשֶׁךְ כִּי־הַרְבֵּה יִהְיוּ כָּל־שֶׁבָּא הָבֶל:
and he remembers days – that the darkness the many – like they be that comes – all vanity

8. And if many years lives a man, let him rejoice in them all; yet let him remember the days of darkness; for they shall be many. All that comes is vanity.

שְׂמַח בָּחוּר בְּיַלְדוּתֶיךָ וִיטִיבְךָ לִבְּךָ בִּימֵי בְחוּרוֹתֶךָ
be happy young man in your childhood and cheer you your heart in days your youth

וְהַלֵּךְ בְּדַרְכֵי לִבְּךָ וּבְמַרְאֵי עֵינֶיךָ
and walk in ways your heart and in sights your eyes

וְדָע כִּי עַל־כָּל־אֵלֶּה יְבִיאֲךָ הָאֱלֹהִים בַּמִּשְׁפָּט:
and know like upon these – all he brings you the Elohim in judgment

9. (K) Rejoice, O young man, in your youth; and let your heart cheer you in the days of your youth, and walk in the ways of your heart, and in the sight of your eyes; but know, that for all these things God will bring you into judgment.

וְהָסֵר כַּעַס מִלִּבֶּךָ וְהַעֲבֵר רָעָה מִבְּשָׂרֶךָ
and remove vexation from your heart and the perish bad from your flesh

כִּי־הַיַּלְדוּת וְהַשַּׁחֲרוּת הָבֶל:
the childhoods – like and the teenagers vanity

10. And remove sorrow from your heart, and put away evil from your flesh; for childhood and youth are vanity.

Chapter 12

מגילת קהלת פרק יב

וּזְכֹר֙ אֶת־בּ֣וֹרְאֶ֔יךָ בִּימֵ֖י בְּחוּרֹתֶ֑יךָ
and remember   your creator – that   in days   your youth

עַ֚ד אֲשֶׁ֣ר לֹא־יָבֹ֔אוּ יְמֵ֖י הָרָעָ֑ה
until   which   they come – not   days   the evil

וְהִגִּ֣יעוּ שָׁנִ֔ים אֲשֶׁ֣ר תֹּאמַ֔ר אֵֽין־לִ֥י בָהֶ֖ם חֵֽפֶץ׃
and they touch you   years   which   you will say   isn't - to me   in them   purpose

1. Remember now your Creator in the days of your youth, before the evil days come, and the years draw near, when you shall say, I have no pleasure in them;

עַ֣ד אֲשֶׁ֤ר לֹא־תֶחְשַׁךְ֙ הַשֶּׁ֣מֶשׁ וְהָא֔וֹר וְהַיָּרֵ֖חַ וְהַכּוֹכָבִ֑ים
until   which   it darkened – not   the sun   and the light   and the moon   and the stars

וְשָׁ֥בוּ הֶעָבִ֖ים אַחַ֥ר הַגָּֽשֶׁם׃
and they return   the clouds   after   the rain

2. Before the sun, and the light, and the moon, and the stars are darkened, and the clouds return after the rain;

בַּיּ֗וֹם שֶׁיָּזֻ֙עוּ֙ שֹׁמְרֵ֣י הַבַּ֔יִת וְהִֽתְעַוְּת֖וּ אַנְשֵׁ֣י הֶחָ֑יִל
in day   that it trembles   heeders   the house   and they bow   peoples   the force

וּבָטְל֤וּ הַטֹּֽחֲנוֹת֙ כִּ֣י מִעֵ֔טוּ וְחָשְׁכ֥וּ הָרֹא֖וֹת בָּאֲרֻבּֽוֹת׃
and they ceased   the grinders   like   they few   and they have darken   the seeings   in cracks

3. In the day when the keepers of the house tremble, and the strong men bow themselves, and the grinders cease because they are few, and those who look out of the windows are dimmed,

וְסֻגְּר֤וּ דְלָתַ֙יִם֙ בַּשּׁ֔וּק בִּשְׁפַ֖ל ק֣וֹל הַֽטַּחֲנָ֑ה
and they shut   doors   in market   in lowly   voice   the mill

וְיָקוּם֙ לְק֣וֹל הַצִּפּ֔וֹר וְיִשַּׁ֖חוּ כָּל־בְּנ֥וֹת הַשִּֽׁיר׃
and he rises   to voice   the bird   and they prostrate   all – daughters   the song

4. And the doors are shut on the streets, when the sound of the grinding is low, and one rises up at the voice of the bird, and all the daughters of song are brought low;

גַּ֣ם מִגָּבֹ֤הַּ יִרָ֙אוּ֙ וְחַתְחַתִּ֣ים בַּדֶּ֔רֶךְ
also   from haughty   they feared   and cut off ones   in the way

וְיָנֵ֤אץ הַשָּׁקֵד֙ וְיִסְתַּבֵּ֣ל הֶֽחָגָ֔ב
and it spurns   the almond tree   and he will burden   the grasshopper

וְתָפֵ֖ר הָֽאֲבִיּוֹנָ֑ה כִּֽי־הֹלֵ֤ךְ הָאָדָם֙ אֶל־בֵּ֣ית עוֹלָמ֔וֹ
and it fail   the fatherhood   like – walks   the Adam   unto – house   his forever

וְסָבְבוּ בַשּׁוּק הַסּוֹפְדִים׃
                  the mourning ones   in market and they go around

5. Also when they are afraid of that which is high, and fears are in the way, and the almond tree blossoms, and the grasshopper drags itself along, and desire fails; because man goes to his eternal home, and the mourners go about the streets;

עַד אֲשֶׁר לֹא־יֵרָתֵק [יֵרָחֵק] חֶבֶל הַכֶּסֶף וְתָרֻץ גֻּלַּת הַזָּהָב
the gold globe and it broken the silver cord he distances - not which until

וְתִשָּׁבֶר כַּד עַל־הַמַּבּוּעַ וְנָרֹץ הַגַּלְגַּל אֶל־הַבּוֹר׃
        cistern – unto the wheel and broken the fountain - upon jug and it broken

6. (K) Before the silver cord is removed, or the golden bowl is broken, or the pitcher is broken at the fountain, or the wheel broken at the cistern.

וְיָשֹׁב הֶעָפָר עַל־הָאָרֶץ כְּשֶׁהָיָה
       like that it was the earth – upon the dust and it returns

וְהָרוּחַ תָּשׁוּב אֶל־הָאֱלֹהִים אֲשֶׁר נְתָנָהּ׃
gave it which the Elohim - unto it returns and the spirit

7. And the dust returns to the earth as it was; and the spirit returns to God who gave it.

הֲבֵל הֲבָלִים אָמַר הַקּוֹהֶלֶת הַכֹּל הָבֶל׃
vanity the all the Kohelet said the vanities vanity

8. Vanity of vanities, said Kohelet; all is vanity.

וְיֹתֵר שֶׁהָיָה קֹהֶלֶת חָכָם עוֹד לִמַּד־דַּעַת אֶת־הָעָם
people – that knowledge – taught again wisdom Kohelet that it was and another

וְאִזֵּן וְחִקֵּר תִּקֵּן מְשָׁלִים הַרְבֵּה׃
the many proverbs established and penetrated and gave ear

9. And besides being wise, Kohelet also taught the people knowledge; for he weighed, and sought out, and set in order many proverbs.

בִּקֵּשׁ קֹהֶלֶת לִמְצֹא דִּבְרֵי־חֵפֶץ וְכָתוּב יֹשֶׁר דִּבְרֵי אֱמֶת׃
truth speakings upright and wrote pleasing – speech to find Kohelet searched

10. Kohelet sought to find out acceptable words; and words of truth written in proper form.

דִּבְרֵי חֲכָמִים כַּדָּרְבֹנוֹת
like goad points wise ones speech

וּכְמַשְׂמְרוֹת נְטוּעִים בַּעֲלֵי אֲסֻפּוֹת נִתְּנוּ מֵרֹעֶה אֶחָד׃
one from shepherd given it collected sayings masters planted ones and like nails

11. The words of the wise are like goads, and like nails firmly fixed are the collected sayings, which are given by one shepherd.

וְיֹתֵר מֵהֵמָּה בְּנִי הִזָּהֵר עֲשׂוֹת סְפָרִים הַרְבֵּה אֵין קֵץ
ending isn't the many books doings be warned my son from them and another

ECCLESIASTES - CHAPTER 12

וְלַהַג הַרְבֵּה יְגִעַת בָּשָׂר׃
and to study   the much   fatigues   flesh

12. And furthermore, by these, my son, be admonished; of making many books there is no end; and much study is a weariness of the flesh.

סוֹף דָּבָר הַכֹּל נִשְׁמָע אֶת־הָאֱלֹהִים יְרָא
end   speak   the all   heard   the Elohim – that   you fear

וְאֶת־מִצְוֹתָיו שְׁמוֹר כִּי־זֶה כָּל־הָאָדָם׃
and that - his commandments   heed   like – this   all– the Adam

13. The end of the matter, all has been heard. Fear God, and keep his commandments; for this is the whole duty of man.

כִּי אֶת־כָּל־מַעֲשֶׂה הָאֱלֹהִים יָבִא בְמִשְׁפָּט עַל כָּל־נֶעְלָם
like   that -all- works   the Elohim   it comes   judgment   upon   all – concealed

אִם־טוֹב וְאִם־רָע׃
if – good   and if – bad

14. For God shall bring every deed into judgment, with every secret thing, whether it is good, or whether it is evil.

Proverbs

Chapter 1

ספר משלי פרק א

מִשְׁלֵ֗י שְׁלֹמֹ֥ה בֶן־דָּוִ֑ד מֶ֝֗לֶךְ יִשְׂרָאֵֽל׃

proverbs   Solomon   son – David   king   Israel

1. The proverbs of Solomon the son of David, king of Israel;

לָדַ֣עַת חָכְמָ֣ה וּמוּסָ֑ר לְ֝הָבִ֗ין אִמְרֵ֥י בִינָֽה׃

to know   wisdom   and instruction   to the understanding   words   understanding

2. To know wisdom and instruction; to perceive the words of understanding;

לָ֭קַחַת מוּסַ֣ר הַשְׂכֵּ֑ל צֶ֥דֶק וּ֝מִשְׁפָּ֗ט וּמֵישָׁרִֽים׃

to take   discipline   the intelligence   righteous   and judgment   and fairness

3. To receive the instruction of wisdom, justice, and judgment, and equity;

לָתֵ֣ת לִפְתָאיִ֣ם עָרְמָ֑ה לְ֝נַ֗עַר דַּ֣עַת וּמְזִמָּֽה׃

to give   to simple ones   prudence   to young man   knowledge   and discretion

4. To give prudence to the simple, to the young man knowledge and discretion.

יִשְׁמַ֣ע חָ֭כָם וְי֣וֹסֶף לֶ֑קַח וְ֝נָב֗וֹן תַּחְבֻּל֥וֹת יִקְנֶֽה׃

he hears   wise   and he increases   to take   and understand   guidance's   he acquires

5. A wise man will hear, and will increase learning; and a man of understanding shall attain to wise counsels;

לְהָבִ֣ין מָ֭שָׁל וּמְלִיצָ֑ה דִּבְרֵ֥י חֲ֝כָמִ֗ים וְחִידֹתָֽם׃

to the understand   proverb   and parable   speakings   wise ones   and their riddles

6. To understand a proverb, and a figure; the words of the wise, and their riddles.

יִרְאַ֣ת יְ֭הוָה רֵאשִׁ֣ית דָּ֑עַת חָכְמָ֥ה וּ֝מוּסָ֗ר אֱוִילִ֥ים בָּֽזוּ׃

fears   ihvh   beginning   knowledge   wisdom   and discipline   fools   they despise

7. The fear of the Lord is the beginning of knowledge; but fools despise wisdom and instruction.

שְׁמַ֣ע בְּ֭נִי מוּסַ֣ר אָבִ֑יךָ וְאַל־תִּ֝טֹּ֗שׁ תּוֹרַ֥ת אִמֶּֽךָ׃

hear   my son   instruction   your father   and don't – forsake your   Torah   your mother

8. My son, hear the instruction of your father, and forsake not the Torah of your mother;

כִּ֤י ׀ לִוְיַ֤ת חֵ֓ן הֵ֬ם לְרֹאשֶׁ֑ךָ וַ֝עֲנָקִ֗ים לְגַרְגְּרֹתֶֽיךָ׃

like   ornament   grace   them   to your head   and chains   to your neck base

9. For they shall be an ornament of grace to your head, and chains around your neck.

בְּנִ֡י אִם־יְפַתּ֥וּךָ חַ֝טָּאִ֗ים אַל־תֹּבֵֽא׃

my son   he entice you – if   sinner ones   don't – you consent

10. My son, if sinners entice you, do not consent.

אִם־יֹאמְרוּ֮ לְכָ֪ה אִ֫תָּ֥נוּ נֶאֶרְבָ֥ה לְדָ֑ם נִצְפְּנָ֖ה לְנָקִ֣י חִנָּֽם׃

if – they say   go   with us   we lay in wait   to blood   we hide   to innocent   without cause

11. If they say, Come with us, let us lay in wait for blood, let us lurk for the innocent without cause;

נִבְלָעֵם כִּשְׁאוֹל חַיִּים וּתְמִימִים כְּיוֹרְדֵי בוֹר׃
pit　like descending　and blameless ones　alive　like Sheol　we swallow them

12. Let us swallow them up alive like Sheol; and whole, like those who go down into the pit;

כָּל־הוֹן יָקָר נִמְצָא נְמַלֵּא בָתֵּינוּ שָׁלָל׃
plunder　our houses　we fill　we find　precious　wealth - all

13. We shall find all precious goods, we shall fill our houses with plunder;

גּוֹרָלְךָ תַּפִּיל בְּתוֹכֵנוּ כִּיס אֶחָד יִהְיֶה לְכֻלָּנוּ׃
to all us　it be　one　purse　in among us　throw　your lot

14. Cast in your lot among us; let us all have one purse;

בְּנִי אַל־תֵּלֵךְ בְּדֶרֶךְ אִתָּם מְנַע רַגְלְךָ מִנְּתִיבָתָם׃
from it their coming　your feet　refrain　with them　in way　you walk – don't　my son

15. My son, do not walk in the way with them; refrain your foot from their path;

כִּי רַגְלֵיהֶם לָרַע יָרוּצוּ וִימַהֲרוּ לִשְׁפָּךְ־דָּם׃
blood – to shed　and they hurry　they run　to bad　their feet　like

16. For their feet run to evil, and make haste to shed blood.

כִּי־חִנָּם מְזֹרָה הָרָשֶׁת בְּעֵינֵי כָל־בַּעַל כָּנָף׃
bird　master – all　in eye　the net　from spread　without cause – like

17. Surely in vain the net is spread in the sight of any bird.

וְהֵם לְדָמָם יֶאֱרֹבוּ יִצְפְּנוּ לְנַפְשֹׁתָם׃
to their souls　they hide　they lie in wait　to their blood　and them

18. And they lay in wait for their own blood; they lurk secretly for their own lives.

כֵּן אָרְחוֹת כָּל־בֹּצֵעַ בָּצַע אֶת־נֶפֶשׁ בְּעָלָיו יִקָּח׃
he takes　in upon him　soul – that　ill-gotten gain　one gaining – all　roads　thus

19. So are the ways of every one who is greedy of gain; it takes away the life of its owners.

חָכְמוֹת בַּחוּץ תָּרֹנָּה בָּרְחֹבוֹת תִּתֵּן קוֹלָהּ׃
her voice　she gives　in roads　she calls aloud　in outside　wisdom

20. Wisdom cries aloud in the street; she utters her voice in the squares;

בְּרֹאשׁ הֹמִיּוֹת תִּקְרָא בְּפִתְחֵי שְׁעָרִים בָּעִיר אֲמָרֶיהָ תֹאמֵר׃
she says　her sayings　in city　gates　in entrances　she cries out　noisy ones　in head

21. She cries in the chief place of concourse, at the entrance of the gates; in the city she utters her words, saying,

עַד־מָתַי פְּתָיִם תְּאֵהֲבוּ פֶתִי
simple　you love it　simple ones　when - till

Proverbs - Chapter 1

וְלֵצִ֗ים לָ֭צוֹן חָמְד֣וּ לָהֶ֑ם וּ֝כְסִילִ֗ים יִשְׂנְאוּ־דָֽעַת׃

knowledge – they hate   and fool ones   to them   they delight   mockery   and mocking ones

22. How long, you simple ones, will you love being simple? And how long will scorners delight in their scorning? And fools hate knowledge?

תָּשׁ֗וּבוּ לְֽתוֹכַ֫חְתִּ֥י הִנֵּ֤ה אַבִּ֣יעָה לָכֶ֣ם רוּחִ֑י

my spirit   to you   I will pour out   here   to my rebuke   you return it

אוֹדִ֖יעָה דְבָרַ֣י אֶתְכֶֽם׃

that them   my speaking   I will make known

23. Turn at my reproof; behold, I will pour out my spirit to you, I will make known my words to you.

יַ֣עַן קָ֭רָאתִי וַתְּמָאֵ֑נוּ נָטִ֥יתִי יָ֝דִ֗י וְאֵ֣ין מַקְשִֽׁיב׃

<u>regard</u>   and isn't   my hand   I stretched   and you refused it   my call   he answers

24. Because I have called, and you refused; I have stretched out my hand, and no man regarded.

וַתִּפְרְע֥וּ כָל־עֲצָתִ֑י וְ֝תוֹכַחְתִּ֗י לֹ֣א אֲבִיתֶֽם׃

you accepted   not   and my rebuke   my counsel – all   and you ignored

25. But you have ignored all my counsel, and would have none of my reproof;

גַּם־אֲ֭נִי בְּאֵידְכֶ֣ם אֶשְׂחָ֑ק אֶ֝לְעַ֗ג בְּבֹ֣א פַחְדְּכֶֽם׃

your fear   in coming   I will mock   I will laugh   in your disaster   I – also

26. I also will laugh at your calamity; I will mock when your fear comes;

בְּבֹ֤א כְשׁוֹאָ֨ה [כְּשׁוֹאָ֨ה] פַּחְדְּכֶ֗ם

your fright   like storm   in coming

וְֽ֭אֵידְכֶם כְּסוּפָ֣ה יֶאֱתֶ֑ה בְּבֹ֥א עֲ֝לֵיכֶ֗ם צָרָ֥ה וְצוּקָֽה׃

and anguish   distress   upon you   in coming   it sweeps over   like whirlwind   and your disaster

27. (K) When your fear comes like a storm, and your calamity comes like a stormy wind; when distress and anguish comes upon you.

אָ֣ז יִ֭קְרָאֻנְנִי וְלֹ֣א אֶעֱנֶ֑ה יְ֝שַׁחֲרֻ֗נְנִי וְלֹ֣א יִמְצָאֻֽנְנִי׃

they will find me   and not   they will seek me   I will answer   and not   they will call on me   then

28. Then shall they call on me, but I will not answer; they shall seek me early, but they shall not find me;

תַּ֭חַת כִּי־שָׂ֣נְאוּ דָ֑עַת וְיִרְאַ֥ת יְ֝הֹוָ֗ה לֹ֣א בָחָֽרוּ׃

they choose   not   ihvh   and fear   knowledge   they hated – like   under

29. For they hated knowledge, and did not choose the fear of the Lord;

לֹא־אָב֥וּ לַעֲצָתִ֑י נָ֝אֲצ֗וּ כָּל־תּוֹכַחְתִּֽי׃

my rebuke – all   they spurned   to my counsel   they come – not

30. They would have none of my counsel; they despised all my reproof.

וְֽ֭יֹאכְלוּ מִפְּרִ֣י דַרְכָּ֑ם וּֽמִמֹּעֲצ֖וֹתֵיהֶ֣ם יִשְׂבָּֽעוּ׃

they will fill   and from schemes of them   their way   from fruit   and they will eat

31. Therefore they shall eat of the fruit of their own way, and be filled with their own

devices.

כִּי	מְשׁוּבַת	פְּתָיִם	תַּהַרְגֵם	וְשַׁלְוַת	כְּסִילִים	תְּאַבְּדֵם:
like	from turnings	simple ones	will the slay them	and prosperity	fool ones	it will destroy them

32. For the turning away of the simple shall slay them, and the prosperity of fools shall destroy them.

וְשֹׁמֵעַ	לִי	יִשְׁכָּן־בֶּטַח	וְשַׁאֲנַן	מִפַּחַד	רָעָה:
and hearer	to me	in safety – he will dwell	and ease	from fright	bad

33. But whoever listens to me shall dwell safely, and shall be at ease without fear of evil.

Chapter 2

ספר משלי פרק ב

בְּנִי אִם־תִּקַּח אֲמָרָי וּמִצְוֹתַי תִּצְפֹּן אִתָּךְ:
with you   you store up   and my commandments   my words   you will take – if   my son

1. My son, if you will receive my words, and treasure my commandments;

לְהַקְשִׁיב לַחָכְמָה אָזְנֶךָ תַּטֶּה לִבְּךָ לַתְּבוּנָה:
to understanding   your heart   you apply   your ear   to wisdom   to the incline

2. So that you incline your ear to wisdom, and apply your heart to understanding;

כִּי אִם לַבִּינָה תִקְרָא לַתְּבוּנָה תִּתֵּן קוֹלֶךָ:
your voice   you give   to understanding   you call   to understanding   if   like

3. Indeed, if you cry after knowledge, and lift up your voice for understanding;

אִם־תְּבַקְשֶׁנָּה כַכָּסֶף וְכַמַּטְמוֹנִים תַּחְפְּשֶׂנָּה:
you search her   and like hidden treasures   like silver   you seek her - if

4. If you seek her like silver, and search for her as for hidden treasures;

אָז תָּבִין יִרְאַת יְהֹוָה וְדַעַת אֱלֹהִים תִּמְצָא:
you will find   Elohim   and knowledge   ihvh   fears   you will understand   then

5. Then shall you understand the fear of the Lord, and find the knowledge of God.

כִּי־יְהֹוָה יִתֵּן חָכְמָה מִפִּיו דַּעַת וּתְבוּנָה:
and understanding   knowledge   from his mouth   wisdom   gives   ihvh - like

6. For the Lord gives wisdom; from his mouth comes knowledge and understanding.

וְצָפַן [יִצְפֹּן] לַיְשָׁרִים תּוּשִׁיָּה מָגֵן לְהֹלְכֵי תֹם:
perfectly   to walkers   shield   sound wisdom   to upright ones   and stores

7. (K) He lays up sound wisdom for the righteous; he is a shield to those who walk uprightly.

לִנְצֹר אָרְחוֹת מִשְׁפָּט וְדֶרֶךְ חֲסִידָו [חֲסִידָיו] יִשְׁמֹר:
he heeds   his pious   and way   commandments   paths   to guard

8. He keeps the paths of judgment, and preserves the way of his pious ones.

אָז תָּבִין צֶדֶק וּמִשְׁפָּט וּמֵישָׁרִים כָּל־מַעְגַּל־טוֹב:
good – steps - all   and fair ones   and judgment   righteousness   you understand   then

9. Then shall you understand righteousness, and judgment, and equity; every good path.

כִּי־תָבוֹא חָכְמָה בְלִבֶּךָ וְדַעַת לְנַפְשְׁךָ יִנְעָם:
it be pleasant   to your soul   and knowledge   in your heart   wisdom   you come - like

10. When wisdom enters into your heart, and knowledge is precious to your soul;

מְזִמָּה תִּשְׁמֹר עָלֶיךָ תְּבוּנָה תִנְצְרֶכָּה:
she guards you   understanding   upon you   you heed   discretion

11. Discretion shall preserve you, understanding shall keep you;

לְהַצִּילְךָ מִדֶּרֶךְ רָע מֵאִישׁ מְדַבֵּר תַּהְפֻּכוֹת:

12. To save you from the way of the evil man, from the man who speaks perverse things;

הַעֹזְבִים אָרְחוֹת יֹשֶׁר לָלֶכֶת בְּדַרְכֵי־חֹשֶׁךְ:

13. Who leave the paths of uprightness, to walk in the ways of darkness;

הַשְּׂמֵחִים לַעֲשׂוֹת רָע יָגִילוּ בְּתַהְפֻּכוֹת רָע:

14. Who rejoice to do evil, and delight in the perverseness of the wicked;

אֲשֶׁר אָרְחֹתֵיהֶם עִקְּשִׁים וּנְלוֹזִים בְּמַעְגְּלוֹתָם:

15. Whose ways are crooked, and who are devious in their paths;

לְהַצִּילְךָ מֵאִשָּׁה זָרָה מִנָּכְרִיָּה אֲמָרֶיהָ הֶחֱלִיקָה:

16. To save you from the alien woman, from the stranger who speaks smoothly;

הַעֹזֶבֶת אַלּוּף נְעוּרֶיהָ וְאֶת־בְּרִית אֱלֹהֶיהָ שָׁכֵחָה:

17. Who forsakes the companion of her youth, and forgets the covenant of her God.

כִּי שָׁחָה אֶל־מָוֶת בֵּיתָהּ וְאֶל־רְפָאִים מַעְגְּלֹתֶיהָ:

18. For her house inclines to death, and her paths to the dead.

כָּל־בָּאֶיהָ לֹא יְשׁוּבוּן וְלֹא־יַשִּׂיגוּ אָרְחוֹת חַיִּים:

19. None that go to her come back, nor do they regain the paths of life.

לְמַעַן תֵּלֵךְ בְּדֶרֶךְ טוֹבִים וְאָרְחוֹת צַדִּיקִים תִּשְׁמֹר:

20. That you may walk in the way of good men, and keep the paths of the righteous.

כִּי־יְשָׁרִים יִשְׁכְּנוּ־אָרֶץ וּתְמִימִים יִוָּתְרוּ בָהּ:

21. For the upright shall dwell in the land, and the innocent shall remain in it.

וּרְשָׁעִים מֵאֶרֶץ יִכָּרֵתוּ וּבוֹגְדִים יִסְּחוּ מִמֶּנָּה:

22. But the wicked shall be cut off from the earth, and the transgressors shall be rooted out of it.

Chapter 3

ספר משלי פרק ג

בְּנִי תּוֹרָתִי אַל־תִּשְׁכָּח וּמִצְוֹתַי יִצֹּר לִבֶּךָ:
your heart　keep　and my commandments　forget – don't　my Torah　my son

1. My son, forget not my Torah; but let your heart keep my commandments;

כִּי אֹרֶךְ יָמִים וּשְׁנוֹת חַיִּים וְשָׁלוֹם יוֹסִיפוּ לָךְ:
to you　they add　and peace　life　and years　days　length　like

2. For length of days, and long life, and peace, shall they add to you.

חֶסֶד וֶאֱמֶת אַל־יַעַזְבֻךָ
you forsake – don't　and truth　mercy

קָשְׁרֵם עַל־גַּרְגְּרוֹתֶיךָ כָּתְבֵם עַל־לוּחַ לִבֶּךָ:
your heart　tablet – upon　write them　your neck – upon　bind them

3. Let not grace and truth forsake you; bind them around your neck; write them on the tablet of your heart;

וּמְצָא־חֵן וְשֵׂכֶל־טוֹב בְּעֵינֵי אֱלֹהִים וְאָדָם:
and Adam　Elohim　in eyes　good – and intelligence　grace – and find

4. So shall you find favor and good understanding in the sight of God and man.

בְּטַח אֶל־יְהֹוָה בְּכָל־לִבֶּךָ וְאֶל־בִּינָתְךָ אַל־תִּשָּׁעֵן:
you lean – don't　your understanding – and unto　your heart – in all　ihvh – unto　trust

5. Trust in the Lord with all your heart; and lean not on your own understanding.

בְּכָל־דְּרָכֶיךָ דָעֵהוּ וְהוּא יְיַשֵּׁר אֹרְחֹתֶיךָ:
your roads　he will straighten　and he　you acknowledge him　your path – in all

6. In all your ways acknowledge him, and he shall direct your paths.

אַל־תְּהִי חָכָם בְּעֵינֶיךָ יְרָא אֶת־יְהֹוָה וְסוּר מֵרָע:
from bad and depart　ihvh – that　fear　in your eyes　wise　you be – don't

7. Be not wise in your own eyes; fear the Lord, and depart from evil.

רִפְאוּת תְּהִי לְשָׁרֶּךָ וְשִׁקּוּי לְעַצְמוֹתֶיךָ:
to your bones　and marrow　to your navel　you will be　healthy

8. It shall be health to your navel, and marrow to your bones.

כַּבֵּד אֶת־יְהֹוָה מֵהוֹנֶךָ וּמֵרֵאשִׁית כָּל־תְּבוּאָתֶךָ:
your produce – all　and from beginning　from your wealth　ihvh – that　honor

9. Honor the Lord with your possessions, and with the first fruits of all your produce;

וְיִמָּלְאוּ אֲסָמֶיךָ שָׂבָע וְתִירוֹשׁ יְקָבֶיךָ יִפְרֹצוּ:
they will overflow　your vats　and it new wine　plenty　your barns　and they will fill

10. So shall your barns be filled with plenty, and your vats shall burst out with new wine.

מוּסַר יְהֹוָה בְּנִי אַל־תִּמְאָס וְאַל־תָּקֹץ בְּתוֹכַחְתּוֹ:
in his rebuke　weary – and don't　despise – don't　my son　ihvh　discipline

11. My son, despise not the chastening of the Lord; nor be weary of his correction;

כִּי אֶת אֲשֶׁר יֶאֱהַב יְהוָה יוֹכִיחַ וּכְאָב אֶת־בֵּן יִרְצֶה:
like   that   which   he loves   ihvh   he corrects   and like father   son – that   he delights

12. For whom the Lord loves he corrects; like a father does with a son in whom he delights.

אַשְׁרֵי אָדָם מָצָא חָכְמָה וְאָדָם יָפִיק תְּבוּנָה:
happy   Adam   find   wisdom   and Adam   he gains   understanding

13. Happy is the man who finds wisdom, and the man who gets understanding.

כִּי טוֹב סַחְרָהּ מִסְּחַר־כָּסֶף וּמֵחָרוּץ תְּבוּאָתָהּ:
like   good   her profit   silver – from profit   and from fine gold   her gain

14. For the merchandise of it is better than the merchandise of silver, and its gain than fine gold.

יְקָרָה הִיא מִפְּנִיִּים [מִפְּנִינִים] וְכָל־חֲפָצֶיךָ לֹא יִשְׁווּ־בָהּ:
precious   she   from rubies   your desires – and all   not   in her – they compare

15. (K) She is more precious than rubies; and all the things you can desire are not to be compared to her.

אֹרֶךְ יָמִים בִּימִינָהּ בִּשְׂמֹאולָהּ עֹשֶׁר וְכָבוֹד:
length   days   in her right hand   in her left   riches   and honor

16. Length of days is in her right hand; and in her left hand riches and honor.

דְּרָכֶיהָ דַרְכֵי־נֹעַם וְכָל־נְתִיבוֹתֶיהָ שָׁלוֹם:
her paths   pleasant – paths   her paths - and all   peace

17. Her ways are ways of pleasantness, and all her paths are peace.

עֵץ־חַיִּים הִיא לַמַּחֲזִיקִים בָּהּ וְתֹמְכֶיהָ מְאֻשָּׁר:
life - tree   she   to embracing one   in her   and you lay hold her   from happy

18. She is a tree of life to those who lay hold on her; and happy is every one who holds her fast.

יְהוָה בְּחָכְמָה יָסַד־אָרֶץ כּוֹנֵן שָׁמַיִם בִּתְבוּנָה:
ihvh   in wisdom   earth – foundation   establishing   heavens   in understanding

19. The Lord by wisdom has founded the earth; by understanding has he established the heavens.

בְּדַעְתּוֹ תְּהוֹמוֹת נִבְקָעוּ וּשְׁחָקִים יִרְעֲפוּ־טָל:
in his knowledge   depths   they were divided   and clouds   dew - they dropped

20. By his knowledge the depths were broken up, and the clouds drop down dew.

בְּנִי אַל־יָלֻזוּ מֵעֵינֶיךָ נְצֹר תֻּשִׁיָּה וּמְזִמָּה:
my son   it depart you – don't   from your eyes   preserve   sound wisdom   and discernment

21. My son, let not them depart from your eyes; keep sound wisdom and discretion;

וְיִהְיוּ חַיִּים לְנַפְשֶׁךָ וְחֵן לְגַרְגְּרֹתֶיךָ:
and they be   life   to your soul   and grace   to your neck

22. So shall they be life to your soul, and grace to your neck.

אָז תֵּלֵךְ לָבֶטַח דַּרְכֶּךָ וְרַגְלְךָ לֹא תִגּוֹף׃
stumble not and your feet your way to safety you walk then

23. Then shall you walk in your way safely, and your foot shall not stumble.

אִם־תִּשְׁכַּב לֹא־תִפְחָד וְשָׁכַבְתָּ וְעָרְבָה שְׁנָתֶךָ׃
your sleep and she sweet and you lie down you be afraid – not you lie down

24. When you lie down, you shall not be afraid; indeed, you shall lie down, and your sleep shall be sweet.

אַל־תִּירָא מִפַּחַד פִּתְאֹם וּמִשֹּׁאַת רְשָׁעִים כִּי תָבֹא׃
it comes like wicked ones and from ruin sudden from fright you be afraid – don't

25. Be not afraid of sudden fear, nor of the ruin of the wicked, when it comes.

כִּי־יְהֹוָה יִהְיֶה בְכִסְלֶךָ וְשָׁמַר רַגְלְךָ מִלָּכֶד׃
from snare your foot and heed in your confidence will be ihvh - like

26. For the Lord shall be your confidence, and shall keep your foot from being caught.

אַל־תִּמְנַע־טוֹב מִבְּעָלָיו בִּהְיוֹת לְאֵל יָדֶיךָ [יָדְךָ] לַעֲשׂוֹת׃
to doings your hand to power in due from you master good – withhold – don't

27. (K) Withhold not good from them to whom it is due, when it is in the power of your hand to do it.

אַל־תֹּאמַר לְרֵעֶיךָ [לְרֵעֲךָ] לֵךְ וָשׁוּב וּמָחָר אֶתֵּן וְיֵשׁ אִתָּךְ׃
with you and it is I will give and tomorrow and return go to your neighbor say – don't

28. (K) Say not to your neighbor, Go, and come back, and tomorrow I will give, when you have it by you.

אַל־תַּחֲרֹשׁ עַל־רֵעֲךָ רָעָה וְהוּא־יוֹשֵׁב לָבֶטַח אִתָּךְ׃
with you to trust dwells - and he bad your neighbor - upon plot – don't

29. Do not plot evil against your neighbor, seeing he dwells securely by you.

אַל־תָּרוֹב [תָּרִיב] עִם־אָדָם חִנָּם אִם־לֹא גְמָלְךָ רָעָה׃
bad your harm not - if with out cause Adam – with accuse – don't

30. (K) Do not strive without cause with a man, if he has done you no harm.

אַל־תְּקַנֵּא בְּאִישׁ חָמָס וְאַל־תִּבְחַר בְּכָל־דְּרָכָיו׃
his ways – in all you choose – and don't violence in man envy – don't

31. Do not envy the oppressor, and choose none of his ways.

כִּי תוֹעֲבַת יְהֹוָה נָלוֹז וְאֶת־יְשָׁרִים סוֹדוֹ׃
his foundation upright ones = and that preserved ihvh detestable like

32. For the perverse is abomination to the Lord; but the righteous are in his confidence.

מְאֵרַת יְהֹוָה בְּבֵית רָשָׁע וּנְוֵה צַדִּיקִים יְבָרֵךְ׃
he blesses righteous ones and habitation wicked in house ihvh from curse

33. The curse of the Lord is in the house of the wicked; but he blesses the habitation of the just.

אִם־לַלֵּצִים הוּא יָלִיץ וְלַעֲנָיִים [וְלַעֲנָוִים] יִתֶּן־חֵן:
to mocking ones - if   he   he mocks   and to humble ones   he gives – grace

34. (K) Surely he scorns the scorners; but he gives grace to the humble.

כָּבוֹד חֲכָמִים יִנְחָלוּ וּכְסִילִים מֵרִים קָלוֹן:
honor   wise ones   they inherit   and fool ones   holding up   shame

35. The wise shall inherit honor; but fools shall get shame.

Chapter 4

ספר משלי פרק ד

שִׁמְעוּ בָנִים מוּסַר אָב וְהַקְשִׁיבוּ לָדַעַת בִּינָה:
_{understanding to know and the you pay attention father discipline sons you hear}

1. Hear, you children, the instruction of a father, and attend to know understanding.

כִּי לֶקַח טוֹב נָתַתִּי לָכֶם תּוֹרָתִי אַל־תַּעֲזֹבוּ:
_{you forsake it – don't my Torah to you I give good to take like}

2. For I give you good doctrine, do not forsake my Torah.

כִּי־בֵן הָיִיתִי לְאָבִי רַךְ וְיָחִיד לִפְנֵי אִמִּי:
_{my mother before and only one tender to my father I was son - like}

3. For I was my father's son, tender and the only one in the sight of my mother.

וַיֹּרֵנִי וַיֹּאמֶר לִי יִתְמָךְ־דְּבָרַי לִבֶּךָ שְׁמֹר מִצְוֹתַי וֶחְיֵה:
_{and live my commandments heed your heart my speaking – you retain to me and said and he taught me}

4. He taught me also, and said to me, Let your heart retain my words; keep my commandments, and live.

קְנֵה חָכְמָה קְנֵה בִינָה אַל־תִּשְׁכַּח וְאַל־תֵּט מֵאִמְרֵי־פִי:
_{my mouth - from words turn away – and don't forget – don't understand acquire wisdom acquire}

5. Get wisdom, acquire understanding; forget it not; nor turn away from the words of my mouth.

אַל־תַּעַזְבֶהָ וְתִשְׁמְרֶךָּ אֱהָבֶהָ וְתִצְּרֶךָּ:
_{and she will keep you love her and it will heed you forsake her – don't}

6. Forsake her not, and she shall preserve you; love her, and she shall keep you.

רֵאשִׁית חָכְמָה קְנֵה חָכְמָה וּבְכָל־קִנְיָנְךָ קְנֵה בִינָה:
_{understanding acquire your buying - and in all wisdom acquire wisdom beginning}

7. The beginning of Wisdom is: Get Wisdom; therefore use all your means to acquire understanding.

סַלְסְלֶהָ וּתְרוֹמְמֶךָּ תְּכַבֵּדְךָ כִּי תְחַבְּקֶנָּה:
_{you will embrace her like she will honor you and she will exalt you esteem her}

8. Exalt her, and she shall promote you; she shall bring you to honor, when you embrace her.

תִּתֵּן לְרֹאשְׁךָ לִוְיַת־חֵן עֲטֶרֶת תִּפְאֶרֶת תְּמַגְּנֶךָּ:
_{she will bestows you beauty crown grace - ornament to your head she will give}

9. She shall give to your head an ornament of grace; a crown of glory shall she bestow on you.

שְׁמַע בְּנִי וְקַח אֲמָרָי וְיִרְבּוּ לְךָ שְׁנוֹת חַיִּים:
_{lives years to you and be many my words and take my son hear}

10. Hear, O my son, and receive my sayings; and the years of your life shall be many.

בְּדֶרֶךְ חָכְמָה הֹרֵתִיךָ הִדְרַכְתִּיךָ בְּמַעְגְּלֵי־יֹשֶׁר:
    upright – in steps   I led you   I guided you   wisdom   in way

11. I have taught you in the way of wisdom; I have led you in paths of rectitude.

בְּלֶכְתְּךָ לֹא־יֵצַר צַעֲדֶךָ וְאִם־תָּרוּץ לֹא תִכָּשֵׁל:
    you will stumble not you run – and if your step will go out – not in your going

12. When you go, your steps shall not be hampered; and when you run, you shall not stumble.

הַחֲזֵק בַּמּוּסָר אַל־תֶּרֶף נִצְּרֶהָ כִּי־הִיא חַיֶּיךָ:
    your life she – like guard her tear off – don't in instruction the latch on

13. Take fast hold of instruction; let her not go; keep her; for she is your life.

בְּאֹרַח רְשָׁעִים אַל־תָּבֹא וְאַל־תְּאַשֵּׁר בְּדֶרֶךְ רָעִים:
    bad ones in way you do – and don't you go – don't wicked ones in road

14. Enter not into the path of the wicked, and go not in the way of evil men.

פְּרָעֵהוּ אַל־תַּעֲבָר־בּוֹ שְׂטֵה מֵעָלָיו וַעֲבוֹר:
    and past by from upon him turn in him – travel – don't avoid him

15. Avoid it, pass not by it, turn from it, and pass away.

כִּי לֹא יִשְׁנוּ אִם־לֹא יָרֵעוּ
    they do bad not – if they sleep not like

וְנִגְזְלָה שְׁנָתָם אִם־לֹא יַכְשׁוֹלוּ [יַכְשִׁילוּ]:
    they to fall not – if their sleep and to robbed

16. (K) For they cannot sleep unless they have done evil deeds; and their sleep is taken away, unless they cause someone to fall.

כִּי לָחֲמוּ לֶחֶם רֶשַׁע וְיֵין חֲמָסִים יִשְׁתּוּ:
    they drink violent ones and wine wicked bread they eat it like

17. For they eat the bread of wickedness, and drink the wine of violence.

וְאֹרַח צַדִּיקִים כְּאוֹר נֹגַהּ הוֹלֵךְ וָאוֹר עַד־נְכוֹן הַיּוֹם:
    the day correct – till and light goes shining like light righteous ones and road

18. But the path of the just is like the shining light, that shines more and more until full day.

דֶּרֶךְ רְשָׁעִים כָּאֲפֵלָה לֹא יָדְעוּ בַּמֶּה יִכָּשֵׁלוּ:
    they stumble in what they know not like deep darkness wicked ones path

19. The way of the wicked is like darkness; they know not at what they stumble.

בְּנִי לִדְבָרַי הַקְשִׁיבָה לַאֲמָרַי הַט אָזְנֶךָ:
    your ear incline to my saying the pay attention to my speaking my son

20. My son, attend to my words; incline your ear to my sayings.

אַל־יַלִּיזוּ מֵעֵינֶיךָ שָׁמְרֵם בְּתוֹךְ לְבָבֶךָ:
    your heart in midst heed them from your eyes they depart – don't

21. Let them not depart from your eyes; keep them in the midst of your heart.

Proverbs - Chapter 4

כִּי־חַיִּים הֵם לְמֹצְאֵיהֶם וּלְכָל־בְּשָׂרוֹ מַרְפֵּא׃
      health   his flesh – and to all   to find them   them   life - like

22. For they are life to those who find them, and health to all their flesh.

מִכָּל־מִשְׁמָר נְצֹר לִבֶּךָ כִּי־מִמֶּנּוּ תּוֹצְאוֹת חַיִּים׃
    life   well springs   from it – like   you heart   guard   watching – from all

23. Keep your heart with all diligence; for out of it are the issues of life.

הָסֵר מִמְּךָ עִקְּשׁוּת פֶּה וּלְזוּת שְׂפָתַיִם הַרְחֵק מִמֶּךָּ׃
    from you   the far   lips   and to corruption   mouth   perverse   from you   remove

24. Put away from you a dissembling mouth, and perverse lips put far from you.

עֵינֶיךָ לְנֹכַח יַבִּיטוּ וְעַפְעַפֶּיךָ יַיְשִׁרוּ נֶגְדֶּךָ׃
    before you   they be straight   and your eyelids   they look   to ahead   your eyes

25. Let your eyes look right on, and let your eyelids look straight before you.

פַּלֵּס מַעְגַּל רַגְלֶךָ וְכָל־דְּרָכֶיךָ יִכֹּנוּ׃
    you establish   your ways – and all   your feet   steps   make level

26. Ponder the path of your feet, and let all your ways be firm.

אַל־תֵּט יָמִין וּשְׂמֹאול הָסֵר רַגְלְךָ מֵרָע׃
    from bad   your feet   remove   and left   right hand   incline - don't

27. Turn not to the right hand nor to the left; remove your foot from evil.

Chapter 5

ספר משלי פרק ה

בְּנִי לְחָכְמָתִי הַקְשִׁיבָה לִתְבוּנָתִי הַט־אָזְנֶךָ:
_{your ear – incline   to my understanding   the pay attention   to my wisdom   my son}

1. My son, attend to my wisdom, and bow your ear to my understanding.

לִשְׁמֹר מְזִמּוֹת וְדַעַת שְׂפָתֶיךָ יִנְצֹרוּ:
_{they preserve   your lips   and knowledge   discretions   to heed}

2. That you may regard discretion, and that your lips may keep knowledge.

כִּי נֹפֶת תִּטֹּפְנָה שִׂפְתֵי זָרָה וְחָלָק מִשֶּׁמֶן חִכָּהּ:
_{her inside mouth   form oil   and smooth   stranger woman   lips   they drip   honey   like}

3. For the lips of a strange woman drip honey, and her mouth is smoother than oil;

וְאַחֲרִיתָהּ מָרָה כַלַּעֲנָה חַדָּה כְּחֶרֶב פִּיּוֹת:
_{edges   like sword   sharp   like gall   bitter   and after her}

4. But her end is bitter like wormwood, sharp like a two edged sword.

רַגְלֶיהָ יֹרְדוֹת מָוֶת שְׁאוֹל צְעָדֶיהָ יִתְמֹכוּ:
_{they lead   her steps   Sheol   death   descends   her feet}

5. Her feet go down to death; her steps take hold of Sheol.

אֹרַח חַיִּים פֶּן־תְּפַלֵּס נָעוּ מַעְגְּלֹתֶיהָ לֹא תֵדָע:
_{she knows   not   her steps   wanders   you give way – lest   life   road}

6. She does not take heed to her way of life; her paths wander, and she does not know it.

וְעַתָּה בָנִים שִׁמְעוּ־לִי וְאַל־תָּסוּרוּ מֵאִמְרֵי־פִי:
_{my mouth – from my words   you depart – and don't   to me – you listen   sons   and now}

7. And now listen to me, O you children, and depart not from the words of my mouth.

הַרְחֵק מֵעָלֶיהָ דַרְכֶּךָ וְאַל־תִּקְרַב אֶל־פֶּתַח בֵּיתָהּ:
_{her house   opening – unto   you near – and don't   your way   from upon her   the far}

8. Remove your way far from her, and come not near the door of her house;

פֶּן־תִּתֵּן לַאֲחֵרִים הוֹדֶךָ וּשְׁנֹתֶיךָ לְאַכְזָרִי:
_{to cruel ones   and your years   you honor   to others   you give – lest}

9. Lest you give your honor to others, and your years to the cruel;

פֶּן־יִשְׂבְּעוּ זָרִים כֹּחֶךָ וַעֲצָבֶיךָ בְּבֵית נָכְרִי:
_{another   in house   and your toils   your power   strange ones   they fill – lest}

10. Lest strangers be filled with your wealth; and your labors go to the house of a stranger;

וְנָהַמְתָּ בְאַחֲרִיתֶךָ בִּכְלוֹת בְּשָׂרְךָ וּשְׁאֵרֶךָ:
_{and your body   in your flesh   in his all   in you after   and you will groan}

11. And you groan when your end comes, when your flesh and your body are consumed.

Proverbs - Chapter 5

וְאָמַרְתָּ אֵיךְ שָׂנֵאתִי מוּסָר וְתוֹכַחַת נָאַץ לִבִּי׃
my heart · despised · and correction · discipline · I hated · how · and you say

12. And say, How have I hated instruction, and my heart despised reproof!

וְלֹא־שָׁמַעְתִּי בְּקוֹל מוֹרָי וְלִמְלַמְּדַי לֹא־הִטִּיתִי אָזְנִי׃
my ear · I turned – not · and to my learning · my teacher · in voice · I listened – and not

13. And I have not obeyed the voice of my teachers, nor inclined my ear to those who instructed me!

כִּמְעַט הָיִיתִי בְכָל־רָע בְּתוֹךְ קָהָל וְעֵדָה׃
and congregation · assembly · in midst · bad – in all · I was · like little

14. I was almost in all evil in the midst of the assembled congregation.

שְׁתֵה־מַיִם מִבּוֹרֶךָ וְנֹזְלִים מִתּוֹךְ בְּאֵרֶךָ׃
your well · from midst · and running waters · from your cistern · waters - drink

15. Drink waters out of your own cistern, and running waters out of your own well.

יָפוּצוּ מַעְיְנֹתֶיךָ חוּצָה בָּרְחֹבוֹת פַּלְגֵי־מָיִם׃
waters – streams · in roads · flow out · from your springs · they overflow

16. Should your springs be dispersed abroad, and streams of waters flow in the streets?

יִהְיוּ־לְךָ לְבַדֶּךָ וְאֵין לְזָרִים אִתָּךְ׃
with you · to strangers · and isn't · your alone · to you – they will be

17. Let them be for you alone, and not for strangers with you.

יְהִי־מְקוֹרְךָ בָרוּךְ וּשְׂמַח מֵאֵשֶׁת נְעוּרֶךָ׃
your youth · from wife · and be happy · blessed · your fountain – it be

18. Let your fountain be blessed; and rejoice with the wife of your youth.

אַיֶּלֶת אֲהָבִים וְיַעֲלַת־חֵן דַּדֶּיהָ יְרַוֻּךָ בְכָל־עֵת
season – in all · your satisfaction · her breasts · grace – and roe · loving ones · does

בְּאַהֲבָתָהּ תִּשְׁגֶּה תָמִיד׃
always · you captivated · in her love

19. Let her be like the loving hind and pleasant roe; let her breasts satisfy you at all times; and be you ravished always with her love.

וְלָמָּה תִשְׁגֶּה בְנִי בְזָרָה וּתְחַבֵּק חֵק נָכְרִיָּה׃
alien · bosom · and you embrace · in strange woman · my son · captivated · and why

20. And why will you, my son, be ravished with a strange woman, and embrace the bosom of an alien?

כִּי נֹכַח עֵינֵי יְהוָה דַּרְכֵי־אִישׁ וְכָל־מַעְגְּלֹתָיו מְפַלֵּס׃
from examining · his steps – and all · man – ways · ihvh · eye · front · like

21. For the ways of man are before the eyes of the Lord, and he ponders all his goings.

עֲוֹנוֹתָיו יִלְכְּדֻנוֹ אֶת־הָרָשָׁע וּבְחַבְלֵי חַטָּאתוֹ יִתָּמֵךְ׃
he held fast · his sin · and in cords · the wicked – that · ensnares him · his inequities

22. His own iniquities shall take the wicked himself, and he shall be caught fast in the cords of his sins.

הוּא יָמוּת בְּאֵין מוּסָר וּבְרֹב אִוַּלְתּוֹ יִשְׁגֶּה:
<small>he led astray　his folly　and in much　discipline　in isn't　will die　he</small>

23. He shall die for lack of instruction; and in the greatness of his folly he shall go astray.

Chapter 6

ספר משלי פרק ו

בְּנִי אִם־עָרַבְתָּ לְרֵעֶךָ תָּקַעְתָּ לַזָּר כַּפֶּיךָ:

my son you put up security – if to you neighbor you struck pledge your palms

1. My son, if you give surety for your friend, if you have given your pledge for a stranger,

נוֹקַשְׁתָּ בְאִמְרֵי־פִיךָ נִלְכַּדְתָּ בְּאִמְרֵי־פִיךָ:

you were trapped your mouth – in words ensnared you mouth – in words

2. If you are trapped with the words of your mouth; if you are taken with the words of your mouth,

עֲשֵׂה זֹאת אֵפוֹא בְּנִי וְהִנָּצֵל כִּי בָאתָ בְכַף־רֵעֶךָ לֵךְ

do this how my son and free yourself like you come your neighbor – in palm to you

הִתְרַפֵּס וּרְהַב רֵעֶיךָ:

become humble and plead your neighbor

3. Do this now, my son, and save yourself, when you come into the hand of your neighbor; go, humble yourself, and importune your neighbor.

אַל־תִּתֵּן שֵׁנָה לְעֵינֶיךָ וּתְנוּמָה לְעַפְעַפֶּיךָ:

give – don't sleep to your eyes and slumber to your eyelids

4. Give no sleep to your eyes, nor slumber to your eyelids.

הִנָּצֵל כִּצְבִי מִיָּד וּכְצִפּוֹר מִיַּד יָקוּשׁ:

free yourself like gazelle from hand and like bird from hand fowler

5. Save yourself like a gazelle from the hand of the hunter, and like a bird from the hand of the fowler.

לֵךְ־אֶל־נְמָלָה עָצֵל רְאֵה דְרָכֶיהָ וַחֲכָם:

go – unto – ant sluggard see its ways and be wise

6. Go to the ant, you sluggard; consider her ways, and be wise;

אֲשֶׁר אֵין־לָהּ קָצִין שֹׁטֵר וּמֹשֵׁל:

which isn't – to her commander over seer and ruler

7. Which having no guide, overseer, or ruler,

תָּכִין בַּקַּיִץ לַחְמָהּ אָגְרָה בַקָּצִיר מַאֲכָלָהּ:

she stores in summer bread she gathers in harvest to food

8. Provides her bread in the summer, and gathers her food in the harvest.

עַד־מָתַי עָצֵל תִּשְׁכָּב מָתַי תָּקוּם מִשְּׁנָתֶךָ:

when – till sluggard you lie when you rise from your sleep

9. How long will you sleep, O sluggard? When will you arise from your sleep?

מְעַט שֵׁנוֹת מְעַט תְּנוּמוֹת מְעַט חִבֻּק יָדַיִם לִשְׁכָּב:

little sleeps little slumbers little folding hands to nap

10. A little sleep, a little slumber, a little folding of the hands to sleep,

וּבָא־כִמְהַלֵּךְ רֵאשֶׁךָ וּמַחְסֹרְךָ כְּאִישׁ מָגֵן:
shield   like man   and your scarcity   your poverty   like bandit - comes

11. So shall poverty come upon you like a vagabond, and want like an armed man.

אָדָם בְּלִיַּעַל אִישׁ אָוֶן הוֹלֵךְ עִקְּשׁוּת פֶּה:
mouth   corruptness   walks   inequity   man   in scoundrel   Adam

12. A base person, a wicked man, walks with a crooked mouth.

קֹרֵץ בְּעֵינָו מֹלֵל בְּרַגְלָו מֹרֶה בְּאֶצְבְּעֹתָיו:
in his finger   teacher   in his feet   signaling   in his eye   winking

13. He winks with his eyes, he taps with his feet, he points with his fingers;

תַּהְפֻּכוֹת בְּלִבּוֹ חֹרֵשׁ רָע בְּכָל־עֵת מִדָנִים [מְדָנִים] יְשַׁלֵּחַ:
he sends   dissensions   season – in all   bad   plotting   in his heart   deceits

14. (K) Perverseness is in his heart, he plots evil continually; he sows discord.

עַל־כֵּן פִּתְאֹם יָבוֹא אֵידוֹ פֶּתַע יִשָּׁבֵר וְאֵין מַרְפֵּא:
remedy   and isn't   he destroyed   suddenly   his disaster   he comes   suddenly   thus - upon

15. Therefore shall his calamity come suddenly; suddenly shall he be broken beyond remedy.

שֶׁשׁ־הֵנָּה שָׂנֵא יְהֹוָה וְשֶׁבַע תּוֹעֲבוֹת [תּוֹעֲבַת] נַפְשׁוֹ:
his soul   abomination   and seven   ihvh   hate   here - six

16. (K) There are six things which the Lord hates, seven which are an abomination to him;

עֵינַיִם רָמוֹת לְשׁוֹן שָׁקֶר וְיָדַיִם שֹׁפְכוֹת דָּם־נָקִי:
innocent – blood   sheddings   and their hands   lie   tongue   haughty   eyes

17. An arrogant look, a lying tongue, and hands that shed innocent blood,

לֵב חֹרֵשׁ מַחְשְׁבוֹת אָוֶן רַגְלַיִם מְמַהֲרוֹת לָרוּץ לָרָעָה:
to bad   to run   from quick ones   feet   inequity   schemes   devising   heart

18. A heart that plots wicked plans, feet that swiftly run to evil.

יָפִיחַ כְּזָבִים עֵד שָׁקֶר וּמְשַׁלֵּחַ מְדָנִים בֵּין אַחִים:
brothers   between   dissensions   and from sending   lie   till   false witnesses   he pours out

19. A false witness who speaks lies, and he who sows discord among brothers.

נְצֹר בְּנִי מִצְוַת אָבִיךָ וְאַל־תִּטֹּשׁ תּוֹרַת אִמֶּךָ:
your mother   Torah   forsake – and not   your father   commandment   my son   keep

20. My son, keep your father's commandment, and forsake not the Torah of your mother;

קָשְׁרֵם עַל־לִבְּךָ תָמִיד עָנְדֵם עַל־גַּרְגְּרֹתֶךָ:
your neck – upon   fasten them   always   your heart – upon   bind them

21. Bind them continually on your heart, and tie them around your neck.

בְּהִתְהַלֶּכְךָ תַּנְחֶה אֹתָךְ בְּשָׁכְבְּךָ תִּשְׁמֹר עָלֶיךָ
upon you   she watches   in your lying down   to you   she guides   in causing you to go

וַהֲקִיצ֗וֹתָ הִ֣יא תְשִׂיחֶֽךָ׃
it takes you   it   and the awake

22. When you walk, it shall lead you; when you sleep, it shall keep you; and when you awake, it shall talk with you.

כִּ֤י נֵ֣ר מִ֭צְוָה וְת֣וֹרָה א֑וֹר וְדֶ֥רֶךְ חַ֝יִּ֗ים תּוֹכְח֥וֹת מוּסָֽר׃
discipline   corrections   life   and way   light   and Torah   commandment   lamp   like

23. For the commandment is a lamp; and the Torah is light; and reproofs of instruction are the way of life;

לִ֭שְׁמָרְךָ מֵאֵ֣שֶׁת רָ֑ע מֵ֝חֶלְקַ֗ת לָשׁ֥וֹן נָכְרִיָּֽה׃
stranger woman   tongue   smoothness   bad   from woman   to keep you

24. To keep you from the evil woman, from the smoothness of the tongue of a strange woman.

אַל־תַּחְמֹ֣ד יָ֭פְיָהּ בִּלְבָבֶ֑ךָ וְאַל־תִּ֝קָּחֲךָ֗ בְּעַפְעַפֶּֽיהָ׃
in her eye lids   you take – and don't   in your heart   her beauty   you trust – don't

25. Lust not after her beauty in your heart; nor let her take you with her eyelids.

כִּ֤י בְעַד־אִשָּׁ֥ה זוֹנָ֗ה עַֽד־כִּכַּ֫ר לָ֥חֶם
bread   piece – till   harlot   woman - in side   like

וְאֵ֥שֶׁת אִ֑ישׁ נֶ֖פֶשׁ יְקָרָ֣ה תָצֽוּד׃
preys   dear her   soul   man   and fire ones

26. For by means of a harlot a man is brought to a piece of bread; and the adulteress will hunt for the precious life.

הֲיַחְתֶּ֤ה אִ֓ישׁ אֵ֬שׁ בְּחֵיק֑וֹ וּ֝בְגָדָ֗יו לֹ֣א תִשָּׂרַֽפְנָה׃
you towards burned   not   and his clothes   in his lap   fire   man   the scoop

27. Can a man take fire in his bosom, and his clothes not be burned?

אִם־יְהַלֵּ֣ךְ אִ֭ישׁ עַל־הַגֶּחָלִ֑ים וְ֝רַגְלָ֗יו לֹ֣א תִכָּוֶֽינָה׃
you scorch   not   and his feet   the coals – upon   man   he go - if

28. Can one go on hot coals, and his feet not be scorched?

כֵּ֗ן הַ֭בָּא אֶל־אֵ֣שֶׁת רֵעֵ֑הוּ לֹ֥א יִ֝נָּקֶ֗ה כָּֽל־הַנֹּגֵ֥עַ בָּֽהּ׃
in her   the touching – all   he unpunished   not   their neighbor   wife – unto   to coming   thus

29. So he who goes in to his neighbor's wife; whoever touches her shall not go unpunished.

לֹא־יָב֣וּזוּ לַ֭גַּנָּב כִּ֣י יִגְנ֑וֹב לְמַלֵּ֥א נַ֝פְשׁ֗וֹ כִּ֣י יִרְעָֽב׃
he hungry   like   his soul   to fill   he steals   like   to thief   they despise - not

30. Do not men despise a thief, even if he steals to satisfy his soul when he is hungry?

וְ֭נִמְצָא יְשַׁלֵּ֣ם שִׁבְעָתָ֑יִם אֶת־כָּל־ה֖וֹן בֵּית֣וֹ יִתֵּֽן׃
he gives   his house   wealth – all – that   seven ones   he pays   and caught

31. And if he is caught, he shall restore seven fold; he shall give all the goods of his house.

נֹאֵף אִשָּׁה חֲסַר־לֵב מַשְׁחִית נַפְשׁוֹ הוּא יַעֲשֶׂנָּה:
    she does so   he his soul destroying heart – lack woman adulterous

32. But whoever commits adultery with a woman lacks understanding; he who does it destroys his own soul.

נֶגַע־וְקָלוֹן יִמְצָא וְחֶרְפָּתוֹ לֹא תִמָּחֶה:
    you wipe away not and his shame he fins and disgrace - blow

33. A wound and dishonor shall he get; and his reproach shall not be wiped away.

כִּי־קִנְאָה חֲמַת־גָּבֶר וְלֹא יַחְמוֹל בְּיוֹם נָקָם:
    revenge in day he shows mercy and not gentlemen – rage jealousy - like

34. For jealousy is the rage of a man; and he will not spare in the day of vengeance.

לֹא־יִשָּׂא פְּנֵי כָל־כֹּפֶר וְלֹא־יֹאבֶה כִּי תַרְבֶּה־שֹׁחַד:
    bribe – you much like he accepts – and not compensate – all before he lifts eyes - not

35. He will not regard any ransom; nor will he rest content, though you give many gifts.

Chapter 7

ספר משלי פרק ז

בְּנִי שְׁמֹר אֲמָרָי וּמִצְוֹתַי תִּצְפֹּן אִתָּךְ:

with you   you store up   and my commandments   my word   heed   my son

1. My son, keep my words, and lay up my commandments with you.

שְׁמֹר מִצְוֹתַי וֶחְיֵה וְתוֹרָתִי כְּאִישׁוֹן עֵינֶיךָ:

your eye   like apple   and my Torah   and live   my commandments   heed

2. Keep my commandments, and live; and my Torah like the apple of your eye.

קָשְׁרֵם עַל־אֶצְבְּעֹתֶיךָ כָּתְבֵם עַל־לוּחַ לִבֶּךָ:

your heart   tablet – upon   write them   your fingers – upon   bind them

3. Bind them on your fingers, write them on the tablet of your heart.

אֱמֹר לַחָכְמָה אֲחֹתִי אָתְּ וּמֹדָע לַבִּינָה תִקְרָא:

you call   to understanding   and kinsman   you   my sister   to wisdom   say

4. Say to wisdom, You are my sister; and call understanding your kinswoman;

לִשְׁמָרְךָ מֵאִשָּׁה זָרָה מִנָּכְרִיָּה אֲמָרֶיהָ הֶחֱלִיקָה:

the seductive   her word   from foreign   adulteress   from woman   to your heeding

5. That they may keep you from the strange woman, from the stranger with her smooth words.

כִּי בְּחַלּוֹן בֵּיתִי בְּעַד אֶשְׁנַבִּי נִשְׁקָפְתִּי:

I looked out   my lattice   in side   my house   in window   like

6. For at the window of my house I looked through my lattice,

וָאֵרֶא בַפְּתָאיִם אָבִינָה בַבָּנִים נַעַר חֲסַר־לֵב:

heart – removed   youth   in sons   I understood   in simple ones   and I saw

7. And beheld among the simple ones, I discerned among the youths, a young man void of understanding,

עֹבֵר בַּשּׁוּק אֵצֶל פִּנָּהּ וְדֶרֶךְ בֵּיתָהּ יִצְעָד:

he strolled   her house   and way   her corner   near   in market   serving

8. Passing through the street near her corner; and he went the road to her house,

בְּנֶשֶׁף־בְּעֶרֶב יוֹם בְּאִישׁוֹן לַיְלָה וַאֲפֵלָה:

and darkness   night   in middle   day – in evening – in twilight

9. In the twilight, in the evening, in the black and dark night;

וְהִנֵּה אִשָּׁה לִקְרָאתוֹ שִׁית זוֹנָה וּנְצֻרַת לֵב:

heart   and crafty   prostitute   dress   to his meet   woman   and see

10. And, behold, there met him a woman dressed as a harlot, and wily of heart.

הֹמִיָּה הִיא וְסֹרָרֶת בְּבֵיתָהּ לֹא־יִשְׁכְּנוּ רַגְלֶיהָ:

her feet   they remain – not   in her house   and defiant   she   one being loud

11. She is loud and stubborn; her feet do not remain in her house;

פַּעַם בַּחוּץ פַּעַם בָּרְחֹבוֹת וְאֵצֶל כָּל־פִּנָּה תֶאֱרֹב:

12. Now is she outside, now in the streets, and lies in wait at every corner.

וְהֶחֱזִיקָה בּוֹ וְנָשְׁקָה־לּוֹ הֵעֵזָה פָנֶיהָ וַתֹּאמַר לוֹ:

13. So she caught hold of him, and kissed him, and with an impudent face said to him,

זִבְחֵי שְׁלָמִים עָלָי הַיּוֹם שִׁלַּמְתִּי נְדָרָי:

14. I have had to sacrifice peace offerings; this day have I paid my vows.

עַל־כֵּן יָצָאתִי לִקְרָאתֶךָ לְשַׁחֵר פָּנֶיךָ וָאֶמְצָאֶךָּ:

15. Therefore came I forth to meet you, diligently to seek your face, and I have found you.

מַרְבַדִּים רָבַדְתִּי עַרְשִׂי חֲטֻבוֹת אֵטוּן מִצְרָיִם:

16. I have decked my bed with coverings, with tapestry of fine linen from Egypt.

נַפְתִּי מִשְׁכָּבִי מֹר אֲהָלִים וְקִנָּמוֹן:

17. I have perfumed my bed with myrrh, aloes, and cinnamon.

לְכָה נִרְוֶה דֹדִים עַד־הַבֹּקֶר נִתְעַלְּסָה בָּאֳהָבִים:

18. Come, let us take our fill of love until the morning; let us delight ourselves with love.

כִּי אֵין הָאִישׁ בְּבֵיתוֹ הָלַךְ בְּדֶרֶךְ מֵרָחוֹק:

19. For my husband is not at home, he has gone on a long journey;

צְרוֹר־הַכֶּסֶף לָקַח בְּיָדוֹ לְיוֹם הַכֵּסֶא יָבֹא בֵיתוֹ:

20. He has taken a bag of money with him, and will return home at the full moon.

הִטַּתּוּ בְּרֹב לִקְחָהּ בְּחֵלֶק שְׂפָתֶיהָ תַּדִּיחֶנּוּ:

21. With her very pretty speech she seduces him, with her smooth talk she compels him.

הוֹלֵךְ אַחֲרֶיהָ פִּתְאֹם כְּשׁוֹר אֶל־טָבַח

יָבוֹא וּכְעֶכֶס אֶל־מוּסַר אֱוִיל:

22. He goes after her at once, like an ox goes to the slaughter, or like a man in chains to the chastisement of a fool.

Proverbs - Chapter 7

עַד יְפַלַּח חֵץ כְּבֵדוֹ כְּמַהֵר צִפּוֹר אֶל־פָּח
snare – unto bird like hurried his liver arrow he pierces till

וְלֹא יָדַע כִּי־בְנַפְשׁוֹ הוּא׃
he in his soul – like knows and not

23. Till an arrow pierces his liver; like a bird rushes to the trap, and knows not that it is for his life.

וְעַתָּה בָנִים שִׁמְעוּ־לִי וְהַקְשִׁיבוּ לְאִמְרֵי־פִי׃
my mouth – to my words and you attend to me – you listen sons and time

24. Listen to me now, O you children, and attend to the words of my mouth.

אַל־יֵשְׂטְ אֶל־דְּרָכֶיהָ לִבֶּךָ אַל־תֵּתַע בִּנְתִיבוֹתֶיהָ׃
into her path you stray – don't your heart her way – unto let him turn – don't

25. Let not your heart decline to her ways, do not go astray in her paths.

כִּי־רַבִּים חֲלָלִים הִפִּילָה וַעֲצֻמִים כָּל־הֲרֻגֶיהָ׃
her slain ones – all and mighty ones wounded cast down ones many ones - like

26. For she has cast down many wounded; indeed, many strong men have been slain by her.

דַּרְכֵי שְׁאוֹל בֵּיתָהּ יֹרְדוֹת אֶל־חַדְרֵי־מָוֶת׃
death – rooms – unto goings down her house Sheol ways

27. Her house is the way to Sheol, going down to the chambers of death.

Chapter 8

ספר משלי פרק ח

הֲלֹא־חָכְמָה תִקְרָא וּתְבוּנָה תִּתֵּן קוֹלָהּ:
her voice   gives   and she understanding   she call   wisdom – the not

1. Does not wisdom call? And understanding put forth her voice?

בְּרֹאשׁ־מְרֹמִים עֲלֵי־דָרֶךְ בֵּית נְתִיבוֹת נִצָּבָה:
she takes stand   paths   house   way – upon   high places - in tops

2. She stands at the top of high places by the way, where the paths meet.

לְיַד־שְׁעָרִים לְפִי־קָרֶת מְבוֹא פְתָחִים תָּרֹנָּה:
cries aloud   entrances   from coming   cries – to mouth   gates – to hand

3. She cries at the gates, at the entry of the city, at the entrance of the doors.

אֲלֵיכֶם אִישִׁים אֶקְרָא וְקוֹלִי אֶל־בְּנֵי אָדָם:
Adam   sons – unto   and my voice   I call   men   unto you

4. To you, O men, I call; and my voice is to the sons of man.

הָבִינוּ פְתָאיִם עָרְמָה וּכְסִילִים הָבִינוּ לֵב:
heart   gain   and fool ones   prudence   simple ones   the gain

5. O you simple, understand wisdom; and, you fools, be you of an understanding heart.

שִׁמְעוּ כִּי־נְגִידִים אֲדַבֵּר וּמִפְתַּח שְׂפָתַי מֵישָׁרִים:
fairness ones   my lips   and from opening   I speak   we tellings - like   you hear

6. Hear; for I will speak of excellent things; and the opening of my lips shall be right things.

כִּי־אֱמֶת יֶהְגֶּה חִכִּי וְתוֹעֲבַת שְׂפָתַי רֶשַׁע:
wicked   my lips   abomination   my palate   he tells   truth - like

7. For my mouth shall speak truth; and wickedness is an abomination to my lips.

בְּצֶדֶק כָּל־אִמְרֵי־פִי אֵין בָּהֶם נִפְתָּל וְעִקֵּשׁ:
and perverse   being crooked   in them   isn't   my mouth – words – all   in righteous

8. All the words of my mouth are in righteousness; there is nothing crooked or perverse in them.

כֻּלָּם נְכֹחִים לַמֵּבִין וִישָׁרִים לְמֹצְאֵי דָעַת:
knowledge   to find   and upright ones   to discerning   right ones   all them

9. They are all plain to him who understands, and right to those who find knowledge.

קְחוּ־מוּסָרִי וְאַל־כָּסֶף וְדַעַת מֵחָרוּץ נִבְחָר:
you choose   from choice gold   and knowledge   silver – and don't   my instruction – you take

10. Receive my instruction, and not silver; and knowledge rather than choice gold.

כִּי־טוֹבָה חָכְמָה מִפְּנִינִים וְכָל־חֲפָצִים לֹא יִשְׁווּ־בָהּ:
in it – they compare   not   desires – and all   from rubies   wisdom   better - like

11. For wisdom is better than rubies; and all the things that may be desired are not to be compared to it.

Proverbs - Chapter 8

אֲנִי־חָכְמָה שָׁכַנְתִּי עָרְמָה וְדַעַת מְזִמּוֹת אֶמְצָא׃
<small>I find   discretions   and knowledge   prudence   my dwelling   wisdom - I</small>

12. I, wisdom, dwell with prudence, and find knowledge and discretion.

יִרְאַת יְהֹוָה שְׂנֹאת רָע גֵּאָה וְגָאוֹן
<small>and arrogance   pride   bad   hate   ihvh   fear</small>

וְדֶרֶךְ רָע וּפִי תַהְפֻּכוֹת שָׂנֵאתִי׃
<small>my hate   perversities   and mouth   bad   and path</small>

13. The fear of the Lord is to hate evil; pride, and arrogance, and the evil way, and the perverse mouth, do I hate.

לִי־עֵצָה וְתוּשִׁיָּה אֲנִי בִינָה לִי גְבוּרָה׃
<small>might   to me   understanding   I   and sound judgment   counsel – to me</small>

14. Counsel is mine, and sound wisdom; I am understanding; I have strength.

בִּי מְלָכִים יִמְלֹכוּ וְרוֹזְנִים יְחֹקְקוּ צֶדֶק׃
<small>righteous   they decree   and ones ruling   they reign   kings   in me</small>

15. By me kings reign, and princes decree justice.

בִּי שָׂרִים יָשֹׂרוּ וּנְדִיבִים כָּל־שֹׁפְטֵי צֶדֶק׃
<small>right   judge - all   and noble ones   they rule   princes   in me</small>

16. By me princes rule, and nobles, even all the judges of the earth.

אֲנִי אֹהֲבֶיהָ [אֹהֲבַי] אֵהָב וּמְשַׁחֲרַי יִמְצָאֻנְנִי׃
<small>they find me   and my seekers   love   my loved ones   I</small>

17. (K) I love those who love me; and those who seek me early shall find me.

עֹשֶׁר־וְכָבוֹד אִתִּי הוֹן עָתֵק וּצְדָקָה׃
<small>and righteousness   enduring   wealth   with me   and honor - richness</small>

18. Riches and honor are with me; enduring wealth and righteousness.

טוֹב פִּרְיִי מֵחָרוּץ וּמִפָּז וּתְבוּאָתִי מִכֶּסֶף נִבְחָר׃
<small>choice   from silver   and my production   and from fine gold   from choice gold   my fruit   good</small>

19. My fruit is better than gold, better than fine gold; and my produce than choice silver.

בְּאֹרַח צְדָקָה אֲהַלֵּךְ בְּתוֹךְ נְתִיבוֹת מִשְׁפָּט׃
<small>judgment   paths   in midst   I walk   righteousness   in road</small>

20. I walk in the way of righteousness, in the midst of the paths of judgment;

לְהַנְחִיל אֹהֲבַי יֵשׁ וְאֹצְרֹתֵיהֶם אֲמַלֵּא׃
<small>I fill   and their treasures   wealth   my love   to bestow</small>

21. That I may cause those who love me to inherit wealth; and I will fill their treasures.

יְהֹוָה קָנָנִי רֵאשִׁית דַּרְכּוֹ קֶדֶם מִפְעָלָיו מֵאָז׃
<small>from old   from his acts   before   his way   beginning   acquired me   ihvh</small>

22. The Lord created me at the beginning of his way, the first of his acts of old.

מֵעוֹלָם נִסַּכְתִּי מֵרֹאשׁ מִקַּדְמֵי־אָרֶץ׃
<small>earth – from before   from head   I was appointed   from forever</small>

23. I was set up from everlasting, from the beginning, even before the earth.

בְּאֵין־תְּהֹמוֹת חוֹלָלְתִּי בְּאֵין מַעְיָנוֹת נִכְבַּדֵּי־מָיִם׃
   waters – abounding   springs   in isn't   I was born   depths – in isn't

24. When there were no depths, I was brought forth; when there were no fountains abounding with water.

בְּטֶרֶם הָרִים הָטְבָּעוּ לִפְנֵי גְבָעוֹת חוֹלָלְתִּי׃
   I was born   hills   before   they were settled   the mountains   in before

25. Before the mountains were settled, before the hills was I brought forth;

עַד־לֹא עָשָׂה אֶרֶץ וְחוּצוֹת וְרֹאשׁ עַפְרוֹת תֵּבֵל׃
   inhabited world   dusts   and head   and fields   earth   made   not - till

26. While as yet he had not made the earth, nor the fields, nor the highest part of the dust of the world.

בַּהֲכִינוֹ שָׁמַיִם שָׁם אָנִי בְּחוּקוֹ חוּג עַל־פְּנֵי תְהוֹם׃
   deep   face – upon   horizon   in his mark   I   there   heavens   in his established

27. When he established the heavens, I was there; when he drew a circle on the face of the deep;

בְּאַמְּצוֹ שְׁחָקִים מִמָּעַל בַּעֲזוֹז עִינוֹת תְּהוֹם׃
   deep   fountains   in secure   from above   clouds   in his established

28. When he established the clouds above; when he strengthened the fountains of the deep;

בְּשׂוּמוֹ לַיָּם חֻקּוֹ
   his statute   to day   in give him

וּמַיִם לֹא יַעַבְרוּ־פִיו בְּחוּקוֹ מוֹסְדֵי אָרֶץ׃
   earth   foundation   his mark   his mouth – they pass   not   and water

29. When he gave to the sea his decree, that the waters should not pass his commandment; when he appointed the foundations of the earth;

וָאֶהְיֶה אֶצְלוֹ אָמוֹן וָאֶהְיֶה שַׁעֲשׁוּעִים יוֹם
   day   delights   and it was   craftsman   his side   and it was

יוֹם מְשַׂחֶקֶת לְפָנָיו בְּכָל־עֵת׃
   time – in all   before him   one rejoicing   day

30. Then I was by him, like a little child; and I was daily his delight, rejoicing always before him;

מְשַׂחֶקֶת בְּתֵבֵל אַרְצוֹ וְשַׁעֲשֻׁעַי אֶת־בְּנֵי אָדָם׃
   Adam   sons – that   and my delights   his land   in whole world   one rejoicing

31. Rejoicing in his inhabited world; and my delights were with the sons of men.

וְעַתָּה בָנִים שִׁמְעוּ־לִי וְאַשְׁרֵי דְּרָכַי יִשְׁמֹרוּ׃
   they heed   my ways   and blessed   to me – you listen   sons   and now

32. Now therefore listen to me, O you children; for happy are they who keep my ways.

Proverbs - Chapter 8

שִׁמְעוּ מוּסָר וַחֲכָמוּ וְאַל־תִּפְרָעוּ:
you ignore – and don't   and you wise   instruction   you hear

33. Hear instruction, and be wise, and refuse it not.

אַשְׁרֵי אָדָם שֹׁמֵעַ לִי
to me   hears   Adam   blessed

לִשְׁקֹד עַל־דַּלְתֹתַי יוֹם יוֹם לִשְׁמֹר מְזוּזֹת פְּתָחָי:
my openings   door posts   to heed   day   day   my doors – upon   to watch

34. Happy is the man who hears me, watching daily at my gates, waiting at the posts of my doors.

כִּי מֹצְאִי מָצָא [מָצָא] חַיִּים וַיָּפֶק רָצוֹן מֵיהוָה:
from ihvh   favor   and he receives   life   he finds   finding me   like

35. (K) For whoever finds me finds life, and shall obtain favor from the Lord.

וְחֹטְאִי חֹמֵס נַפְשׁוֹ כָּל־מְשַׂנְאַי אָהֲבוּ מָוֶת:
death   they love   from hating – all   his soul   violence   and sinner

36. But he who sins against me wrongs his own soul; all those who hate me love death.

Chapter 9

ספר משלי פרק ט

חָכְמוֹת בָּנְתָה בֵיתָהּ חָצְבָה עַמּוּדֶיהָ שִׁבְעָה׃
    seven   pillars   hewed out her house build wisdoms

1. Wisdom has build her house, she has hewn out her seven pillars;

טָבְחָה טִבְחָהּ מָסְכָה יֵינָהּ אַף עָרְכָה שֻׁלְחָנָהּ׃
 her table she set then wine her mixed her meat prepared

2. She has killed her beasts; she has mixed her wine; she has also set her table.

שָׁלְחָה נַעֲרֹתֶיהָ תִקְרָא עַל־גַּפֵּי מְרֹמֵי קָרֶת׃
  city high places heights–upon she calls her young girls she sent

3. She has sent forth her maidens; she calls on the highest places of the city,

מִי־פֶתִי יָסֻר הֵנָּה חֲסַר־לֵב אָמְרָה לּוֹ׃
 to him she says heart–removed here turn simple–who

4. Whoever is simple, let him turn in here; as for him who lacks understanding, she says to him:

לְכוּ לַחֲמוּ בְלַחֲמִי וּשְׁתוּ בְּיַיִן מָסָכְתִּי׃
 from mixed in wine and you drink in my bread you bread go

5. Come, eat of my bread, and drink of the wine which I have mixed.

עִזְבוּ פְתָאיִם וִחְיוּ וְאִשְׁרוּ בְּדֶרֶךְ בִּינָה׃
 understanding in way and they do and you live simple ones leave

6. Forsake the foolish, and live; and go in the way of understanding.

יֹסֵר לֵץ לֹקֵחַ לוֹ קָלוֹן וּמוֹכִיחַ לְרָשָׁע מוּמוֹ׃
 his abuse to wicked and rebuking insult to him inviting mocking correcting

7. He who corrects a scorner brings shame on himself; and he who rebukes a wicked man brings on himself a blemish.

אַל־תּוֹכַח לֵץ פֶּן־יִשְׂנָאֶךָּ הוֹכַח לְחָכָם וְיֶאֱהָבֶךָּ׃
 and he loves you to wise rebuke he hate you–lest mocking you rebuke–don't

8. Reprove not a scorner, lest he hate you; rebuke a wise man, and he will love you.

תֵּן לְחָכָם וְיֶחְכַּם־עוֹד הוֹדַע לְצַדִּיק וְיוֹסֶף לֶקַח׃
 learning he adds to righteous teach still–and he wise to wise give

9. Give instruction to a wise man, and he will be yet wiser; teach a just man, and he will increase in learning.

תְּחִלַּת חָכְמָה יִרְאַת יְהוָה וְדַעַת קְדֹשִׁים בִּינָה׃
 understanding holy ones and knowledge ihvh fear wisdom start

10. The fear of the Lord is the beginning of wisdom; and the knowledge of holy matters is understanding.

כִּי־בִי יִרְבּוּ יָמֶיךָ וְיוֹסִיפוּ לְּךָ שְׁנוֹת חַיִּים׃
 life years to you and they add your days they many in me–like

11. For by me your days shall be multiplied, and the years of your life shall be increased.

אִם־חָכַ֗מְתָּ חָכַ֥מְתָּ לָּ֑ךְ וְלַ֥צְתָּ לְבַדְּךָ֥ תִשָּֽׂא׃
      you suffer   you alone and you mock to you   you wise   you wise - if

12. If you are wise, you shall be wise for yourself; but if you scorn, you alone shall bear it.

אֵ֣שֶׁת כְּ֭סִילוּת הֹמִיָּ֑ה פְּ֝תַיּ֗וּת וּבַל־יָ֥דְעָה־מָּֽה׃
   what – she knows – and without simple ones being loud   fools   woman

13. A foolish woman is noisy; she is simple, and knows nothing.

וְֽ֭יָשְׁבָה לְפֶ֣תַח בֵּיתָ֑הּ עַל־כִּ֝סֵּ֗א מְרֹ֣מֵי קָֽרֶת׃
     city   heights   chair – upon   her house to opening and she sits

14. For she sits at the door of her house, on a seat in the high places of the city,

לִ֭קְרֹא לְעֹבְרֵי־דָ֑רֶךְ הַֽ֝מְיַשְּׁרִ֗ים אֹֽרְחוֹתָֽם׃
     their way   the fairness ones way – passers by   to call

15. To call passers by who go right on their ways;

מִי־פֶ֭תִי יָסֻ֣ר הֵ֑נָּה וַחֲסַר־לֵ֝֗ב וְאָ֣מְרָה לּֽוֹ׃
   to him and she says heart – removed here turn in simple - who

16. Whoever is simple, let him turn in here; and as for him who lacks understanding, she says to him,

מַֽיִם־גְּנוּבִ֥ים יִמְתָּ֑קוּ וְלֶ֖חֶם סְתָרִ֣ים יִנְעָֽם׃
  pleasant secret ones and bread they sweet   stolen ones - waters

17. Stolen waters are sweet, and bread eaten in secret is pleasant.

וְֽלֹא־יָ֭דַע כִּֽי־רְפָאִ֣ים שָׁ֑ם בְּעִמְקֵ֖י שְׁא֣וֹל קְרֻאֶֽיהָ׃
  her guests   Sheol in depths there healing ones – like he knows – and not

18. But he knows not that the dead are there; and that her guests are in the depths of Sheol.

Chapter 10

ספר משלי פרק י

מִשְׁלֵי שְׁלֹמֹה
    Solomon Proverbs

בֵּן חָכָם יְשַׂמַּח־אָב וּבֵן כְּסִיל תּוּגַת אִמּוֹ׃
his mother grief fool and son father – will be happy wise son

1. The proverbs of Solomon. A wise son makes a father glad; but a foolish son is the grief of his mother.

לֹא־יוֹעִילוּ אוֹצְרוֹת רֶשַׁע וּצְדָקָה תַּצִּיל מִמָּוֶת׃
from deaths he delivers and righteous wicked treasures they valuable - not

2. Treasures of wickedness profit nothing; but righteousness saves from death.

לֹא־יַרְעִיב יְהוָה נֶפֶשׁ צַדִּיק וְהַוַּת רְשָׁעִים יֶהְדֹּף׃
he thwarts wicked ones and craving righteous soul ihvh he suffers – and not

3. The Lord will not suffer the soul of the righteous to famish; but he thwarts the craving of the wicked.

רָאשׁ עֹשֶׂה כַף־רְמִיָּה וְיַד חָרוּצִים תַּעֲשִׁיר׃
she rich diligent ones and hand laziness – palm does poor

4. A slack hand causes poverty; but the hand of the diligent makes rich.

אֹגֵר בַּקַּיִץ בֵּן מַשְׂכִּיל נִרְדָּם בַּקָּצִיר בֵּן מֵבִישׁ׃
from disgrace son in harvest one sleeping from wise son in summer gathering

5. He who gathers in summer is a wise son; but a son who sleeps during the harvest brings shame.

בְּרָכוֹת לְרֹאשׁ צַדִּיק וּפִי רְשָׁעִים יְכַסֶּה חָמָס׃
violence he covered wicked and mouth righteous to head blessings

6. Blessings are upon the head of the just; but violence covers the mouth of the wicked.

זֵכֶר צַדִּיק לִבְרָכָה וְשֵׁם רְשָׁעִים יִרְקָב׃
will rot wicked ones and name to blessing righteous memory

7. The memory of the just is blessed; but the name of the wicked shall rot.

חֲכַם־לֵב יִקַּח מִצְוֹת וֶאֱוִיל שְׂפָתַיִם יִלָּבֵט׃
will ruin lips and prating fool commandments will take heart - wise

8. The wise in heart will heed commandments; but a prating fool will come to ruin.

הוֹלֵךְ בַּתֹּם יֵלֵךְ בֶּטַח וּמְעַקֵּשׁ דְּרָכָיו יִוָּדֵעַ׃
he found out his way and crooked securely he walks in integrity walk

9. He who walks uprightly walks surely; but he who perverts his ways shall be found out.

קֹרֵץ עַיִן יִתֵּן עַצָּבֶת וֶאֱוִיל שְׂפָתַיִם יִלָּבֵט׃
to ruin chattering ones and prating fool grief will give eye winking

10. He who winks the eye causes trouble; but a prating fool will come to ruin.

Proverbs - Chapter 10

מְקוֹר חַיִּים פִּי צַדִּיק וּפִי רְשָׁעִים יְכַסֶּה חָמָס׃
violence he covers wicked ones and mouth righteous mouth life fountain

11. The mouth of a righteous man is a well of life; but violence covers the mouth of the wicked.

שִׂנְאָה תְּעוֹרֵר מְדָנִים וְעַל כָּל־פְּשָׁעִים תְּכַסֶּה אַהֲבָה׃
love you cover transgressions – all and upon dissensions stirs up hate

12. Hatred stirs up quarrels; but love covers all sins.

בְּשִׂפְתֵי נָבוֹן תִּמָּצֵא חָכְמָה וְשֵׁבֶט לְגֵו חֲסַר־לֵב׃
heart – lack to back and rod wisdom you find discerning in lips

13. In the lips of him who has understanding wisdom is found; but a rod is for the back of him who is void of understanding.

חֲכָמִים יִצְפְּנוּ־דָעַת וּפִי־אֱוִיל מְחִתָּה קְרֹבָה׃
near ruin fool – and mouth knowledge – they store up wise ones

14. Wise men lay up knowledge; but the mouth of the fool brings ruin near.

הוֹן עָשִׁיר קִרְיַת עֻזּוֹ מְחִתַּת דַּלִּים רֵישָׁם׃
their poverty poor ones ruin his fornication city rich wealth

15. The rich man's wealth is his strong city; the destruction of the poor is their poverty.

פְּעֻלַּת־צַדִּיק לְחַיִּים תְּבוּאַת רָשָׁע לְחַטָּאת׃
to punishments wicked she come to life righteous - wage

16. The wage of the righteous leads to life; the gain of the wicked to sin.

אֹרַח לְחַיִּים שׁוֹמֵר מוּסָר וְעוֹזֵב תּוֹכַחַת מַתְעֶה׃
leading astray correction and ignoring discipline heeding to life road

17. He who keeps instruction is in the way of life; but he who refuses reproof goes astray.

מְכַסֶּה שִׂנְאָה שִׂפְתֵי־שָׁקֶר וּמוֹצִא דִבָּה הוּא כְסִיל׃
fool he slander and comer out lie – lips hate concealing

18. He who hides hatred has lying lips, and he who utters a slander is a fool.

בְּרֹב דְּבָרִים לֹא יֶחְדַּל־פָּשַׁע וְחוֹשֵׂךְ שְׂפָתָיו מַשְׂכִּיל׃
from wise his lips and holding sin – he absent not speakings in many

19. In the multitude of words sin is not lacking; but he who restrains his lips is wise.

כֶּסֶף נִבְחָר לְשׁוֹן צַדִּיק לֵב רְשָׁעִים כִּמְעָט׃
like little wicked ones heart righteous tongue we choice silver

20. The tongue of the just is like choice silver; the heart of the wicked is little worth.

שִׂפְתֵי צַדִּיק יִרְעוּ רַבִּים וֶאֱוִילִים בַּחֲסַר־לֵב יָמוּתוּ׃
they die heart – in lack and fools many they nourish righteous lips

21. The lips of the righteous feed many; but fools die for lack of wisdom.

בִּרְכַּת יְהוָה הִיא תַעֲשִׁיר וְלֹא־יוֹסִף עֶצֶב עִמָּהּ׃
with her trouble he adds – and not her wealth she ihvh blessings

22. The blessing of the Lord makes rich, and he adds no sorrow with it.

כִּשְׂחוֹק לִכְסִיל עֲשׂוֹת זִמָּה וְחָכְמָה לְאִישׁ תְּבוּנָה׃
he understand to man and wisdom mischief doings to fool like pleasure

23. It is like sport to a fool to do wrong; likewise it is to a man of understanding to practice wisdom.

מְגוֹרַת רָשָׁע הִיא תְבוֹאֶנּוּ וְתַאֲוַת צַדִּיקִים יִתֵּן׃
he gives righteous ones and desire she overtake him she wicked dread

24. What the wicked fears shall come upon him; but the desire of the righteous shall be granted.

כַּעֲבוֹר סוּפָה וְאֵין רָשָׁע וְצַדִּיק יְסוֹד עוֹלָם׃
forever foundation and righteous wicked and isn't storm like past

25. As the stormy wind which passes, so is the wicked no more; but the righteous is an everlasting foundation.

כַּחֹמֶץ לַשִּׁנַּיִם וְכֶעָשָׁן לָעֵינָיִם כֵּן הֶעָצֵל לְשֹׁלְחָיו׃
to his senders the sluggard thus to eyes and like smoke to teeth like vinegar

26. As vinegar to the teeth, and as smoke to the eyes, so is the sluggard to those who send him.

יִרְאַת יְהוָה תּוֹסִיף יָמִים וּשְׁנוֹת רְשָׁעִים תִּקְצֹרְנָה׃
cut short wicked ones and years days she prolong ihvh fears

27. The fear of the Lord prolongs days; but the years of the wicked shall be shortened.

תּוֹחֶלֶת צַדִּיקִים שִׂמְחָה וְתִקְוַת רְשָׁעִים תֹּאבֵד׃
perishes wicked ones and hope happy righteous ones prospect

28. The hope of the righteous shall be gladness; but the expectation of the wicked shall perish.

מָעוֹז לַתֹּם דֶּרֶךְ יְהוָה וּמְחִתָּה לְפֹעֲלֵי אָוֶן׃
iniquity to workers and ruin ihvh way to blameless refuge

29. The way of the Lord is a fortress to the upright; but it is destruction to the workers of iniquity.

צַדִּיק לְעוֹלָם בַּל־יִמּוֹט וּרְשָׁעִים לֹא יִשְׁכְּנוּ־אָרֶץ׃
earth – they remain not wicked ones uprooted – without to forever righteous

30. The righteous shall never be removed; but the wicked shall not inhabit the earth.

פִּי־צַדִּיק יָנוּב חָכְמָה וּלְשׁוֹן תַּהְפֻּכוֹת תִּכָּרֵת׃
it cut off perversenesses and tongue wisdom he producing righteous - mouth

31. The mouth of the just brings forth wisdom; but the perverse tongue shall be cut out.

שִׂפְתֵי צַדִּיק יֵדְעוּן רָצוֹן וּפִי רְשָׁעִים תַּהְפֻּכוֹת׃
will be perverse wicked ones and mouth favor he be knowing righteous lips

32. The lips of the righteous know what is acceptable; but the mouth of the wicked speaks what is perverse.

Chapter 11

ספר משלי פרק יא

מֹאזְנֵי מִרְמָה תּוֹעֲבַת יְהֹוָה וְאֶבֶן שְׁלֵמָה רְצוֹנוֹ׃

1. A false scale is an abomination to the Lord; but a just weight is his delight.

בָּא זָדוֹן וַיָּבֹא קָלוֹן וְאֶת־צְנוּעִים חָכְמָה׃

2. When pride comes, then comes shame; but with the humble is wisdom.

תֻּמַּת יְשָׁרִים תַּנְחֵם וְסֶלֶף בֹּגְדִים וְשָׁדָם [יְשָׁדֵּם]׃

3. (K) The integrity of the upright shall guide them; but the perverseness of the faithless shall destroy them.

לֹא־יוֹעִיל הוֹן בְּיוֹם עֶבְרָה וּצְדָקָה תַּצִּיל מִמָּוֶת׃

4. Riches profit not in the day of wrath; but righteousness saves from death.

צִדְקַת תָּמִים תְּיַשֵּׁר דַּרְכּוֹ וּבְרִשְׁעָתוֹ יִפֹּל רָשָׁע׃

5. The righteousness of the innocent shall direct his way; but the wicked shall fall by his own wickedness.

צִדְקַת יְשָׁרִים תַּצִּילֵם וּבְהַוַּת בֹּגְדִים יִלָּכֵדוּ׃

6. The righteousness of the upright shall save them; but transgressors shall be caught by their own lust.

בְּמוֹת אָדָם רָשָׁע תֹּאבַד תִּקְוָה וְתוֹחֶלֶת אוֹנִים אָבָדָה׃

7. When a wicked man dies, his expectation shall perish; and the hope of unjust men perishes.

צַדִּיק מִצָּרָה נֶחֱלָץ וַיָּבֹא רָשָׁע תַּחְתָּיו׃

8. The righteous is saved from trouble, and the wicked gets into it instead.

בְּפֶה חָנֵף יַשְׁחִת רֵעֵהוּ וּבְדַעַת צַדִּיקִים יֵחָלֵצוּ׃

9. A hypocrite with his mouth destroys his neighbor; but through knowledge shall the just be saved.

בְּטוּב צַדִּיקִים תַּעֲלֹץ קִרְיָה וּבַאֲבֹד רְשָׁעִים רִנָּה׃

10. When it goes well with the righteous, the city rejoices; and when the wicked perish, there is jubilation.

בְּבִרְכַּת יְשָׁרִים תָּרוּם קָרֶת וּבְפִי רְשָׁעִים תֵּהָרֵס׃

destroyed   wicked ones   and in mouth   city   exalted   upright ones   in blessings

11. By the blessing of the upright the city is exalted; but it is overthrown by the mouth of the wicked.

בָּז־לְרֵעֵהוּ חֲסַר־לֵב וְאִישׁ תְּבוּנוֹת יַחֲרִישׁ׃

he holds tongue   understandings   and man   heart – lacking   to his neighbor - derides

12. He who is void of wisdom despises his neighbor; but a man of understanding holds his peace.

הוֹלֵךְ רָכִיל מְגַלֶּה־סּוֹד וְנֶאֱמַן־רוּחַ מְכַסֶּה דָבָר׃

matter   keeping secret   spirit - and trustworthy   confidence – betraying   gossip   he goes

13. A talebearer reveals secrets; but he who is of a faithful spirit conceals the matter.

בְּאֵין תַּחְבֻּלוֹת יִפָּל־עָם וּתְשׁוּעָה בְּרֹב יוֹעֵץ׃

he advises   in many   and victory   people - falls   guidances   in isn't

14. Where there is no counsel, the people fall; but in the multitude of counsellors there is safety.

רַע־יֵרוֹעַ כִּי־עָרַב זָר וְשֹׂנֵא תֹקְעִים בּוֹטֵחַ׃

being safe   strikings   and hates   stranger   security – like   he suffer - bad

15. He who gives surety for a stranger shall smart for it; and he who hates suretyship is secure.

אֵשֶׁת חֵן תִּתְמֹךְ כָּבוֹד וְעָרִיצִים יִתְמְכוּ־עֹשֶׁר׃

wealth – they gain   and ruthless men   honor   gains   grace   woman

16. A gracious woman obtains honor; and strong men obtain riches.

גֹּמֵל נַפְשׁוֹ אִישׁ חָסֶד וְעֹכֵר שְׁאֵרוֹ אַכְזָרִי׃

cruel man   his self   and harming   mercy   man   his soul   benefiting

17. The merciful man does good to his own soul; but he who is cruel troubles his own flesh.

רָשָׁע עֹשֶׂה פְעֻלַּת־שָׁקֶר וְזֹרֵעַ צְדָקָה שֶׂכֶר אֱמֶת׃

truth   reward   righteousness   and one seeding   lie – wage   doing   wicked

18. The wicked works a deceitful deed; but to him who sows righteousness shall be a sure reward.

כֵּן־צְדָקָה לְחַיִּים וּמְרַדֵּף רָעָה לְמוֹתוֹ׃

to his death   evil   and pursuing   to life   righteous - thus

19. He who is firm in righteousness will life; so he who pursues evil comes to his own death.

תּוֹעֲבַת יְהוָה עִקְּשֵׁי־לֵב וּרְצוֹנוֹ תְּמִימֵי דָרֶךְ׃

way   blameless   and his delight   heart – perverse   ihvh   abomination

20. Those who are of a perverse heart are an abomination to the Lord; but those who are upright in their way are his delight.

יָד לְיָד לֹא־יִנָּקֶה רָע וְזֶרַע צַדִּיקִים נִמְלָט׃

go free   righteous ones   and seed   bad   unpunished – not   to hand   hand

21. Though who join hands for wicked ends shall not go unpunished; but the seed of the righteous shall be saved.

נֶ֣זֶם זָ֭הָב בְּאַ֣ף חֲזִ֑יר אִשָּׁ֥ה יָ֝פָ֗ה וְסָ֣רַת טָֽעַם׃

discretion and withdrawing beautiful woman pig in nose gold ring

22. As a jewel of gold in a swine's snout, so is a pretty woman who lacks discretion.

תַּאֲוַ֣ת צַדִּיקִ֣ים אַךְ־ט֑וֹב תִּקְוַ֖ת רְשָׁעִ֣ים עֶבְרָֽה׃

wrath wicked ones hope good - surely righteous ones desire

23. The desire of the righteous is only good; but the expectation of the wicked is wrath.

יֵ֣שׁ מְ֭פַזֵּר וְנוֹסָ֥ף ע֑וֹד וְחוֹשֵׂ֥ךְ מִ֝יֹּ֗שֶׁר אַךְ־לְמַחְסֽוֹר׃

to poverty – surely from upright and withholdin again and added giving freely there is

24. There is one who gives freely, and yet increases; another one withholds what he should give, and only comes to want.

נֶֽפֶשׁ־בְּרָכָ֥ה תְדֻשָּׁ֑ן וּ֝מַרְוֶ֗ה גַּם־ה֥וּא יוֹרֶֽא׃

will be refreshed he – also and refreshin prosper blessed - soul

25. The liberal soul shall be made rich; and he who waters shall be himself be watered.

מֹ֣נֵֽעַ בָּ֭ר יִקְּבֻ֣הוּ לְא֑וֹם וּ֝בְרָכָ֗ה לְרֹ֣אשׁ מַשְׁבִּֽיר׃

seller to head and blessing to people they curse him grain hoarding

26. He who withholds grain, the people shall curse him; but blessing shall be upon the head of him who sells it.

שֹׁ֣חֵֽר ט֭וֹב יְבַקֵּ֣שׁ רָצ֑וֹן וְדֹרֵ֖שׁ רָעָ֣ה תְבוֹאֶֽנּוּ׃

come to him bad and searching favor he seeks good early seeker

27. He who diligently seeks good procures favor; but evil comes to him who searches for it.

בּוֹטֵ֣חַ בְּ֭עָשְׁרוֹ ה֣וּא יִפֹּ֑ל וְ֝כֶעָלֶ֗ה צַדִּיקִ֥ים יִפְרָֽחוּ׃

they thrive righteous ones and like green leaf he falls he in his riches trusting

28. He who trusts in his riches shall fall; but the righteous shall flourish like a green leaf.

עוֹכֵ֣ר בֵּ֭יתוֹ יִנְחַל־ר֑וּחַ וְעֶ֥בֶד אֱ֝וִ֗יל לַחֲכַם־לֵֽב׃

heart – to wise fool and servant wind – he inherits his house troubling

29. He who troubles his own house shall inherit the wind; and the fool shall be servant to the wise of heart.

פְּרִֽי־צַ֭דִּיק עֵ֣ץ חַיִּ֑ים וְלֹקֵ֖חַ נְפָשׁ֣וֹת חָכָֽם׃

wise souls and wins life tree righteous - fruit

30. The fruit of the righteous is a tree of life; and he who wins souls is wise.

הֵ֣ן צַ֭דִּיק בָּאָ֣רֶץ יְשֻׁלָּ֑ם אַ֝֗ף כִּֽי־רָשָׁ֥ע וְחוֹטֵֽא׃

and sinner wicked – like so he be rewarded in earth righteous thus

31. Behold, if the righteous is rewarded on earth, how much more the wicked and the sinner!

Chapter 12

ספר משלי פרק יב

אֹהֵב מוּסָר אֹהֵב דָּעַת וְשׂוֹנֵא תוֹכַחַת בָּעַר׃
lover   discipline   lover   knowledge   and hater   correction   stupid

1. Whoever loves discipline loves knowledge; but he who hates reproof is stupid.

טוֹב יָפִיק רָצוֹן מֵיְהוָה וְאִישׁ מְזִמּוֹת יַרְשִׁיעַ׃
good   obtains   favor   from ihvh   and man   craftinesses   he condemns

2. A good man obtains favor from the Lord; but a man of wicked devices will he condemn.

לֹא־יִכּוֹן אָדָם בְּרֶשַׁע וְשֹׁרֶשׁ צַדִּיקִים בַּל־יִמּוֹט׃
establish - not   Adam   in wickedness   and root   righteous ones   he be moved – without

3. A man shall not be established by wickedness; but the root of the righteous shall not be moved.

אֵשֶׁת־חַיִל עֲטֶרֶת בַּעְלָהּ וּכְרָקָב בְּעַצְמוֹתָיו מְבִישָׁה׃
nobility - wife   crown   her husband   and like decay   in his bones   brings disgrace

4. A virtuous woman is a crown to her husband; but she who acts shamefully is as rottenness in his bones.

מַחְשְׁבוֹת צַדִּיקִים מִשְׁפָּט תַּחְבֻּלוֹת רְשָׁעִים מִרְמָה׃
thoughts   righteous ones   judgment   advisers   wicked ones   deceit

5. The thoughts of the righteous are right; but the counsels of the wicked are deceit.

דִּבְרֵי רְשָׁעִים אֱרָב־דָּם וּפִי יְשָׁרִים יַצִּילֵם׃
speakings   wicked ones   blood – lie in wait   and mouth   upright ones   rescues them

6. The words of the wicked lie in wait for blood; but the mouth of the upright saves them.

הָפוֹךְ רְשָׁעִים וְאֵינָם וּבֵית צַדִּיקִים יַעֲמֹד׃
the over throw   wicked ones   and isn't them   and house   righteous ones   he stand

7. The wicked are overthrown, and are no more; but the house of the righteous shall stand.

לְפִי־שִׂכְלוֹ יְהֻלַּל־אִישׁ וְנַעֲוֵה־לֵב יִהְיֶה לָבוּז׃
his wisdom – to mouth   man – he praised   heart – and perverse   will be   despised

8. A man shall be commended according to his wisdom; but he who is of a perverse heart shall be despised.

טוֹב נִקְלֶה וְעֶבֶד לוֹ מִמִּתְכַּבֵּד וַחֲסַר־לָחֶם׃
good   nobody   and servant   to him   from pretending greatness   bread – and lacking

9. Better is a man lightly esteemed who has a servant, than he who honors himself but lacks bread.

יוֹדֵעַ צַדִּיק נֶפֶשׁ בְּהֶמְתּוֹ וְרַחֲמֵי רְשָׁעִים אַכְזָרִי׃
knows   righteous   soul   his beast   and kindness   wicked ones   cruel

10. A righteous man regards the life of his beast; but the heart of the wicked is cruel.

עֹבֵד אַדְמָתוֹ יִשְׂבַּע־לָחֶם וּמְרַדֵּף רֵיקִים חֲסַר־לֵב׃

working his soil — he be satisfied — bread and one chasing fantasies lacks — heart

11. He who tills his land shall have plenty of bread; but he who follows vain persons is void of understanding.

חָמַד רָשָׁע מְצוֹד רָעִים וְשֹׁרֶשׁ צַדִּיקִים יִתֵּן׃

desires wicked ones plunder evil ones and root righteous ones he gives

12. The wicked craves, he is snared by evil; but the righteous strike root.

בְּפֶשַׁע שְׂפָתַיִם מוֹקֵשׁ רָע וַיֵּצֵא מִצָּרָה צַדִּיק׃

in sinfulness lips trap bad and he comes out from trouble righteous

13. The wicked is trapped by the transgression of his lips; but the just shall come out of trouble.

מִפְּרִי פִי־אִישׁ יִשְׂבַּע־טוֹב

from fruit mouth — man he be filled — good

וּגְמוּל יְדֵי־אָדָם יָשׁוּב [יָשִׁיב] לוֹ׃

and reward hand — Adam he returned to him

14. (K) A man shall be satisfied with good by the fruit of his mouth; and the reward of a man's hands shall be rendered to him.

דֶּרֶךְ אֱוִיל יָשָׁר בְּעֵינָיו וְשֹׁמֵעַ לְעֵצָה חָכָם׃

way fool upright in his eyes and hearing to advice wise

15. The way of a fool is right in his own eyes; but he who listens to counsel is wise.

אֱוִיל בַּיּוֹם יִוָּדַע כַּעְסוֹ וְכֹסֶה קָלוֹן עָרוּם׃

fool in day known his anger and overlooking insult prudent

16. A fool's wrath is immediately known; but a prudent man conceals disgrace.

יָפִיחַ אֱמוּנָה יַגִּיד צֶדֶק וְעֵד שְׁקָרִים מִרְמָה׃

he mouths truth he tells righteous and witness fallacies deceits

17. He who speaks truth gives just evidence; but a false witness deceits.

יֵשׁ בּוֹטֶה כְּמַדְקְרוֹת חָרֶב וּלְשׁוֹן חֲכָמִים מַרְפֵּא׃

there is speak recklessly like piercing sword and tongue wise ones health

18. There is one who speaks like the piercing of a sword; but the tongue of the wise is health.

שְׂפַת־אֱמֶת תִּכּוֹן לָעַד וְעַד־אַרְגִּיעָה לְשׁוֹן שָׁקֶר׃

truth - lip established to ever and till — be momentary tongue lie

19. The lip of truth shall be established for ever; but a lying tongue is but for a moment.

מִרְמָה בְּלֶב־חֹרְשֵׁי־רָע וּלְיֹעֲצֵי שָׁלוֹם שִׂמְחָה׃

deceit in heart — plotting — bad and to promoting peace happiness

20. Deceit is in the heart of those who plot evil; but the counsellors of peace have joy.

לֹא־יְאֻנֶּה לַצַּדִּיק כָּל־אָוֶן וּרְשָׁעִים מָלְאוּ רָע׃
bad   they fill   and wicked ones   inequity - all   to righteous   befalls - not

21. No evil shall happen to the just; but the wicked shall be filled with trouble.

תּוֹעֲבַת יְהוָה שִׂפְתֵי־שָׁקֶר וְעֹשֵׂי אֱמוּנָה רְצוֹנוֹ׃
his favor   truth   and doings   lie – lips   ihvh   abomination

22. Lying lips are an abomination to the Lord; but those who deal truly are his delight.

אָדָם עָרוּם כֹּסֶה דָּעַת וְלֵב כְּסִילִים יִקְרָא אִוֶּלֶת׃
folly   he calls   fool ones   and heart   knowledge   keeping   prudent   Adam

23. A prudent man conceals knowledge; but the heart of fools proclaims his foolishness.

יַד־חָרוּצִים תִּמְשׁוֹל וּרְמִיָּה תִּהְיֶה לָמַס׃
slave labor   he be   and laziness   he rules   diligent ones - hand

24. The hand of the diligent man shall bear rule; but the lazy man shall be under tribute.

דְּאָגָה בְלֶב־אִישׁ יַשְׁחֶנָּה וְדָבָר טוֹב יְשַׂמְּחֶנָּה׃
he happies her   good   and speech   weighs down   man – in heart   anxiety

25. Anxiety in the heart of a man weighs him down; but a good word makes him glad.

יָתֵר מֵרֵעֵהוּ צַדִּיק וְדֶרֶךְ רְשָׁעִים תַּתְעֵם׃
leads them astray   wicked ones   and way   righteous   from his neighbor   cautions

26. The righteous guides his neighbor aright; but the way of the wicked leads them astray.

לֹא־יַחֲרֹךְ רְמִיָּה צֵידוֹ וְהוֹן־אָדָם יָקָר חָרוּץ׃
diligent   precious   Adam – and possession   his game   lazy man   roasts - not

27. The lazy man does not roast his catch; but the diligent man will get precious wealth.

בְּאֹרַח־צְדָקָה חַיִּים וְדֶרֶךְ נְתִיבָה אַל־מָוֶת׃
death – unto   worn path   and way   life   righteous – in road

28. In the way of righteousness is life; and in its path there is no death.

Chapter 13

ספר משלי פרק יג

בֵּן חָכָם מוּסַר אָב וְלֵץ לֹא־שָׁמַע גְּעָרָה:
rebuke   hears-not   and mocking   father   instruction   wise   son

1. A wise son hears his father's instruction; but a scorner does not accept rebuke.

מִפְּרִי פִי־אִישׁ יֹאכַל טוֹב וְנֶפֶשׁ בֹּגְדִים חָמָס:
violence   unfaithful one   and soul   good   he eats   man-mouth   from fruit

2. A man shall eat good from the fruit of his mouth; but the desire of the transgressors is for violence.

נֹצֵר פִּיו שֹׁמֵר נַפְשׁוֹ פֹּשֵׂק שְׂפָתָיו מְחִתָּה־לוֹ:
to him-ruin   his lips   opening wide   his soul   heed   his mouth   guarding

3. He who guards his mouth keeps his life; but he who opens wide his lips shall have destruction.

מִתְאַוָּה וָאַיִן נַפְשׁוֹ עָצֵל וְנֶפֶשׁ חָרֻצִים תְּדֻשָּׁן:
satisfied   diligent ones   and soul   sluggard   his soul   and isn't   craving

4. The soul of the sluggard desires, and has nothing; but the soul of the diligent shall be richly supplied.

דְּבַר־שֶׁקֶר יִשְׂנָא צַדִּיק וְרָשָׁע יַבְאִישׁ וְיַחְפִּיר:
and he disgrace   he shame   and wicked   righteous   he hates   lie-speak

5. A righteous man hates lying; but a wicked man is loathsome, and comes to shame.

צְדָקָה תִּצֹּר תָּם־דָּרֶךְ וְרִשְׁעָה תְּסַלֵּף חַטָּאת:
sinner   overthrows   and towards wickedness   way-integrity   guards   righteous

6. Righteousness keeps him who is upright in the way; but wickedness overthrows the sinner.

יֵשׁ מִתְעַשֵּׁר וְאֵין כֹּל מִתְרוֹשֵׁשׁ וְהוֹן רָב:
much   and rich   pretending poverty   all   and isn't   one pretending rich   there is

7. There is one who pretends to be rich, yet has nothing; there is one who pretends to be poor, yet has great riches.

כֹּפֶר נֶפֶשׁ־אִישׁ עָשְׁרוֹ וְרָשׁ לֹא־שָׁמַע גְּעָרָה:
threat   hear-not   and poor   his wealth   man-soul   ransom

8. The ransom of a man's life are his riches; but the poor hears no threat.

אוֹר־צַדִּיקִים יִשְׂמָח וְנֵר רְשָׁעִים יִדְעָךְ:
snuffed out   wicked ones   and lamp   happy   righteous ones-light

9. The light of the righteous rejoices; but the lamp of the wicked shall be put out.

רַק־בְּזָדוֹן יִתֵּן מַצָּה וְאֶת־נוֹעָצִים חָכְמָה:
wisdom   advised ones-and that   quarrel   he gives   in pride-only

10. Only by pride comes quarrel; but with the well advised is wisdom.

הוֹן מֵהֶבֶל יִמְעָט וְקֹבֵץ עַל־יָד יַרְבֶּה:
he increases hand – upon and gathering he be little from dishonesty wealth

11. Wealth acquired by vanity shall be diminished; but he who gathers by labor shall increase.

תּוֹחֶלֶת מְמֻשָּׁכָה מַחֲלָה־לֵב וְעֵץ חַיִּים תַּאֲוָה בָאָה:
comes longing life and tree heart sick deferred hope

12. Hope deferred makes the heart sick; but desire fulfilled is a tree of life.

בָּז לְדָבָר יֵחָבֶל לוֹ וִירֵא מִצְוָה הוּא יְשֻׁלָּם:
he be paid he commandment and fear to him will pay to speak scorning

13. Whoever despises the word shall be destroyed; but he who fears the commandment shall be rewarded.

תּוֹרַת חָכָם מְקוֹר חַיִּים לָסוּר מִמֹּקְשֵׁי מָוֶת:
death snares to close life fountain wise Torah

14. The Torah of the wise is a fountain of life, to depart from the traps of death.

שֵׂכֶל־טוֹב יִתֶּן־חֵן וְדֶרֶךְ בֹּגְדִים אֵיתָן:
hard unfaithful ones and way favor – he gives good – intellect

15. Good understanding gives grace; but the way of the transgressors is hard.

כָּל־עָרוּם יַעֲשֶׂה בְדָעַת וּכְסִיל יִפְרֹשׂ אִוֶּלֶת:
follies he exposes and fool in knowledge he does prudent – all

16. In everything a prudent man acts with knowledge; but a fool lays bare his folly.

מַלְאָךְ רָשָׁע יִפֹּל בְּרָע וְצִיר אֱמוּנִים מַרְפֵּא:
health trusting ones and envoy in bad he falls wicked messenger

17. A bad messenger falls into mischief; but a faithful envoy brings healing.

רֵישׁ וְקָלוֹן פּוֹרֵעַ מוּסָר וְשׁוֹמֵר תּוֹכַחַת יְכֻבָּד:
he be honored correction and heeder instruction ignoring and shame poverty

18. Poverty and shame come to him who refuses instruction; but he who heeds reproof shall be honored.

תַּאֲוָה נִהְיָה תֶעֱרַב לְנָפֶשׁ וְתוֹעֲבַת כְּסִילִים סוּר מֵרָע:
from evil depart fool ones and abomination to soul sweet fulfilled longing

19. A desire fulfilled is sweet to the soul; but it is abomination to fools to depart from evil.

הֹלֵךְ [הוֹלֵךְ] אֶת־חֲכָמִים וֶחָכָם [יֶחְכָּם] וְרֹעֶה כְסִילִים יֵרוֹעַ:
he suffer harm fool ones and companions he be wise wise ones – that you walk

20. (K) He who walks with wise men shall be wise; but a companion of fools will suffer harm.

חַטָּאִים תְּרַדֵּף רָעָה וְאֶת־צַדִּיקִים יְשַׁלֶּם־טוֹב:
good – he is paid righteous ones – and that evil pursues sinner ones

21. Evil pursues sinners; but to the righteous good shall be repaid.

טוֹב יַנְחִיל בְּנֵי־בָנִים וְצָפוּן לַצַּדִּיק חֵיל חוֹטֵא׃
<small>sinner wealth to righteous and stored   sons – son he inheritance good</small>

22. A good man leaves an inheritance to his grandchildren; but the wealth of the sinner is laid up for the just.

רָב־אֹכֶל נִיר רָאשִׁים וְיֵשׁ נִסְפֶּה בְּלֹא מִשְׁפָּט׃
<small>judgment without swept away and there is poor ones tilled field food - much</small>

23. Much food is in the well tilled acre of the poor; but sometimes ruin comes for lack of judgment.

חוֹשֵׂךְ שִׁבְטוֹ שׂוֹנֵא בְנוֹ וְאֹהֲבוֹ שִׁחֲרוֹ מוּסָר׃
<small>instruction his careful and his love his son hates his rod sparing</small>

24. He who spares his rod hates his son; but he who loves him disciplines him early.

צַדִּיק אֹכֵל לְשֹׂבַע נַפְשׁוֹ וּבֶטֶן רְשָׁעִים תֶּחְסָר׃
<small>lacks wicked and stomach his soul to fill eats righteous</small>

25. The righteous eats to satisfy his soul; but the belly of the wicked suffers want.

Chapter 14

ספר משלי פרק יד

חַכְמוֹת נָשִׁים בָּנְתָה בֵיתָהּ וְאִוֶּלֶת בְּיָדֶיהָ תֶהֶרְסֶנּוּ:

_{she tears down   in her hands   and foolish   her house   she builds   women   wise ones}

1. The wisdom of women builds her house; but folly plucks it down with her hands.

הוֹלֵךְ בְּיָשְׁרוֹ יְרֵא יְהֹוָה וּנְלוֹז דְּרָכָיו בּוֹזֵהוּ:

_{despising him   his ways   and devious   ihvh   fear   in his upright   walk}

2. He who walks in his uprightness fears the Lord; but he who is perverse in his ways despises him.

בְּפִי־אֱוִיל חֹטֶר גַּאֲוָה וְשִׂפְתֵי חֲכָמִים תִּשְׁמוּרֵם:

_{she protects them   wise ones   and lips   proud   rod   fool – in mouth}

3. In the mouth of the foolish is a rod of pride; but the lips of the wise shall preserve them.

בְּאֵין אֲלָפִים אֵבוּס בָּר וְרָב־תְּבוּאוֹת בְּכֹחַ שׁוֹר:

_{ox   in strength   produces – and much   clean   stall   oxen   in isn't}

4. Where no oxen are, the crib is clean; but much increase comes by the strength of the ox.

עֵד אֱמוּנִים לֹא יְכַזֵּב וְיָפִיחַ כְּזָבִים עֵד שָׁקֶר:

_{lie   witness   false ones   and he pours out   he deceives   not   honest ones   witness}

5. A trusty witness will not lie; but a false witness will utter lies.

בִּקֶּשׁ־לֵץ חָכְמָה וָאָיִן וְדַעַת לְנָבוֹן נָקָל:

_{comes easily   to discerning   and knowledge   and isn't   wisdom   mocking - seeks}

6. A scorner seeks wisdom, and does not find it; but knowledge is easy to him who understands.

לֵךְ מִנֶּגֶד לְאִישׁ כְּסִיל וּבַל־יָדַעְתָּ שִׂפְתֵי־דָעַת:

_{knowledge – lips   you know – and without   fool   to man   from near   go}

7. Go from the presence of a foolish man, for in him you do not perceive the lips of knowledge.

חָכְמַת עָרוּם הָבִין דַּרְכּוֹ וְאִוֶּלֶת כְּסִילִים מִרְמָה:

_{deception   fool ones   and follys   his way   the understanding   prudent   wisdom}

8. The wisdom of the prudent is to understand his way; but the folly of fools is deceit.

אֱוִלִים יָלִיץ אָשָׁם וּבֵין יְשָׁרִים רָצוֹן:

_{favor   upright ones   and among   amends   mocks   fool ones}

9. Fools mock sin; but among the righteous there is favor.

לֵב יוֹדֵעַ מָרַּת נַפְשׁוֹ וּבְשִׂמְחָתוֹ לֹא־יִתְעָרַב זָר:

_{stranger   he share – not   and his happiness   his soul   bitterness   knows   heart}

10. The heart knows his own bitterness; and no stranger shares its joy.

Proverbs - Chapter 14

בֵּית רְשָׁעִים יִשָּׁמֵד וְאֹהֶל יְשָׁרִים יַפְרִיחַ׃
he flourishes   upright ones   and tent   he be destroyed   wicked ones   house

11. The house of the wicked shall be overthrown; but the tent of the upright shall flourish.

יֵשׁ דֶּרֶךְ יָשָׁר לִפְנֵי־אִישׁ וְאַחֲרִיתָהּ דַּרְכֵי־מָוֶת׃
death – way   and after   man – before   upright   way   there is

12. There is a way which seems right to a man, but its end are the ways of death.

גַּם־בִּשְׂחוֹק יִכְאַב־לֵב וְאַחֲרִיתָהּ שִׂמְחָה תוּגָה׃
grief   happy   and her after   heart – he aches   in laughter - also

13. Even in laughter the heart aches; and the end of that mirth is grief.

מִדְּרָכָיו יִשְׂבַּע סוּג לֵב וּמֵעָלָיו אִישׁ טוֹב׃
good   man   and his ___   heart   faithless   he filled   from his way

14. The dissembler shall have enough of his own ways; and a good man shall find satisfaction in himself.

פֶּתִי יַאֲמִין לְכָל־דָּבָר וְעָרוּם יָבִין לַאֲשֻׁרוֹ׃
to his step   he understand   and prudent   speech – to all   he believes   simple

15. The simpleton believes every word; but the prudent man looks well where he is going.

חָכָם יָרֵא וְסָר מֵרָע וּכְסִיל מִתְעַבֵּר וּבוֹטֵחַ׃
and reckless   rages   and fool   from bad   and departs   fear   wise

16. A wise man fears, and departs from evil; but the fool rages, and is confident.

קְצַר־אַפַּיִם יַעֲשֶׂה אִוֶּלֶת וְאִישׁ מְזִמּוֹת יִשָּׂנֵא׃
he be hated   craftiness   and man   folly   does   angers - quick

17. He who is soon angry deals foolishly; and a man of wicked devices is hated.

נָחֲלוּ פְתָאיִם אִוֶּלֶת וַעֲרוּמִים יַכְתִּרוּ דָעַת׃
knowledge   they crown   and prudent ones   folly   simple ones   they inherit

18. The simple inherit folly; but the prudent are crowned with knowledge.

שַׁחוּ רָעִים לִפְנֵי טוֹבִים וּרְשָׁעִים עַל־שַׁעֲרֵי צַדִּיק׃
righteous   gates – upon   and wicked ones   good ones   before   evil ones   they bow

19. The evil bow before the good; and the wicked at the gates of the righteous.

גַּם־לְרֵעֵהוּ יִשָּׂנֵא רָשׁ וְאֹהֲבֵי עָשִׁיר רַבִּים׃
many   rich   and loved   poor   he hated   to neighbor - also

20. The poor is hated even by his own neighbor; but the rich has many friends.

בָּז־לְרֵעֵהוּ חוֹטֵא וּמְחוֹנֵן עֲנָיִים [עֲנָוִים] אַשְׁרָיו׃
his blessed   needy ones   and kind   sin   to his neighbor - despising

21. (K) He who despises his neighbor sins; but happy is he who is kind to the humble.

הֲלוֹא־יִתְעוּ חֹרְשֵׁי רָע וְחֶסֶד וֶאֱמֶת חֹרְשֵׁי טוֹב׃
good   planning   and truth   and mercy   evil   plotting   they astray – the not

22. Do not those who plan evil go astray? But those who plan good shall enjoy loyalty

and truth.

בְּכָל־עֶצֶב יִהְיֶה מוֹתָר וּדְבַר־שְׂפָתַיִם אַךְ־לְמַחְסוֹר:
   poverty – only   lips – and speaking   profit   will be   hard work – in all

23. In all labor there is profit; but the talk of the lips tends only to penury.

עֲטֶרֶת חֲכָמִים עָשְׁרָם אִוֶּלֶת כְּסִילִים אִוֶּלֶת:
   follies   fool ones   follies   their wealth   wise ones   crown

24. The crown of the wise is their riches; but the foolishness of fools is folly.

מַצִּיל נְפָשׁוֹת עֵד אֱמֶת וְיָפִחַ כְּזָבִים מִרְמָה:
   deceitful   falsehoods and witness   truth   witness   souls   saving

25. A true witness saves lives; but a deceitful witness speaks lies.

בְּיִרְאַת יְהוָה מִבְטַח־עֹז וּלְבָנָיו יִהְיֶה מַחְסֶה:
   refuge   will be   and to his sons   strength – security   ihvh   in fear

26. In the fear of the Lord is strong confidence; and his children shall have a place of refuge.

יִרְאַת יְהוָה מְקוֹר חַיִּים לָסוּר מִמֹּקְשֵׁי מָוֶת:
   death   from snares   to depart   life   fountain   ihvh   fear

27. The fear of the Lord is a fountain of life, to depart from the traps of death.

בְּרָב־עָם הַדְרַת־מֶלֶךְ וּבְאֶפֶס לְאֹם מְחִתַּת רָזוֹן:
   prince   ruin   to people   and in lack   king – the glory   people – in much

28. In the multitude of people is the king's glory; but in the lack of people is the downfall of the prince.

אֶרֶךְ אַפַּיִם רַב־תְּבוּנָה וּקְצַר־רוּחַ מֵרִים אִוֶּלֶת:
   folly   displaying   spirit – and hasty   understanding – many   angers   long

29. He who is slow to wrath is of great understanding; but he who is hasty of spirit exalts folly.

חַיֵּי בְשָׂרִים לֵב מַרְפֵּא וּרְקַב עֲצָמוֹת קִנְאָה:
   envy   bones   and rot   health   heart   in flesh   life

30. A sound heart is the life of the flesh; but envy is the rottenness of the bones.

עֹשֵׁק דָּל חֵרֵף עֹשֵׂהוּ וּמְכַבְּדוֹ חֹנֵן אֶבְיוֹן:
   needy   kind and his hovering lips   his maker   showing contempt   poor   oppressing

31. He who oppresses the poor blasphemes his maker; but he who has mercy on the poor honors him.

בְּרָעָתוֹ יִדָּחֶה רָשָׁע וְחֹסֶה בְמוֹתוֹ צַדִּיק:
   righteous   in his death   and refuge   wicked   brought down   in his evil

32. The wicked is overthrown through his evil doing; but the righteous has hope in his death.

בְּלֵב נָבוֹן תָּנוּחַ חָכְמָה וּבְקֶרֶב כְּסִילִים תִּוָּדֵעַ:
   you be known   fool ones   and in near   wisdom   reposes   discerning   in heart

33. Wisdom rests in the heart of him who has understanding; but that which is in the

midst of fools is made known.

צְדָקָה תְרוֹמֵם־גּוֹי וְחֶסֶד לְאֻמִּים חַטָּאת׃
righteous   nations – exalts   and mercy   to peoples   sin

34. Righteousness exalts a nation; but sin is a reproach to any people.

רְצוֹן־מֶלֶךְ לְעֶבֶד מַשְׂכִּיל וְעֶבְרָתוֹ תִּהְיֶה מֵבִישׁ׃
king - favor   to servant   being wise   and his wrath   will be   bringing shame

35. The king's favor is turned towards a wise servant; but his wrath is against him who causes shame.

Chapter 15

ספר משלי פרק טו

מַעֲנֶה־רַּךְ יָשִׁיב חֵמָה וּדְבַר־עֶצֶב יַעֲלֶה־אָף׃
<small>anger – he raises   harshness – and speech   wrath   he turns away   soft – answer</small>

1. A soft answer turns away wrath; but grievous words stir up anger.

לְשׁוֹן חֲכָמִים תֵּיטִיב דָּעַת וּפִי כְסִילִים יַבִּיעַ אִוֶּלֶת׃
<small>follies   anguishes   fool ones   and mouth   knowledge   commends   wise ones   tongue</small>

2. The tongue of the wise dispenses knowledge; but the mouth of fools pours out foolishness.

בְּכָל־מָקוֹם עֵינֵי יְהוָה צֹפוֹת רָעִים וְטוֹבִים׃
<small>and good ones   evil ones   watchings   ihvh   eyes   place – in all</small>

3. The eyes of the Lord are in every place, beholding the evil and the good.

מַרְפֵּא לָשׁוֹן עֵץ חַיִּים וְסֶלֶף בָּהּ שֶׁבֶר בְּרוּחַ׃
<small>in spirit   breaks   in her   and deceit   life   tree   tongue   healing</small>

4. A wholesome tongue is a tree of life; but perverseness in it breaks the spirit.

אֱוִיל יִנְאַץ מוּסַר אָבִיו וְשֹׁמֵר תּוֹכַחַת יַעְרִם׃
<small>he shows prudence   corrections   and heeder   his father   discipline   spurns   fool</small>

5. A fool despises his father's instruction; but he who heeds reproof is prudent.

בֵּית צַדִּיק חֹסֶן רָב וּבִתְבוּאַת רָשָׁע נֶעְכָּרֶת׃
<small>will be troubles   wicked   and incomes   much   treasure   righteous   house</small>

6. In the house of the righteous there is much treasure; but in the income of the wicked there is trouble.

שִׂפְתֵי חֲכָמִים יְזָרוּ דָּעַת וְלֵב כְּסִילִים לֹא־כֵן׃
<small>thus – not   fools   and heart   knowledge   they spread   wise ones   lips</small>

7. The lips of the wise spread knowledge; but the heart of the foolish does not do so.

זֶבַח רְשָׁעִים תּוֹעֲבַת יְהוָה וּתְפִלַּת יְשָׁרִים רְצוֹנוֹ׃
<small>his favor   upright ones   and prayers   ihvh   abomination   wicked ones   sacrifice</small>

8. The sacrifice of the wicked is an abomination to the Lord; but the prayer of the upright is his delight.

תּוֹעֲבַת יְהוָה דֶּרֶךְ רָשָׁע וּמְרַדֵּף צְדָקָה יֶאֱהָב׃
<small>he loves   righteousness   and perusing   wicked   way   ihvh   abomination</small>

9. The way of the wicked is an abomination to the Lord; but he loves him who follows after righteousness.

מוּסָר רָע לְעֹזֵב אֹרַח שׂוֹנֵא תוֹכַחַת יָמוּת׃
<small>he dies   correction   hater   road   to leave   bad   discipline</small>

10. Correction is grievous to him who forsakes the way; and he who hates reproof shall die.

Proverbs - Chapter 15

שְׁאוֹל וַאֲבַדּוֹן נֶגֶד יְהֹוָה אַף כִּי־לִבּוֹת בְּנֵי־אָדָם:
Adam – sons   hearts – like   surely   ihvh   before   and Abaddo   Sheol

11. Sheol and destruction are before the Lord; how much more then the hearts of the children of men?

לֹא יֶאֱהַב־לֵץ הוֹכֵחַ לוֹ אֶל־חֲכָמִים לֹא יֵלֵךְ:
he go   not   wise ones – unto   to him   correction   mocking – he loves   not

12. A scorner does not like to be reproved; nor will he go to the wise.

לֵב שָׂמֵחַ יֵיטִב פָּנִים וּבְעַצְּבַת־לֵב רוּחַ נְכֵאָה:
crushed   spirit   heart – and aches   faces   will be good   happy   heart

13. A merry heart makes a cheerful countenance; but by sorrow of the heart the spirit is broken.

לֵב נָבוֹן יְבַקֶּשׁ־דָּעַת וּפְנֵי [וּפִי] כְסִילִים יִרְעֶה אִוֶּלֶת:
follies   he be bad   fool ones   and mouth   knowledge – he seeks   discerning   heart

14. (K) The heart of the judicious seeks knowledge; but the mouth of fools feeds on foolishness.

כָּל־יְמֵי עָנִי רָעִים וְטוֹב־לֵב מִשְׁתֶּה תָמִיד:
continually   feast   heart – and good   bad ones   oppressed   days - all

15. All the days of the afflicted are evil; but he who is of a merry heart has a continual feast.

טוֹב־מְעַט בְּיִרְאַת יְהֹוָה מֵאוֹצָר רָב וּמְהוּמָה בּוֹ:
in it   and turmoil   much   from treasure   ihvh   in fears   little - good

16. Better is little with the fear of the Lord than great treasure and trouble with it.

טוֹב אֲרֻחַת יָרָק וְאַהֲבָה־שָׁם מִשּׁוֹר אָבוּס וְשִׂנְאָה־בוֹ:
in it – and hate   fattened   from ox   there – and love   vegetable   meal   good

17. Better is a dinner of herbs where love is, than a fatted ox and hatred with it.

אִישׁ חֵמָה יְגָרֶה מָדוֹן וְאֶרֶךְ אַפַּיִם יַשְׁקִיט רִיב:
quarrel   he calms   angers   and long   dissension   stirs up   hot   man

18. A wrathful man stirs up quarrel; but he who is slow to anger appeases quarrels.

דֶּרֶךְ עָצֵל כִּמְשֻׂכַת חָדֶק וְאֹרַח יְשָׁרִים סְלֻלָה:
highway   upright ones   and road   thorn   like blocking   lazy   way

19. The way of the lazy man is like a hedge of thorns; but the way of the righteous is level.

בֵּן חָכָם יְשַׂמַּח־אָב וּכְסִיל אָדָם בּוֹזֶה אִמּוֹ:
his mother   despises   Adam   and fool   father - he be happy   wise   son

20. A wise son makes a father glad; but a foolish man despises his mother.

אִוֶּלֶת שִׂמְחָה לַחֲסַר־לֵב וְאִישׁ תְּבוּנָה יְיַשֶּׁר־לָכֶת:
goings – he be upright   understanding   and man   heart – to lacking   happy   follies

21. Folly is joy to him who is destitute of wisdom; but a man of understanding walks uprightly.

הָפֵר מַחֲשָׁבוֹת בְּאֵין סוֹד וּבְרֹב יוֹעֲצִים תָּקוּם:
established · advisor ones · and in much · foundation · in isn't · from thoughts · falls

22. Without counsel purposes are frustrated; but in the multitude of counsellors they are established.

שִׂמְחָה לָאִישׁ בְּמַעֲנֵה־פִיו וְדָבָר בְּעִתּוֹ מַה־טּוֹב:
good – what · in season · and speech · his mouth – in reply · to man · happy

23. A man has joy in the answer of his mouth; and a word spoken in due season, how good it is!

אֹרַח חַיִּים לְמַעְלָה לְמַשְׂכִּיל לְמַעַן סוּר מִשְּׁאוֹל מָטָּה:
downward · from Sheol · close · to end · to wise · to upward · life · road

24. To the wise the way of life leads upward, that he may depart from Sheol beneath.

בֵּית גֵּאִים יִסַּח יְהוָה וְיַצֵּב גְּבוּל אַלְמָנָה:
widow · boundary · and he keeps intact · ihvh · tears down · proud ones · house

25. The Lord will destroy the house of the proud; but he will establish the border of the widow.

תּוֹעֲבַת יְהוָה מַחְשְׁבוֹת רָע וּטְהֹרִים אִמְרֵי־נֹעַם:
pleasing – words · and pure ones · bad · thoughts · ihvh · abomination

26. The thoughts of the wicked are an abomination to the Lord; but pleasant words are pure.

עֹכֵר בֵּיתוֹ בּוֹצֵעַ בָּצַע וְשׂוֹנֵא מַתָּנֹת יִחְיֶה:
he lives · bribes · and hater · greed · in greedy · his house · troubler

27. He who is greedy of gain troubles his own house; but he who hates bribes shall live.

לֵב צַדִּיק יֶהְגֶּה לַעֲנוֹת וּפִי רְשָׁעִים יַבִּיעַ רָעוֹת:
evils · pours out · wicked ones · and mouth · to answers · he weighs · righteous · heart

28. The heart of the righteous ponders how to answer; but the mouth of the wicked pours out evil things.

רָחוֹק יְהוָה מֵרְשָׁעִים וּתְפִלַּת צַדִּיקִים יִשְׁמָע:
he hears · righteous ones · and prayer · from wicked ones · ihvh · far

29. The Lord is far from the wicked; but he hears the prayer of the righteous.

מְאוֹר־עֵינַיִם יְשַׂמַּח־לֵב שְׁמוּעָה טוֹבָה תְּדַשֶּׁן־עָצֶם:
bones – gives fat · better · news · heart – he be happy · eyes - reflection

30. The light of the eyes rejoices the heart; and a good report makes the bones fat.

אֹזֶן שֹׁמַעַת תּוֹכַחַת חַיִּים בְּקֶרֶב חֲכָמִים תָּלִין:
he spend night · wise ones · in close · life · rebuke · hearings · ear

31. The ear that listens to the reproof of life abides among the wise.

פּוֹרֵעַ מוּסָר מוֹאֵס נַפְשׁוֹ וְשׁוֹמֵעַ תּוֹכַחַת קוֹנֶה לֵּב:
heart · acquires · correction · and heeder · his soul · despising · instruction · ignoring

32. He who refuses instruction despises his own soul; but he who hears reproof gets understanding.

יִרְאַת	יְהוָֹה	מוּסַר	חָכְמָה	וְלִפְנֵי	כָבוֹד	עֲנָוָה׃
fear	ihvh	instruction	wisdom	and before	honor	humility

33. The fear of the Lord is instruction in wisdom; and humility is before honor.

Chapter 16

ספר משלי פרק טז

לְאָדָ֥ם מַֽעַרְכֵי־לֵ֑ב וּ֝מֵיְהֹוָ֗ה מַעֲנֵ֥ה לָשֽׁוֹן׃

tongue from answer and from ihvh heart – plans to Adam

1. The thoughts of the heart are man's, and the answer of the tongue, is from the Lord.

כָּֽל־דַּרְכֵי־אִ֭ישׁ זַ֣ךְ בְּעֵינָ֑יו וְתֹכֵ֖ן רוּח֣וֹת יְהֹוָֽה׃

ihvh spirits and weights in his eyes clean man – paths – all

2. All the ways of a man are clean in his own eyes; but the Lord weighs the spirits.

גֹּ֣ל אֶל־יְהֹוָ֣ה מַעֲשֶׂ֑יךָ וְ֝יִכֹּ֗נוּ מַחְשְׁבֹתֶֽיךָ׃

your thoughts and you establish from your works ihvh – unto commit

3. Commit your deeds to the Lord, and your thoughts shall be established.

כֹּ֤ל פָּעַ֣ל יְ֭הֹוָה לַֽמַּעֲנֵ֑הוּ וְגַם־רָ֝שָׁ֗ע לְי֣וֹם רָעָֽה׃

bad to day wicked – and also to reply him ihvh makings all

4. The Lord has made all things for himself; even the wicked for the day of evil.

תּוֹעֲבַ֣ת יְ֭הֹוָה כָּל־גְּבַהּ־לֵ֑ב יָ֥ד לְ֝יָ֗ד לֹ֣א יִנָּקֶֽה׃

he be unpunished not to hand hand heart – proud – all ihvh abomination

5. Everyone who is proud in heart is an abomination to the Lord; those who join hands in an evil cause shall not go unpunished.

בְּחֶ֣סֶד וֶ֭אֱמֶת יְכֻפַּ֣ר עָוֺ֑ן וּבְיִרְאַ֥ת יְ֝הֹוָ֗ה ס֣וּר מֵרָֽע׃

from bad close ihvh and in fears inequity cover and truth in mercy

6. By loving kindness and truth iniquity is purged; and by the fear of the Lord men depart from evil.

בִּרְצ֣וֹת יְ֭הֹוָה דַּרְכֵי־אִ֑ישׁ גַּם־א֝וֹיְבָ֗יו יַשְׁלִ֥ם אִתּֽוֹ׃

with him be at peace his enemies – also man – way ihvh in pleasings

7. When a man's ways please the Lord, he makes even his enemies be at peace with him.

טוֹב־מְ֭עַט בִּצְדָקָ֑ה מֵרֹ֥ב תְּ֝בוּא֗וֹת בְּלֹ֣א מִשְׁפָּֽט׃

judgment in not gains from much in righteous little – good

8. Better is a little with righteousness than great income without right.

לֵ֣ב אָ֭דָם יְחַשֵּׁ֣ב דַּרְכּ֑וֹ וַ֝יהֹוָ֗ה יָכִ֥ין צַעֲדֽוֹ׃

his steps erects and ihvh his way weaves Adam heart

9. A man's heart devises his way; but the Lord directs his steps.

קֶ֤סֶם ׀ עַֽל־שִׂפְתֵי־מֶ֑לֶךְ בְּ֝מִשְׁפָּ֗ט לֹ֣א יִמְעַל־פִּֽיו׃

his mouth – he betray not in judgment king – lips – upon oracle

10. A divine sentence is in the lips of the king; his mouth does not transgress in judgment.

פֶּ֤לֶס ׀ וּמֹאזְנֵ֣י מִ֭שְׁפָּט לַיהֹוָ֑ה מַ֝עֲשֵׂ֗הוּ כָּל־אַבְנֵי־כִֽיס׃

bag – stones – all works him to ihvh judgment and balances scale

11. A just weight and scale are the Lord's; all the weights in the bag are his work.

Proverbs - Chapter 16

תּוֹעֲבַת מְלָכִים עֲשׂוֹת רֶשַׁע כִּי בִצְדָקָה יִכּוֹן כִּסֵּא׃
throne | he establishes | in righteousness | like | evil | doings | kings | abomination

12. It is an abomination to kings to commit wickedness; for the throne is established by righteousness.

רְצוֹן מְלָכִים שִׂפְתֵי־צֶדֶק וְדֹבֵר יְשָׁרִים יֶאֱהָב׃
he loves | upright ones | and speaker | righteous – lips | kings | delight

13. Righteous lips are the delight of kings; and they love him who speaks right.

חֲמַת־מֶלֶךְ מַלְאֲכֵי־מָוֶת וְאִישׁ חָכָם יְכַפְּרֶנָּה׃
he pacifies | wise | and man | death – messenger | king - wrath

14. The wrath of a king is like messengers of death; but a wise man will pacify it.

בְּאוֹר־פְּנֵי־מֶלֶךְ חַיִּים וּרְצוֹנוֹ כְּעָב מַלְקוֹשׁ׃
spring rain | like cloud | and his favor | lives | king - face - in light

15. In the light of the king's countenance is life; and his favor is like a cloud that brings spring rain.

קְנֹה־חָכְמָה מַה־טּוֹב מֵחָרוּץ וּקְנוֹת בִּינָה נִבְחָר מִכָּסֶף׃
from silver | choose | understanding | and buyings | from gold?? | good – what | wisdom - buy

16. How much better it is to get wisdom than gold; and to get understanding is preferable to silver;

מְסִלַּת יְשָׁרִים סוּר מֵרָע שֹׁמֵר נַפְשׁוֹ נֹצֵר דַּרְכּוֹ׃
his way | preserves | his soul | heed | from evil | close | upright ones | highway

17. The highway of the upright is to depart from evil; he who guards his way preserves his soul.

לִפְנֵי־שֶׁבֶר גָּאוֹן וְלִפְנֵי כִשָּׁלוֹן גֹּבַהּ רוּחַ׃
spirit | haughty | fall | and before | pride | destruction - before

18. Pride goes before destruction, and a haughty spirit before a fall.

טוֹב שְׁפַל־רוּחַ אֶת־עֲנָיִים [עֲנָוִים] מֵחַלֵּק שָׁלָל אֶת־גֵּאִים׃
proud ones – that | spoils | from sharing | oppressed – that | spirit – lowness | good

19. (K) Better it is to be of a humble spirit with the lowly, than to divide the spoil with the proud.

מַשְׂכִּיל עַל־דָּבָר יִמְצָא־טוֹב וּבוֹטֵחַ בַּיהוָה אַשְׁרָיו׃
his blessing | in ihvh | and trust | good – he finds | speaking – upon | considering

20. He who considers his words shall find good; and happy is he who trusts in the Lord.

לַחֲכַם־לֵב יִקָּרֵא נָבוֹן וּמֶתֶק שְׂפָתַיִם יֹסִיף לֶקַח׃
learning | he adds | lips | and sweetness | discerning | he calls | heart – to wise

21. The wise in heart shall be called prudent; and the sweetness of the lips increases learning.

מְקוֹר חַיִּים שֵׂכֶל בְּעָלָיו וּמוּסַר אֱוִלִים אִוֶּלֶת׃
follies | fool ones | and chastisement | his master | intelligence | lives | fountain

22. Intelligence is a fountain of life to him who has it; but the chastisement of fools is folly.

לֵב חָכָם יַשְׂכִּיל פִּיהוּ וְעַל־שְׂפָתָיו יֹסִיף לֶקַח׃
learning | he adds | his lips – and upon | his mouth | he learns | wise | heart

23. The heart of the wise teaches his mouth, and adds learning to his lips.

צוּף־דְּבַשׁ אִמְרֵי־נֹעַם מָתוֹק לַנֶּפֶשׁ וּמַרְפֵּא לָעָצֶם׃
to bones | and health | to soul | sweet | pleasant – words | honey - comb

24. Pleasant words are like a honeycomb, sweet to the soul, and health to the bones.

יֵשׁ דֶּרֶךְ יָשָׁר לִפְנֵי־אִישׁ וְאַחֲרִיתָהּ דַּרְכֵי־מָוֶת׃
death – ways | and its after | man – before | upright | way | there is

25. There is a way which seems right to a man, but its end are the ways of death.

נֶפֶשׁ עָמֵל עָמְלָה לּוֹ כִּי־אָכַף עָלָיו פִּיהוּ׃
mouth of him | upon him | urges - like | to him | labor | laborer | soul

26. The worker's hunger works for him; for his mouth urges him on.

אִישׁ בְּלִיַּעַל כֹּרֶה רָעָה וְעַל־שְׂפָתָיו [שְׂפָתוֹ] כְּאֵשׁ צָרָבֶת׃
scorching | like fire | his lips – and upon | evil | plotting | scoundrel | man

27. (K) A worthless man digs up evil; and in his lips there is a kind of burning fire.

אִישׁ תַּהְפֻּכוֹת יְשַׁלַּח מָדוֹן וְנִרְגָּן מַפְרִיד אַלּוּף׃
close friend | separates | and gossip | dissension | stirs up | perversities | man

28. A perverse man sows quarrels; and a whisperer separates close friends.

אִישׁ חָמָס יְפַתֶּה רֵעֵהוּ וְהוֹלִיכוֹ בְּדֶרֶךְ לֹא־טוֹב׃
good – not | in way | and his lead | neighbor of his | entices | violence | man

29. A violent man entices his neighbor, and leads him into the way that is not good.

עֹצֶה עֵינָיו לַחְשֹׁב תַּהְפֻּכוֹת קֹרֵץ שְׂפָתָיו כִּלָּה רָעָה׃
evil | like towards | his lips | pursuing | perversities | to think | his eye | wink

30. He winks his eyes to plan perverse things; pursing his lips he brings evil to pass.

עֲטֶרֶת תִּפְאֶרֶת שֵׂיבָה בְּדֶרֶךְ צְדָקָה תִּמָּצֵא׃
you find | righteous | in way | gray hair | beauty | crown

31. The hoary head is a crown of glory; it is found in the way of righteousness.

טוֹב אֶרֶךְ אַפַּיִם מִגִּבּוֹר וּמֹשֵׁל בְּרוּחוֹ מִלֹּכֵד עִיר׃
city | from conquering | in his spirit | and from ruling | from mighty | angers | long | good

32. He who is slow to anger is better than the mighty; and he who rules his spirit than he who takes a city.

בַּחֵיק יוּטַל אֶת־הַגּוֹרָל וּמֵיְהוָה כָּל־מִשְׁפָּטוֹ׃
his judgments – all | and from ihvh | the lot – that | he casts | in lap

33. The lot is cast into the lap; but the decision is wholly from the Lord.

Chapter 17

ספר משלי פרק יז

טוֹב פַּת חֲרֵבָה וְשַׁלְוָה־בָהּ מִבַּיִת מָלֵא זִבְחֵי־רִיב׃
strife - sacrifice　　full　from house　in it - and quietness　dry　morsel　good

1. Better is a dry morsel, and quietness with it, than a house full of feasting with quarrels.

עֶבֶד מַשְׂכִּיל יִמְשֹׁל בְּבֵן מֵבִישׁ וּבְתוֹךְ אַחִים יַחֲלֹק נַחֲלָה׃
inheritance　apportion　brothers　and among　embarrassing　in son　will rule　intelligent　servant

2. A wise slave shall have rule over a son who causes shame, and shall have part of the inheritance among the brothers.

מַצְרֵף לַכֶּסֶף וְכוּר לַזָּהָב וּבֹחֵן לִבּוֹת יְהוָה׃
ihvh　hearts　and tests　to gold　and crucible　to silver　refining

3. The refining pot is for silver, and the furnace for gold; but the Lord tests the hearts.

מֵרַע מַקְשִׁיב עַל־שְׂפַת־אָוֶן שֶׁקֶר מֵזִין עַל־לְשׁוֹן הַוֺּת׃
mischief　tongue - upon　from ear　lie　inequity – lips - upon　hearkens　from bad

4. A wicked doer gives heed to false lips; and a liar gives ear to a mischievous tongue.

לֹעֵג לָרָשׁ חֵרֵף עֹשֵׂהוּ שָׂמֵחַ לְאֵיד לֹא יִנָּקֶה׃
he innocent　not　to calamity　happy　does him　shows contempt　to poor　to mock

5. Whoever mocks the poor insults his Maker; and he who is glad at calamities shall not go unpunished.

עֲטֶרֶת זְקֵנִים בְּנֵי בָנִים וְתִפְאֶרֶת בָּנִים אֲבוֹתָם׃
their fathers　sons　and beauty　sons　son　old men　crown

6. Grandchildren are the crown of old men; and the glory of children are their fathers.

לֹא־נָאוָה לְנָבָל שְׂפַת־יֶתֶר אַף כִּי־לְנָדִיב שְׂפַת־שָׁקֶר׃
lie – lips　to prince – like　so　exuberance – lips　to fool　suitable - not

7. Fine speech is not becoming to a fool; still less is lying speech to a prince.

אֶבֶן־חֵן הַשֹּׁחַד בְּעֵינֵי בְעָלָיו אֶל־כָּל־אֲשֶׁר יִפְנֶה יַשְׂכִּיל׃
he intelligent　he faces　which – all – unto　his owner　in eyes　the bribe　favor - stone

8. A bribe is a precious stone in the eyes of him who gives it; wherever it turns, it prospers.

מְכַסֶּה־פֶּשַׁע מְבַקֵּשׁ אַהֲבָה וְשֹׁנֶה בְדָבָר מַפְרִיד אַלּוּף׃
close friend　breaks apart　in matter　and repeater　love　seeks　transgression - covering

9. He who covers a transgression seeks love; but he who repeats a matter separates close friends.

תֵּחַת גְּעָרָה בְמֵבִין מֵהַכּוֹת כְּסִיל מֵאָה׃
one hundred　fool　from strikes　in understand　rebuke　instead

10. A reproof enters more into a wise man than a hundred blows into a fool.

אַךְ־מְרִי יְבַקֶּשׁ־רָע וּמַלְאָךְ אַכְזָרִי יְשֻׁלַּח־בּוֹ:

11. An evil man seeks only rebellion; and a cruel messenger shall be sent against him.

פָּגוֹשׁ דֹּב שַׁכּוּל בְּאִישׁ וְאַל־כְּסִיל בְּאִוַּלְתּוֹ:

12. Let a man meet a bear robbed of her cubs, rather than a fool in his folly.

מֵשִׁיב רָעָה תַּחַת טוֹבָה לֹא־תָמִישׁ [תָמוּשׁ] רָעָה מִבֵּיתוֹ:

13. (K) Whoever rewards evil for good, evil shall not depart from his house.

פּוֹטֵר מַיִם רֵאשִׁית מָדוֹן וְלִפְנֵי הִתְגַּלַּע הָרִיב נְטוֹשׁ:

14. The beginning of a quarrel is like letting out water; therefore quit the dispute, before quarrel breaks out.

מַצְדִּיק רָשָׁע וּמַרְשִׁיעַ צַדִּיק תּוֹעֲבַת יְהֹוָה גַּם־שְׁנֵיהֶם:

15. He who justifies the wicked, and he who condemns the just, both of them are abomination to the Lord.

לָמָּה־זֶּה מְחִיר בְּיַד־כְּסִיל לִקְנוֹת חָכְמָה וְלֶב־אָיִן:

16. Why is the purchase price of wisdom in the hand of a fool, seeing he has no sense?

בְּכָל־עֵת אֹהֵב הָרֵעַ וְאָח לְצָרָה יִוָּלֵד:

17. A friend loves at all times, and a brother is born for adversity.

אָדָם חֲסַר־לֵב תּוֹקֵעַ כָּף עֹרֵב עֲרֻבָּה לִפְנֵי רֵעֵהוּ:

18. A man who strikes the palm is void of understanding, and becomes surety in the presence of his friend.

אֹהֵב פֶּשַׁע אֹהֵב מַצָּה מַגְבִּיהַּ פִּתְחוֹ מְבַקֶּשׁ־שָׁבֶר:

19. He who loves quarrel loves transgression; and he who makes his door high seeks destruction.

עִקֶּשׁ־לֵב לֹא יִמְצָא־טוֹב וְנֶהְפָּךְ בִּלְשׁוֹנוֹ יִפּוֹל בְּרָעָה:

20. He who has a crooked heart finds no good; and he who has a perverse tongue falls into mischief.

יֹלֵד כְּסִיל לְתוּגָה לוֹ וְלֹא־יִשְׂמַח אֲבִי נָבָל:

21. He who begets a fool does it to his sorrow; and the father of a fool has no joy.

Proverbs - Chapter 17

לֵב שָׂמֵחַ יֵיטִב גֵּהָה וְרוּחַ נְכֵאָה תְּיַבֶּשׁ־גָּרֶם:
bone – it dries up   crushed   and spirit   cure   he be good   happy   heart

22. A merry heart is a good medicine; but a broken spirit dries the bones.

שֹׁחַד מֵחֵיק רָשָׁע יִקָּח לְהַטּוֹת אָרְחוֹת מִשְׁפָּט:
judgment   roads   to pervert   he takes   wicked   from bosom   bribe

23. A wicked man takes a bribe out of the bosom to pervert the ways of judgment.

אֶת־פְּנֵי מֵבִין חָכְמָה וְעֵינֵי כְסִיל בִּקְצֵה־אָרֶץ:
earth – in ends   fool   and eyes   wisdom   discerning   faces - that

24. Wisdom is before him who has understanding; but the eyes of a fool are in the ends of the earth.

כַּעַס לְאָבִיו בֵּן כְּסִיל וּמֶמֶר לְיוֹלַדְתּוֹ:
to his begetting one   and bitterness   fool   son   to his father   anger

25. A foolish son is a grief to his father, and bitterness to her who bore him.

גַּם עֲנוֹשׁ לַצַּדִּיק לֹא־טוֹב לְהַכּוֹת נְדִיבִים עַל־יֹשֶׁר:
upright – upon   nobel ones   to the striking   good – not   to righteous   punish   also

26. Also to punish the just is not good, nor to strike blows to noble men for their integrity.

חוֹשֵׂךְ אֲמָרָיו יוֹדֵעַ דָּעַת וְקַר [וִיקַר־] רוּחַ אִישׁ תְּבוּנָה:
understanding   man   spirit   precious   knowledge   he knows   his words   restraining

27. (K) He who has knowledge spares his words; and a man of understanding is slow to anger.

גַּם אֱוִיל מַחֲרִישׁ חָכָם יֵחָשֵׁב אֹטֵם שְׂפָתָיו נָבוֹן:
understanding   his lips   holding   he thinks   wisdom   keeps silent   fool   also

28. Even a fool, when he holds his peace, is counted wise; and he who closes his lips is considered a man of understanding.

Chapter 18

ספר משלי פרק יח

לְתַאֲוָה יְבַקֵּשׁ נִפְרָד בְּכָל־תּוּשִׁיָּה יִתְגַּלָּע׃
he defies   sound judgement – in all   being parted   he asks   to yearning

1. He who keeps himself apart, desires to satisfy his own vanity; he breaks out against all sound judgment.

לֹא־יַחְפֹּץ כְּסִיל בִּתְבוּנָה כִּי אִם־בְּהִתְגַּלּוֹת לִבּוֹ׃
his heart   in cause to reveal – with   like   in understanding   fool   he pleasures - not

2. A fool has no delight in understanding, but only in revealing his heart.

בְּבוֹא־רָשָׁע בָּא גַּם־בּוּז וְעִם־קָלוֹן חֶרְפָּה׃
reproach   shame - and with   contempt - also   come   wicked - in comes

3. When the wicked comes, then comes also contempt, and with ignominy reproach.

מַיִם עֲמֻקִּים דִּבְרֵי פִי־אִישׁ נַחַל נֹבֵעַ מְקוֹר חָכְמָה׃
wisdom   fountain   flowing   river   man – mouth   speakings   deep   water

4. The words of a man's mouth are like deep waters, and the fountain of wisdom like a flowing brook.

שְׂאֵת פְּנֵי־רָשָׁע לֹא־טוֹב לְהַטּוֹת צַדִּיק בַּמִּשְׁפָּט׃
in judgment   righteous   to the deprive   good – not   wicked – face   respect

5. It is not good to favor the wicked man, and to deprive a righteous man of justice.

שִׂפְתֵי כְסִיל יָבֹאוּ בְרִיב וּפִיו לְמַהֲלֻמוֹת יִקְרָא׃
he calls   to beatings   and his mouth   in strife   they come   fool   lips

6. A fool's lips enter into quarrel, and his mouth invites a flogging.

פִּי־כְסִיל מְחִתָּה־לוֹ וּשְׂפָתָיו מוֹקֵשׁ נַפְשׁוֹ׃
his soul   snare   and his lips   to him – undoing   fool - mouth

7. A fool's mouth is his destruction, and his lips are the trap of his soul.

דִּבְרֵי נִרְגָּן כְּמִתְלַהֲמִים וְהֵם יָרְדוּ חַדְרֵי־בָטֶן׃
stomach – chambers   they descend   and them   like choice morsels   talebearer   speakings

8. The words of a talebearer are like delicacies, and they go down into the innermost parts of the body.

גַּם מִתְרַפֶּה בִּמְלַאכְתּוֹ אָח הוּא לְבַעַל מַשְׁחִית׃
destruction   to owner   he   brother   in his work   slack one   also

9. Also, he who is slothful in his work is a brother to him who destroys.

מִגְדַּל־עֹז שֵׁם יְהוָה בּוֹ־יָרוּץ צַדִּיק וְנִשְׂגָּב׃
and he set on high   righteous   he runs – in him   ihvh   name   strength – tower

10. The name of the Lord is a strong tower; the righteous runs into it, and is safe.

הוֹן עָשִׁיר קִרְיַת עֻזּוֹ וּכְחוֹמָה נִשְׂגָּבָה בְּמַשְׂכִּתוֹ׃
in his conceit   impregnable   and like wall   his strength   town   rich   wealth

Proverbs - Chapter 18

11. The rich man's wealth is his strong city, and like a high wall in his imagination.

לִפְנֵי־שֶׁבֶר יִגְבַּהּ לֵב־אִישׁ וְלִפְנֵי כָבוֹד עֲנָוָה׃
humility   honor   and before   man – heart   he proud   destruction - before

12. Before destruction the heart of man is haughty, and before honor goes humility.

מֵשִׁיב דָּבָר בְּטֶרֶם יִשְׁמָע אִוֶּלֶת הִיא־לוֹ וּכְלִמָּה׃
and shame   to him – it   follies   he hears   in before   speaking   responding

13. He who answers a matter before he hears it, it is his folly and shame.

רוּחַ־אִישׁ יְכַלְכֵּל מַחֲלֵהוּ וְרוּחַ נְכֵאָה מִי יִשָּׂאֶנָּה׃
he bears it   who   crushed   and spirit   his sickness   he sustains   man   spirit

14. The spirit of a man will endure his infirmity; but a wounded spirit who can bear?

לֵב נָבוֹן יִקְנֶה־דָּעַת וְאֹזֶן חֲכָמִים תְּבַקֶּשׁ־דָּעַת׃
knowledge - it asks   wise ones   and ear   knowledge - he acquires   prudent   heart

15. The heart of the prudent acquires knowledge; and the ear of the wise seeks knowledge.

מַתָּן אָדָם יַרְחִיב לוֹ וְלִפְנֵי גְדֹלִים יַנְחֶנּוּ׃
he ushers him   great ones   and before   to him   he widens   Adam   gift

16. A man's gift makes room for him, and brings him before great men.

צַדִּיק הָרִאשׁוֹן בְּרִיבוֹ יָבֹא־[וּבָא־]רֵעֵהוּ וַחֲקָרוֹ׃
and examines him   neighbor - and comes   in his contention   the beginning   righteous

17. (K) The one who pleads first seems to be in the right; until the other comes and examines him.

מִדְיָנִים יַשְׁבִּית הַגּוֹרָל וּבֵין עֲצוּמִים יַפְרִיד׃
he separates   powerful ones   and between   the lot   he settles   disputes

18. (K) The lot causes disputes to cease, and it decides between the mighty.

אָח נִפְשָׁע מִקִּרְיַת־עֹז וּמִדְיָנִים [וּמִדְיָנִים] כִּבְרִיחַ אַרְמוֹן׃
citadel   like bar   and disputes   strong – from town   offended   brother

19. A brother offended is harder to be won than a strong city; and their quarrels are like the bars of a castle.

מִפְּרִי פִי־אִישׁ תִּשְׂבַּע בִּטְנוֹ תְּבוּאַת שְׂפָתָיו יִשְׂבָּע׃
he full   his lips   produce   his belly   it satisfied   man – mouth   from fruit

20. A man's belly shall be satisfied with the fruit of his mouth; and with the yield of his lips shall he be filled.

מָוֶת וְחַיִּים בְּיַד־לָשׁוֹן וְאֹהֲבֶיהָ יֹאכַל פִּרְיָהּ׃
it's fruit   will eat   and those who love it   tongue – in hand   and lives   death

21. Death and life are in the power of the tongue; and those who love it shall eat its fruit.

מָצָא אִשָּׁה מָצָא טוֹב וַיָּפֶק רָצוֹן מֵיְהוָה׃
from ihvh   favor   and he obtains   good   finds   wife   find

22. Whoever finds a wife finds a good thing, and obtains favor from the Lord.

תַּחֲנוּנִים יְדַבֶּר־רָשׁ וְעָשִׁיר יַעֲנֶה עַזּוֹת׃

strong ones   answer   and rich   poor – he speaks   entreaties

23. The poor uses entreaties; but the rich answers roughly.

אִישׁ רֵעִים לְהִתְרֹעֵעַ וְיֵשׁ אֹהֵב דָּבֵק מֵאָח׃

from brother   clings   lover   and there is   to it ruined   neighbor ones   man

24. There are men who pretend friendship; and there is a true friend who sticks closer than a brother.

Chapter 19

ספר משלי פרק יט

טוֹב־רָשׁ הוֹלֵךְ בְּתֻמּוֹ מֵעִקֵּשׁ שְׂפָתָיו וְהוּא כְסִיל:
<small>fool   and he   his lips   from perverse   in his integrity   walks   poor - good</small>

1. Better is the poor man who walks in his integrity, than he who is perverse in his lips, and is a fool.

גַּם בְּלֹא־דַעַת נֶפֶשׁ לֹא־טוֹב וְאָץ בְּרַגְלַיִם חוֹטֵא:
<small>sins   in feet   and hasty   good – not   soul   knowledge - without   also</small>

2. Also, it is not good that the soul should be without knowledge; and he who hurries with his feet sins.

אִוֶּלֶת אָדָם תְּסַלֵּף דַּרְכּוֹ וְעַל־יְהוָה יִזְעַף לִבּוֹ:
<small>his heart   he rages   ihvh - and upon   his way   subverts   Adam   folly</small>

3. The foolishness of a man perverts his way; and his heart rages against the Lord.

הוֹן יֹסִיף רֵעִים רַבִּים וְדָל מֵרֵעֵהוּ יִפָּרֵד:
<small>he parted   from his neighbors   and poor man   many ones   neighbors   he adds   wealth</small>

4. Wealth makes many friends; but the poor is deserted by his neighbor.

עֵד שְׁקָרִים לֹא יִנָּקֶה וְיָפִיחַ כְּזָבִים לֹא יִמָּלֵט:
<small>he escape   not   like falsehoods   and he pours out   he innocent   not   lies   witness</small>

5. A false witness shall not go unpunished, and he who speaks lies shall not escape.

רַבִּים יְחַלּוּ פְנֵי־נָדִיב וְכָל־הָרֵעַ לְאִישׁ מַתָּן:
<small>gift   to man   the patron – and all   prince – face   they entreat   many ones</small>

6. Many will entreat the favor of the prince; and every man is a friend to him who gives gifts.

כָּל אֲחֵי־רָשׁ שְׂנֵאֻהוּ אַף כִּי מְרֵעֵהוּ רָחֲקוּ מִמֶּנּוּ
<small>from him   they avoid   companions   like   thus   they hate him   poor – brothers   all</small>

מְרַדֵּף אֲמָרִים לֹא [לוֹ] ־הֵמָּה:
<small>they are – to him   sayings   pursuer</small>

7. (K) All the brothers of the poor hate him; how much more do his friends go far from him? Their word for him is: pursuer.

קֹנֶה־לֵּב אֹהֵב נַפְשׁוֹ שֹׁמֵר תְּבוּנָה לִמְצֹא־טוֹב:
<small>good to find   understanding   heed   his soul   love   heart - acquire</small>

8. He who gets wisdom loves his own soul; he who keeps understanding shall find good.

עֵד שְׁקָרִים לֹא יִנָּקֶה וְיָפִיחַ כְּזָבִים יֹאבֵד:
<small>he perishes   lies   and he pours out   he innocent   not   lies   witness</small>

9. A false witness shall not go unpunished, and he who speaks lies shall perish.

לֹא־נָאוֶה לִכְסִיל תַּעֲנוּג אַף כִּי־לְעֶבֶד מְשֹׁל בְּשָׂרִים:
<small>in chiefs   rule   to servant – like   thus   luxury   to fool   fitting - not</small>

10. Luxury is not seemly for a fool; still less for a servant to have rule over princes.

שֵׂ֣כֶל אָ֭דָם הֶאֱרִ֣יךְ אַפּ֑וֹ וְ֝תִפְאַרְתּ֗וֹ עֲבֹ֣ר עַל־פָּֽשַׁע׃
transgression – upon   passover   and his beauty   his anger   the long   Adam   intelligent

11. The discretion of a man makes him slow to anger; and it is his glory to overlook a transgression.

נַ֣הַם כַּ֭כְּפִיר זַ֣עַף מֶ֑לֶךְ וּכְטַ֖ל עַל־עֵ֣שֶׂב רְצוֹנֽוֹ׃
his favor   grass – upon   and like dew   king   wrath   like young lion   roar

12. The king's wrath is like the roaring of a lion; but his favor is like dew on the grass.

הַוֺּ֣ת לְ֭אָבִיו בֵּ֣ן כְּסִ֑יל וְדֶ֥לֶף טֹ֝רֵ֗ד מִדְיְנֵ֥י אִשָּֽׁה׃
wife   disputes   constant   and dripping   foolish   son   to his father   ruins

13. A foolish son is the calamity of his father; and the disputes of a wife are a continual dropping.

בַּ֣יִת וָ֭הוֹן נַחֲלַ֣ת אָב֑וֹת וּ֝מֵיְהֹוָ֗ה אִשָּׁ֥ה מַשְׂכָּֽלֶת׃
being intelligent   wife   and from ihvh   fathers   inheritance   and wealth   house

14. House and riches are inherited from fathers; but a prudent wife is from the Lord.

עַ֭צְלָה תַּפִּ֣יל תַּרְדֵּמָ֑ה וְנֶ֖פֶשׁ רְמִיָּ֣ה תִרְעָֽב׃
it gives hunger   deceptive   and soul   deep sleep   casts   laziness

15. Laziness casts into a deep sleep; and the idle soul shall suffer hunger.

שֹׁמֵ֣ר מִ֭צְוָה שֹׁמֵ֣ר נַפְשׁ֑וֹ בּוֹזֵ֖ה דְרָכָ֣יו יוּמָֽת [יָמֽוּת]׃
he will die   his ways   despises   his soul   heeder   commandment   heeder

16. (K) He who keeps the commandment keeps his own soul; but he who despises his ways shall die.

מַלְוֵ֣ה יְ֭הֹוָה ח֣וֹנֵֽן דָּ֑ל וּ֝גְמֻל֗וֹ יְשַׁלֶּם־לֽוֹ׃
to him – will pay   and his requital   poor   kind   ihvh   obligating

17. He who gives kindly to the poor lends to the Lord; and that which he has given will he pay him back.

יַסֵּ֣ר בִּ֭נְךָ כִּי־יֵ֣שׁ תִּקְוָ֑ה וְאֶל־הֲ֝מִית֗וֹ אַל־תִּשָּׂ֥א נַפְשֶֽׁךָ׃
your soul   you lift – don't   the his kill – and unto   hope   there is – like   your son   chasten

18. Chasten your son while there is hope, and let not your soul spare for his crying.

גְּרָל־[גְּדָל־] חֵ֭מָה נֹ֣שֵׂא עֹ֑נֶשׁ כִּ֥י אִם־תַּ֝צִּ֗יל וְע֣וֹד תּוֹסִֽף׃
you will add   and again   you rescue – if   like   penalty   bearing   fury   – great

19. (K) A man of great anger shall pay the penalty; for if you save him, you will only have to do it again.

שְׁמַ֣ע עֵ֭צָה וְקַבֵּ֣ל מוּסָ֑ר לְ֝מַ֗עַן תֶּחְכַּ֥ם בְּאַחֲרִיתֶֽךָ׃
in your afterwards   you be wise   to end   instruction   and receive   counsel   hear

20. Hear counsel, and receive instruction, that you may be wise in your latter end.

רַבּ֣וֹת מַחֲשָׁב֣וֹת בְּלֶב־אִ֑ישׁ וַעֲצַ֥ת יְ֝הֹוָ֗ה הִ֣יא תָקֽוּם׃
will stand   it   ihvh   and counsel   man – in heart   designs   many

21. There are many plans in a man's heart; nevertheless the counsel of the Lord shall stand.

Proverbs - Chapter 19

תַּאֲוַת אָדָם חַסְדּוֹ וְטוֹב רָשׁ מֵאִישׁ כָּזָב׃
    liar   from man   poor and good his kindness Adam   desire

22. The attraction of a man is his kindness; and a poor man is better than a liar.

יִרְאַת יְהֹוָה לְחַיִּים וְשָׂבֵעַ יָלִין בַּל־יִפָּקֶד רָע׃
  bad he visited – without he spends night and satisfied to life ihvh   fear

23. The fear of the Lord tends to life; and he who has it shall abide satisfied; he shall not be visited by harm.

טָמַן עָצֵל יָדוֹ בַּצַּלָּחַת גַּם־אֶל־פִּיהוּ לֹא יְשִׁיבֶנָּה׃
  he brings back it not his mouth – unto - also   in dish his hand sluggard buries

24. A lazy man hides his hand in the dish, and will not even bring it back to his mouth.

לֵץ תַּכֶּה וּפֶתִי יַעְרִם וְהוֹכִיחַ לְנָבוֹן יָבִין דָּעַת׃
 knowledge he understands to discerning and rebuke he crafty and simple you strike mocker

25. Strike a scorner, and the simple will beware; and reprove one who has understanding, and he will gain knowledge.

מְשַׁדֶּד־אָב יַבְרִיחַ אֵם בֵּן מֵבִישׁ וּמַחְפִּיר׃
  and disgrace from shame son mother he drives away father – shaming

26. A son who causes shame and brings reproach ruins his father, and chases away his mother.

חֲדַל־בְּנִי לִשְׁמֹעַ מוּסָר לִשְׁגוֹת מֵאִמְרֵי־דָעַת׃
  knowledge – from words to stray instruction to hear my son - cease

27. Cease, my son, to hear the instruction, only to stray from the words of knowledge.

עֵד בְּלִיַּעַל יָלִיץ מִשְׁפָּט וּפִי רְשָׁעִים יְבַלַּע־אָוֶן׃
 inequity - he swallows wicked ones and mouth judgment he mocks corruptness witness

28. A wicked witness scorns judgment; and the mouth of the wicked devours iniquity.

נָכוֹנוּ לַלֵּצִים שְׁפָטִים וּמַהֲלֻמוֹת לְגֵו כְּסִילִים׃
  fool ones to body and beatings judgments to mocking ones they prepared

29. Judgments are prepared for scorners, and flogging for the back of fools.

Chapter 20

ספר משלי פרק כ

לֵץ הַיַּיִן הֹמֶה שֵׁכָר וְכָל־שֹׁגֶה בּוֹ לֹא יֶחְכָּם׃

he wise　not　in it　led astray – and all　liquor　riotous　the wine　mocking

1. Wine is a mocker, strong drink is riotous; and whoever is deceived by it is not wise.

נַהַם כַּכְּפִיר אֵימַת מֶלֶךְ מִתְעַבְּרוֹ חוֹטֵא נַפְשׁוֹ׃

his soul　sins　his provoking　king　wrath　like lion　roar

2. The fear of a king is like the roaring of a lion; whoever provokes him to anger forfeits his life.

כָּבוֹד לָאִישׁ שֶׁבֶת מֵרִיב וְכָל־אֱוִיל יִתְגַּלָּע׃

he quarrels　fool – and all　from contention　avoidance　to man　honor

3. It is an honor for a man to keep aloof from quarrel; but every fool will quarrel.

מֵחֹרֶף עָצֵל לֹא־יַחֲרֹשׁ יִשְׁאַל [וְשָׁאַל] בַּקָּצִיר וָאָיִן׃

and isn't　in harvest　and begs　he plows – not　lazy　from winter

4. (K) The sluggard will not plow because of the cold; therefore shall he beg in harvest, and have nothing.

מַיִם עֲמֻקִּים עֵצָה בְלֶב־אִישׁ וְאִישׁ תְּבוּנָה יִדְלֶנָּה׃

he draws out　understanding　and man　man – in heart　counsel　deep ones　water

5. Counsel in the heart of man is like deep water; but a man of understanding will draw it out.

רָב־אָדָם יִקְרָא אִישׁ חַסְדּוֹ וְאִישׁ אֱמוּנִים מִי יִמְצָא׃

he find　who　faithful ones　and man　his kindness　man　he call　Adam - much

6. Most men will proclaim every one his own goodness; but a faithful man who can find?

מִתְהַלֵּךְ בְּתֻמּוֹ צַדִּיק אַשְׁרֵי בָנָיו אַחֲרָיו׃

after him　his sons　happy　righteous　in his integrity　walking

7. The just man walks in his integrity; happy are his children after him.

מֶלֶךְ יוֹשֵׁב עַל־כִּסֵּא־דִין מְזָרֶה בְעֵינָיו כָּל־רָע׃

bad – all　in his eyes　winnowing out　judgment – chair – upon　he sits　king

8. A king who sits in the throne of judgment scatters away all evil with his eyes.

מִי־יֹאמַר זִכִּיתִי לִבִּי טָהַרְתִּי מֵחַטָּאתִי׃

from my sin　I pure　my heart　I cleaned　he says - who

9. Who can say, I have made my heart clean, I am pure from my sin?

אֶבֶן וָאֶבֶן אֵיפָה וְאֵיפָה תּוֹעֲבַת יְהוָה גַּם־שְׁנֵיהֶם׃

both them – also　ihvh　abomination　and measure　measure　and stone　[standard] stone

10. Different weights, and different measures, both of them are alike an abomination to the Lord.

Proverbs - Chapter 20

גַּם בְּמַעֲלָלָיו יִתְנַכֶּר־נָעַר אִם־זַךְ וְאִם־יָשָׁר פָּעֳלוֹ׃

11. Even a child is known by his doings, whether what he does is pure and right.

אֹזֶן שֹׁמַעַת וְעַיִן רֹאָה יְהֹוָה עָשָׂה גַם־שְׁנֵיהֶם׃

12. The hearing ear, and the seeing eye, the Lord has made them both.

אַל־תֶּאֱהַב שֵׁנָה פֶּן־תִּוָּרֵשׁ פְּקַח עֵינֶיךָ שְֽׂבַע־לָחֶם׃

13. Do not love sleep, lest you come to poverty; open your eyes, and you shall be satisfied with bread.

רַע רַע יֹאמַר הַקּוֹנֶה וְאֹזֵל לוֹ אָז יִתְהַלָּל׃

14. It is bad, it is bad, says the buyer; but when he goes away, then he boasts.

יֵשׁ זָהָב וְרָב־פְּנִינִים וּכְלִי יְקָר שִׂפְתֵי־דָעַת׃

15. There is gold, and a multitude of rubies; but the lips of knowledge are a precious jewel.

לְקַח־בִּגְדוֹ כִּי־עָרַב זָר וּבְעַד נָכְרִים [נָכְרִיָּה] חַבְלֵהוּ׃

16. (K) Take his garment when he has given surety for a stranger; and take his pledge on behalf of an alien woman.

עָרֵב לָאִישׁ לֶחֶם שָׁקֶר וְאַחַר יִמָּלֵא־פִיהוּ חָצָץ׃

17. Bread of deceit is sweet to a man; but afterwards his mouth shall be filled with gravel.

מַחֲשָׁבוֹת בְּעֵצָה תִכּוֹן וּבְתַחְבֻּלוֹת עֲשֵׂה מִלְחָמָה׃

18. Every purpose is established by counsel; and with good advice conduct war.

גּוֹלֶה־סּוֹד הוֹלֵךְ רָכִיל וּלְפֹתֶה שְׂפָתָיו לֹא תִתְעָרָב׃

19. He who goes about as a tale bearer reveals secrets; therefore meddle not with him who flatters with his lips.

מְקַלֵּל אָבִיו וְאִמּוֹ יִדְעַךְ נֵרוֹ בֶּאֱשׁוּן [בֶּאֱשׁוּן] חֹשֶׁךְ׃

20. (K) Whoever curses his father or his mother, his lamp shall be put out in utter darkness.

נַחֲלָה מְבֻחֶלֶת [מְבֹהֶלֶת] בָּרִאשֹׁנָה וְאַחֲרִיתָהּ לֹא תְבֹרָךְ׃

21. (K) An inheritance gotten hastily in the beginning will not be blessed in the end.

אַל־תֹּאמַר אֲשַׁלְּמָה־רָע קַוֵּה לַיהוָה וְיֹשַׁע לָךְ׃
to you   and he will save   to ihvh   wait   bad – I will pay   you say – don't

22. Do not say, I will repay evil; but wait on the Lord, and he shall save you.

תּוֹעֲבַת יְהוָה אֶבֶן וָאָבֶן וּמֹאזְנֵי מִרְמָה לֹא־טוֹב׃
good – not   deceit   and scales   and stone   stone   ihvh   abomination

23. Different weights are an abomination to the Lord; and false scales are not good.

מֵיהוָה מִצְעֲדֵי־גָבֶר וְאָדָם מַה־יָּבִין דַּרְכּוֹ׃
his way   he understands – what   and Adam   gentlemen – steps   from ihvh

24. Man's steps are of the Lord; how can a man then understand his own way?

מוֹקֵשׁ אָדָם יָלַע קֹדֶשׁ וְאַחַר נְדָרִים לְבַקֵּר׃
to ask   vows   and after   holy   he swallows   Adam   trap

25. It is a trap for a man to rashly declare, It is holy, and to inquire only after making his vows.

מְזָרֶה רְשָׁעִים מֶלֶךְ חָכָם וַיָּשֶׁב עֲלֵיהֶם אוֹפָן׃
wheel   upon them   and he returns   wise   king   wicked ones   winnowing out

26. A wise king scatters the wicked, and drives the wheel over them.

נֵר יְהוָה נִשְׁמַת אָדָם חֹפֵשׂ כָּל־חַדְרֵי־בָטֶן׃
belly – chambers – all   searching   Adam   spirit   ihvh   lamp

27. The spirit of man is the candle of the Lord, searching all the inward parts of the belly.

חֶסֶד וֶאֱמֶת יִצְּרוּ־מֶלֶךְ וְסָעַד בַּחֶסֶד כִּסְאוֹ׃
his chair   in kindness   and secure   king – they preserve   and truth   kindness

28. Love and truth preserve the king; and his throne is upheld by loyalty.

תִּפְאֶרֶת בַּחוּרִים כֹּחָם וַהֲדַר זְקֵנִים שֵׂיבָה׃
gray hair   old ones   and splendor   their vigor   young men   beauty

29. The glory of young men is their strength; and the beauty of old men is the grey head.

חַבֻּרוֹת פֶּצַע תַּמְרִיק [תַּמְרוּק] בְּרָע וּמַכּוֹת חַדְרֵי־בָטֶן׃
belly – chambers   and blows   in evil   cleanse   wound   welts

30. (K) Bruises and wounds cleanse away evil; so does flogging the innermost parts.

Chapter 21

ספר משלי פרק כא

פַּלְגֵי־מַיִם לֶב־מֶלֶךְ בְּיַד־יְהֹוָה עַל־כָּל־אֲשֶׁר יַחְפֹּץ יַטֶּנּוּ׃

he turns to   he pleases   which – all – upon   ihvh – in hand   king – heart   water - courses

1. Like water streams is the king's heart in the hand of the Lord; he turns it wherever he wants.

כָּל־דֶּרֶךְ־אִישׁ יָשָׁר בְּעֵינָיו וְתֹכֵן לִבּוֹת יְהֹוָה׃

ihvh   hearts and regulator   in his eyes   upright   man   ways - all

2. Every way of a man is right in his own eyes; but the Lord weighs the hearts.

עָשֹׂה צְדָקָה וּמִשְׁפָּט נִבְחָר לַיהֹוָה מִזָּבַח׃

from [temple] sacrifice   to ihvh   choose   and judgment   righteous   do

3. To do justice and judgment is more acceptable to the Lord than sacrifice.

רוּם־עֵינַיִם וּרְחַב־לֵב נֵר רְשָׁעִים חַטָּאת׃

sins   wicked ones   candle   heart – and pretensions   eyes   highness

4. A haughty look, and a proud heart, are the sinful growth of the wicked.

מַחְשְׁבוֹת חָרוּץ אַךְ־לְמוֹתָר וְכָל־אָץ אַךְ־לְמַחְסוֹר׃

to lack – surely   hastening – and all   to profit – surely   diligent   thoughts

5. The thoughts of the diligent lead surely to abundance; but every one who is hasty comes only to want.

פֹּעַל אוֹצָרוֹת בִּלְשׁוֹן שָׁקֶר הֶבֶל נִדָּף מְבַקְשֵׁי־מָוֶת׃

death – seekers   fleeting   vanity   lie   in tongue   treasures   laboring

6. The acquiring of treasures by a lying tongue is a fleeting vapor; they lead to death.

שֹׁד־רְשָׁעִים יְגוֹרֵם כִּי מֵאֲנוּ לַעֲשׂוֹת מִשְׁפָּט׃

judgment   to do   refusing   like   he will swirl away   wicked ones - devastation

7. The robbery of the wicked shall destroy them; because they refuse to do justice.

הֲפַכְפַּךְ דֶּרֶךְ אִישׁ וָזָר וְזַךְ יָשָׁר פָּעֳלוֹ׃

his work   upright   and innocent   and heavy guilt   man   way   the devious

8. The way of some men is crooked and strange; but as for the pure, his work is right.

טוֹב לָשֶׁבֶת עַל־פִּנַּת־גָּג מֵאֵשֶׁת מִדְיָנִים [מִדְיָנִים] וּבֵית חָבֶר׃

roomy   and house   quarrels   from woman   roof – corner – upon   to dwell   good

9. (K) It is better to dwell in a corner of the housetop, than with a brawling woman in a roomy house.

נֶפֶשׁ רָשָׁע אִוְּתָה־רָע לֹא־יֻחַן בְּעֵינָיו רֵעֵהוּ׃

his neighbor   in his eyes   he graces – not   bad – craves   wicked   soul

10. The soul of the wicked desires evil; his neighbor finds no favor in his eyes.

בַּעֲנָשׁ־לֵץ יֶחְכַּם־פֶּתִי וּבְהַשְׂכִּיל לְחָכָם יִקַּח־דָּעַת׃

knowledge – he takes   to wise   and in the intelligent   simple – he gains wisdom   mocking – in punishment

11. When the scorner is punished, the simple man is made wise; and when the wise is

instructed, he receives knowledge.

מַשְׂכִּיל צַדִּיק לְבֵית רָשָׁע מְסַלֵּף רְשָׁעִים לָרָע:

12. The righteous man who considers the house of the wicked leads the wicked astray to greater evil.

אֹטֵם אָזְנוֹ מִזַּעֲקַת־דָּל גַּם־הוּא יִקְרָא וְלֹא יֵעָנֶה:

13. Whoever stops his ears at the cry of the poor, he also shall cry himself, but shall not be heard.

מַתָּן בַּסֵּתֶר יִכְפֶּה־אָף וְשֹׁחַד בַּחֵק חֵמָה עַזָּה:

14. A gift in secret pacifies anger; and a bribe in the bosom strong wrath.

שִׂמְחָה לַצַּדִּיק עֲשׂוֹת מִשְׁפָּט וּמְחִתָּה לְפֹעֲלֵי אָוֶן:

15. It is joy to the just to do justice; but it is the downfall of the workers of iniquity.

אָדָם תּוֹעֶה מִדֶּרֶךְ הַשְׂכֵּל בִּקְהַל רְפָאִים יָנוּחַ:

16. The man who wanders out of the way of understanding shall remain in the congregation of the dead.

אִישׁ מַחְסוֹר אֹהֵב שִׂמְחָה אֹהֵב יַיִן וָשֶׁמֶן לֹא יַעֲשִׁיר:

17. He who loves pleasure shall be a poor man; he who loves wine and oil shall not be rich.

כֹּפֶר לַצַּדִּיק רָשָׁע וְתַחַת יְשָׁרִים בּוֹגֵד:

18. The wicked shall be a ransom for the righteous, and the transgressor for the upright.

טוֹב שֶׁבֶת בְּאֶרֶץ מִדְבָּר מֵאֵשֶׁת מִדְוָנִים [מִדְיָנִים] וָכָעַס:

19. (K) It is better to live in the desert, than with a quarrelsome and angry woman.

אוֹצָר נֶחְמָד וָשֶׁמֶן בִּנְוֵה חָכָם וּכְסִיל אָדָם יְבַלְּעֶנּוּ:

20. Costly things and oil are treasured in the dwelling of the wise; but a foolish man spends it up.

רֹדֵף צְדָקָה וָחָסֶד יִמְצָא חַיִּים צְדָקָה וְכָבוֹד:

21. He who follows after righteousness and loving kindness finds life, righteousness, and honor.

עִיר גִּבֹּרִים עָלָה חָכָם וַיֹּרֶד עֹז מִבְטֶחָה:

22. A wise man scales the city of the mighty, and brings down the fortress in which it trusts.

שֹׁמֵ֣ר פִּ֭יו וּלְשׁוֹנ֑וֹ שֹׁמֵ֖ר מִצָּר֣וֹת נַפְשֽׁוֹ׃
<small>his soul   troubles   heeds   and his tongue   his mouth   heed</small>

23. Whoever guards his mouth and his tongue keeps his soul from troubles.

זֵ֣ד יָ֭הִיר לֵ֣ץ שְׁמ֑וֹ ע֝וֹשֶׂ֗ה בְּעֶבְרַ֥ת זָדֽוֹן׃
<small>arrogance   in rage   doing   his name   mocks   he haughtily   proud</small>

24. The proud and haughty, scorner is his name, acts in arrogant wrath.

תַּאֲוַ֣ת עָצֵ֣ל תְּמִיתֶ֑נּוּ כִּֽי־מֵאֲנ֖וּ יָדָ֣יו לַעֲשֽׂוֹת׃
<small>to doings   his hands   he refuse - like   it to him to death   sluggard   craving</small>

25. The desire of the lazy man kills him; for his hands refuse to labor.

כָּל־הַ֭יּוֹם הִתְאַוָּ֣ה תַאֲוָ֑ה וְצַדִּ֥יק יִ֝תֵּ֗ן וְלֹ֣א יַחְשֹֽׂךְ׃
<small>he holds back   and not   he gives   and righteous   craved one   causes craving   the day - all</small>

26. He covets greedily all the day long; but the righteous gives and spares not.

זֶ֣בַח רְ֭שָׁעִים תּוֹעֵבָ֑ה אַ֝֗ף כִּֽי־בְזִמָּ֥ה יְבִיאֶֽנּוּ׃
<small>he brings him   in mischief – like   surely   abomination   wicked ones   temple sacrifice</small>

27. The sacrifice of the wicked is an abomination; how much more, when he brings it with evil intent?

עֵד־כְּזָבִ֥ים יֹאבֵ֑ד וְאִ֥ישׁ שׁ֝וֹמֵ֗עַ לָנֶ֥צַח יְדַבֵּֽר׃
<small>he speaks   to victory   hearing   and man   he perishes   falsehoods - witness</small>

28. A false witness shall perish; but the word of a man who pays attention shall endure.

הֵעֵ֬ז אִ֣ישׁ רָשָׁ֣ע בְּפָנָ֑יו וְ֝יָשָׁ֗ר ה֤וּא ׀ יָכִ֬ין [יָבִין] דְּרָכָֽיו [דַּרְכּֽוֹ]׃
<small>his way   he understands   he and upright   in his faces   wicked   man   impudent</small>

29. (K) A wicked man hardens his face; but as for the upright, he considers his way.

אֵ֣ין חָ֭כְמָה וְאֵ֣ין תְּבוּנָ֑ה וְאֵ֥ין עֵ֝צָ֗ה לְנֶ֣גֶד יְהֹוָֽה׃
<small>ihvh   to in front   counsel   and isn't   understanding   and isn't   wisdom   isn't</small>

30. There is no wisdom, nor understanding, nor counsel against the Lord.

ס֗וּס מ֭וּכָן לְי֣וֹם מִלְחָמָ֑ה וְ֝לַֽיהֹוָ֗ה הַתְּשׁוּעָֽה׃
<small>the saving   and to ihvh   war   to day   prepared   horse</small>

31. The horse is prepared for the day of battle; but safety comes from the Lord.

Chapter 22

ספר משלי פרק כב

נִבְחָר שֵׁם מֵעֹשֶׁר רָב מִכֶּסֶף וּמִזָּהָב חֵן טוֹב׃

good grace and from gold from sliver much from riches name chosen

1. A good name is to be chosen rather than great riches, and loving favor rather than silver or gold.

עָשִׁיר וָרָשׁ נִפְגָּשׁוּ עֹשֵׂה כֻלָּם יְהוָה׃

ihvh all them maker they meet up and poor rich

2. The rich and poor meet together; the Lord is the maker of them all.

עָרוּם רָאָה רָעָה וְיִסָּתֵר [וְנִסְתָּר] וּפְתָיִים עָבְרוּ וְנֶעֱנָשׁוּ׃

and they fined they pass and simple ones and he conceals bad sees prudent

3. (K) A prudent man foresees evil, and hides himself; but the simple pass on, and are punished.

עֵקֶב עֲנָוָה יִרְאַת יְהוָה עֹשֶׁר וְכָבוֹד וְחַיִּים׃

and life and honor wealth ihvh fear humility result

4. The reward of humility and the fear of the Lord are riches, and honor, and life.

צִנִּים פַּחִים בְּדֶרֶךְ עִקֵּשׁ שׁוֹמֵר נַפְשׁוֹ יִרְחַק מֵהֶם׃

from them he far his soul heeder perverse in path snares thorns

5. Thorns and traps are in the way of the perverse; he who guards his soul shall be far from them.

חֲנֹךְ לַנַּעַר עַל־פִּי דַרְכּוֹ גַּם כִּי־יַזְקִין לֹא־יָסוּר מִמֶּנָּה׃

from it he turns – not he grows old – like also his way mouth – upon to child dedicate up

6. Train up a child in the way he should go; and when he is old, he will not depart from it.

עָשִׁיר בְּרָשִׁים יִמְשׁוֹל וְעֶבֶד לֹוֶה לְאִישׁ מַלְוֶה׃

lending to man borrowing and servant he rules in destitute ones rich

7. The rich rules over the poor, and the borrower is servant to the lender.

זוֹרֵעַ עַוְלָה יִקְצוֹר [יִקְצָר] ־אָוֶן וְשֵׁבֶט עֶבְרָתוֹ יִכְלֶה׃

he be finished his fury and rod lawless – he reaps iniquity sowing

8. (K) He who sows iniquity shall reap vanity; and the rod of his anger shall fail.

טוֹב־עַיִן הוּא יְבֹרָךְ כִּי־נָתַן מִלַּחְמוֹ לַדָּל׃

to poor from his bread gives – like he blessed he eye - good

9. He who has a generous eye shall be blessed; for he gives of his bread to the poor.

גָּרֵשׁ לֵץ וְיֵצֵא מָדוֹן וְיִשְׁבֹּת דִּין וְקָלוֹן׃

and dishonor adjudication and he rests quarrel and he goes out mocking drive out

10. Cast out the scorner, and dispute shall go out; indeed, quarrel and abuse shall cease.

אֹהֵב טְהוֹר־ [טְהָר־] לֵב חֵן שְׂפָתָיו רֵעֵהוּ מֶלֶךְ׃

king his neighbor his lips grace heart - purity love

11. (K) He who loves purity of heart, and grace is on his lips, the king shall be his friend.

עֵינֵי יְהֹוָה נָצְרוּ דָעַת וַיְסַלֵּף דִּבְרֵי בֹגֵד׃

treacherous speeches   and he subverts   knowledge   they keep   ihvh   eyes

12. The eyes of the Lord preserve knowledge, and he overthrows the words of the transgressor.

אָמַר עָצֵל אֲרִי בַחוּץ בְּתוֹךְ רְחֹבוֹת אֵרָצֵחַ׃

I will be murdered   streets   in midst   outside   lion   sluggard   says

13. The lazy man says, There is a lion outside, I shall be slain in the streets.

שׁוּחָה עֲמֻקָּה פִּי זָרוֹת זְעוּם יְהֹוָה יִפּוֹל־ [יִפָּל־] שָׁם׃

there –   he fall   ihvh   menaced   alien woman   mouth   deep   pit

14. (K) The mouth of an alien women is a deep pit; he with whom the Lord is angry shall fall in it.

אִוֶּלֶת קְשׁוּרָה בְלֶב־נָעַר שֵׁבֶט מוּסָר יַרְחִיקֶנָּה מִמֶּנּוּ׃

from him   he far it   discipline   rod   child – in heart   bound   folly

15. Foolishness is bound in the heart of a child; but the rod of correction shall drive it far from him.

עֹשֵׁק דָּל לְהַרְבּוֹת לוֹ נֹתֵן לְעָשִׁיר אַךְ־לְמַחְסוֹר׃

to lack – surely   to riches   giving to him   to increase   poor   oppresses

16. He who oppresses the poor to increase his riches, and he who gives to the rich, shall surely come to want.

הַט אָזְנְךָ וּשְׁמַע דִּבְרֵי חֲכָמִים וְלִבְּךָ תָּשִׁית לְדַעְתִּי׃

to my knowledge   you set   and your heart   wise ones   speakings   and hear   your ear   stretch out

17. Incline your ear, and hear the words of the wise, and apply your heart to my knowledge.

כִּי־נָעִים כִּי־תִשְׁמְרֵם בְּבִטְנֶךָ יִכֹּנוּ יַחְדָּו עַל־שְׂפָתֶיךָ׃

your lips – upon   together   they establish   in your stomach   you keep them – like   pleasing - like

18. For it is a pleasant thing if you keep them inside you; let them be firmly attached to your lips.

לִהְיוֹת בַּיהֹוָה מִבְטַחֶךָ הוֹדַעְתִּיךָ הַיּוֹם אַף־אָתָּה׃

you – surely   the day   I make known to you   you trustworthy   in ihvh   to be

19. That your trust may be in the Lord, I have made known to you this day, even to you.

הֲלֹא כָתַבְתִּי לְךָ שָׁלִשׁוֹם [שָׁלִישִׁים] בְּמוֹעֵצוֹת וָדָעַת׃

and knowledge   in counsels   thirds   to you   I wrote   the not

20. (K) Have not I written to you excellent things in counsels and knowledge,

לְהוֹדִיעֲךָ קֹשְׁטְ אִמְרֵי אֱמֶת לְהָשִׁיב אֲמָרִים אֱמֶת לְשֹׁלְחֶיךָ׃

to your sender   truth   sayings   to the return   truth   words   certainly   to make you know

21. That I might make you know the certainty of the words of truth; that you might answer the words of truth to those who send you?

אַל־תִּגְזָל־דָּל כִּי דַל־הוּא וְאַל־תְּדַכֵּא עָנִי בַשָּׁעַר׃

22. Rob not the poor, because he is poor; nor oppress the afflicted in the gate;

כִּי־יְהוָה יָרִיב רִיבָם וְקָבַע אֶת־קֹבְעֵיהֶם נָפֶשׁ׃

23. For the Lord will plead their cause, and rob the life of those who rob them.

אַל־תִּתְרַע אֶת־בַּעַל אָף וְאֶת־אִישׁ חֵמוֹת לֹא תָבוֹא׃

24. Make no friendship with an angry man; and with a furious man you shall not go;

פֶּן־תֶּאֱלַף אֹרְחֹתוֹ [אֹרְחֹתָיו] וְלָקַחְתָּ מוֹקֵשׁ לְנַפְשֶׁךָ׃

25. Lest you learn his ways, and get a snare to your soul.

אַל־תְּהִי בְתֹקְעֵי־כָף בַּעֹרְבִים מַשָּׁאוֹת׃

26. Do not be one of those who strike the palm, or of those who are sureties for debts.

אִם־אֵין־לְךָ לְשַׁלֵּם לָמָּה יִקַּח מִשְׁכָּבְךָ מִתַּחְתֶּיךָ׃

27. If you have nothing with which to pay, why should he take away your bed from under you?

אַל־תַּסֵּג גְּבוּל עוֹלָם אֲשֶׁר עָשׂוּ אֲבוֹתֶיךָ׃

28. Remove not the ancient landmark, which your fathers have set.

חָזִיתָ אִישׁ מָהִיר בִּמְלַאכְתּוֹ
לִפְנֵי־מְלָכִים יִתְיַצָּב בַּל־יִתְיַצֵּב לִפְנֵי חֲשֻׁכִּים׃

29. Do you see a man diligent in his business? He shall stand before kings; He shall not stand before obscure men.

Chapter 23

ספר משלי פרק כג

כִּי־תֵשֵׁב לִלְחוֹם אֶת־מוֹשֵׁל בִּין תָּבִין אֶת־אֲשֶׁר לְפָנֶיךָ:

1. When you sit to eat with a ruler, consider diligently what is before you;

וְשַׂמְתָּ שַׂכִּין בְּלֹעֶךָ אִם־בַּעַל נֶפֶשׁ אָתָּה:

2. And put a knife to your throat, if you are a man given to appetite.

אַל־תִּתְאָו לְמַטְעַמּוֹתָיו וְהוּא לֶחֶם כְּזָבִים:

3. Do not desire his delicacies; for they are deceitful food.

אַל־תִּיגַע לְהַעֲשִׁיר מִבִּינָתְךָ חֲדָל:

4. Labor not to be rich; forbear, because you have understanding.

הֲתָעוּף [הֲתָעִיף] עֵינֶיךָ בּוֹ וְאֵינֶנּוּ כִּי עָשֹׂה יַעֲשֶׂה־לּוֹ כְנָפַיִם כְּנֶשֶׁר וָעִיף [יָעוּף] הַשָּׁמָיִם:

5. (K) Will you set your eyes on it? It is already gone; for riches suddenly make themselves wings; they fly away like an eagle towards the sky.

אַל־תִּלְחַם אֶת־לֶחֶם רַע עָיִן וְאַל־תִּתְאָו [תִּתְאָיו] לְמַטְעַמֹּתָיו:

6. Do not eat the bread of him who has an evil eye, nor should you desire his delicacies;

כִּי כְּמוֹ־שָׁעַר בְּנַפְשׁוֹ כֶּן־הוּא אֱכֹל וּשְׁתֵה יֹאמַר לָךְ וְלִבּוֹ בַּל־עִמָּךְ:

7. For he is one who calculates in his heart; Eat and drink, he says to you; but his heart is not with you.

פִּתְּךָ־אָכַלְתָּ תְקִיאֶנָּה וְשִׁחַתָּ דְּבָרֶיךָ הַנְּעִימִים:

8. The morsel which you have eaten shall you vomit up, and lose your sweet words.

בְּאָזְנֵי כְסִיל אַל־תְּדַבֵּר כִּי־יָבוּז לְשֵׂכֶל מִלֶּיךָ:

9. Speak not in the ears of a fool; for he will despise the wisdom of your words.

אַל־תַּסֵּג גְּבוּל עוֹלָם וּבִשְׂדֵי יְתוֹמִים אַל־תָּבֹא:
you come – don't   orphan ones   and in fields   ancient   boundary   relocate – don't

10. Remove not the old landmark; and enter not into the fields of the orphan;

כִּי־גֹאֲלָם חָזָק הוּא־יָרִיב אֶת־רִיבָם אִתָּךְ:
with you   their case - that   will quarrel – he   strong   redeemer - like

11. For their redeemer is mighty; he shall plead their cause with you.

הָבִיאָה לַמּוּסָר לִבֶּךָ וְאָזְנֶךָ לְאִמְרֵי־דָעַת:
knowledge – to words   and your ears   your heart   to instruction   the bring

12. Apply your heart to instruction, and your ears to the words of knowledge.

אַל־תִּמְנַע מִנַּעַר מוּסָר כִּי־תַכֶּנּוּ בַשֵּׁבֶט לֹא יָמוּת:
he die   not   in rod   you strike him – like   discipline   from child   with withhold – don't

13. Withhold not correction from the child; for if you beat him with the rod, he shall not die.

אַתָּה בַּשֵּׁבֶט תַּכֶּנּוּ וְנַפְשׁוֹ מִשְּׁאוֹל תַּצִּיל:
you rescue   from Sheol   and his soul   you strike him   in rod   you

14. If you beat him with the rod, you shall save his soul from Sheol.

בְּנִי אִם־חָכַם לִבֶּךָ יִשְׂמַח לִבִּי גַם־אָנִי:
I – also   my heart   he be happy   your heart   wise – if   my son

15. My son, if your heart is wise, my heart too shall rejoice.

וְתַעְלֹזְנָה כִלְיוֹתָי בְּדַבֵּר שְׂפָתֶיךָ מֵישָׁרִים:
from upright ones   your lips   in speaking   my kidneys   and they rejoice

16. My insides shall rejoice, when your lips speak right things.

אַל־יְקַנֵּא לִבְּךָ בַּחַטָּאִים כִּי אִם־בְּיִרְאַת־יְהוָה כָּל־הַיּוֹם:
the day – all   ihvh – in fear – with   like   in sinner ones   your heart   he jealous – don't

17. Let not your heart envy sinners; but be in the fear of the Lord all the day long.

כִּי אִם־יֵשׁ אַחֲרִית וְתִקְוָתְךָ לֹא תִכָּרֵת:
will be cut off   not   and your hope   afterwards   there is – with   like

18. For surely there is a future; and your expectation shall not be cut off.

שְׁמַע־אַתָּה בְנִי וַחֲכָם וְאַשֵּׁר בַּדֶּרֶךְ לִבֶּךָ:
your heart   in way   and which   and be wise   my son   you - hear

19. Hear you, my son, and be wise, and guide your heart in the way.

אַל־תְּהִי בְסֹבְאֵי־יָיִן בְּזֹלֲלֵי בָשָׂר לָמוֹ:
to them   flesh   in gorging   wine – drunkard   you be – don't

20. Be not among wine bibbers; among riotous eaters of meat;

כִּי־סֹבֵא וְזוֹלֵל יִוָּרֵשׁ וּקְרָעִים תַּלְבִּישׁ נוּמָה:
drowsiness   it clothes   and rags   he be destitute   and glutton   drunkard - like

21. For the drunkard and the glutton shall come to poverty; and drowsiness shall clothe a man with rags.

Proverbs - Chapter 23

שְׁמַע לְאָבִיךָ זֶה יְלָדֶךָ וְאַל־תָּבוּז כִּי־זָקְנָה אִמֶּךָ:
your mother   she old – like   you despise – and don't   begot you   that   to your father   hear

22. Listen to your father who begot you, and despise not your mother when she is old.

אֱמֶת קְנֵה וְאַל־תִּמְכֹּר חָכְמָה וּמוּסָר וּבִינָה:
and understanding   and instruction   wisdom   you sell – and don't   buy   truth

23. Buy the truth, and sell it not; also wisdom, and instruction, and understanding.

גּוֹל [גִּיל] יָגוּל [יָגִיל] אֲבִי צַדִּיק יוֹלֵד [וְיוֹלֵד] חָכָם
wise   and he beget   righteous   fathers   he exults   exult

וְיִשְׂמַח [יִשְׂמַח]־בּוֹ:
in him –   and he be happy

24. (K) The father of the righteous shall greatly rejoice; and he who begets a wise child shall have joy of him.

יִשְׂמַח־אָבִיךָ וְאִמֶּךָ וְתָגֵל יוֹלַדְתֶּךָ:
she bore you   and she exult   and your mother   your father – he be happy

25. Your father and your mother shall be glad, and she who bore you shall rejoice.

תְּנָה בְנִי לִבְּךָ לִי וְעֵינֶיךָ דְּרָכַי תִּרְצֶנָה [תִּצֹּרְנָה]:
you observe   my way   and your eyes   to me   your heart   my son   give

26. (K) My son, give me your heart, and let your eyes observe my ways.

כִּי־שׁוּחָה עֲמֻקָּה זוֹנָה וּבְאֵר צָרָה נָכְרִיָּה:
foreign woman   narrow   and well   prostitute   deep   pit – like

27. For a harlot is a deep ditch; and an alien woman is a narrow pit.

אַף־הִיא כְּחֶתֶף תֶּאֱרֹב וּבוֹגְדִים בְּאָדָם תּוֹסִף:
she adds   in Adam   and treacherous ones   she ambushes   like bandit   she – surely

28. She also lies in wait like a robber, and increases the transgressors among men.

לְמִי אוֹי לְמִי אֲבוֹי לְמִי מִדְיָנִים [מִדְוָנִים]
quarrels   to who   need   to who   woe   to who

לְמִי שִׂיחַ לְמִי פְּצָעִים חִנָּם לְמִי חַכְלִלוּת עֵינָיִם:
eyes   bloodshot   to who   without cause   injuries   to who   complaint   to who

29. (K) Who cries woe? Who cries alas? who has quarrels? Who has complaints? Who has wounds without cause? Who has redness of eyes?

לַמְאַחֲרִים עַל־הַיָּיִן לַבָּאִים לַחְקֹר מִמְסָךְ:
mixed wine   to sample   to coming ones   the wine – upon   to lingering ones

30. Those who tarry long over the wine; those who go to seek mixed wine.

אַל־תֵּרֶא יַיִן כִּי יִתְאַדָּם
it be red   like   wine   you look – don't

כִּי־יִתֵּן בַּכִּיס [בַּכּוֹס] עֵינוֹ יִתְהַלֵּךְ בְּמֵישָׁרִים:
in fairness   it goes   his eye   in cup   he give – like

31. (K) Do not look on the wine when it is red, when it sparkles in the cup, when it goes

down smoothly.

אַחֲרִיתוֹ כְּנָחָשׁ יִשָּׁךְ וּכְצִפְעֹנִי יַפְרִשׁ׃

he spreads and like viper he bites like snake his afterwards

32. At the last it bites like a serpent, and stings like a viper.

עֵינֶיךָ יִרְאוּ זָרוֹת וְלִבְּךָ יְדַבֵּר תַּהְפֻּכוֹת׃

perverseness he speaks and your heart strangeness they see your eyes

33. Your eyes shall behold strange things, and your heart shall utter perverse words.

וְהָיִיתָ כְּשֹׁכֵב בְּלֶב־יָם וּכְשֹׁכֵב בְּרֹאשׁ חִבֵּל׃

mast in top and like one lying sea – in heart like one lying and you be

34. Indeed, you shall be like one who lies down in the midst of the sea, or like one who lies on the top of a mast.

הִכּוּנִי בַל־חָלִיתִי הֲלָמוּנִי בַל־יָדָעְתִּי

my knowing – without the they beat me my hurting – without they struck me

מָתַי אָקִיץ אוֹסִיף אֲבַקְשֶׁנּוּ עוֹד׃

again I will seek it I add will I wake when

35. They struck me, but I was not hurt; they have beaten me, and I did not feel it; When shall I awake? I will seek it yet again.

Chapter 24

ספר משלי פרק כד

אַל־תְּקַנֵּא בְּאַנְשֵׁי רָעָה וְאַל־תִּתְאָו [תִּתְאָיו] לִהְיוֹת אִתָּם:
<small>with them   to be   you desire – and don't   evil   in men   you jealous – don't</small>

1. Do not be envious of evil men, nor desire to be with them.

כִּי־שֹׁד יֶהְגֶּה לִבָּם וְעָמָל שִׂפְתֵיהֶם תְּדַבֵּרְנָה:
<small>it speaks it   their lips   and labor   their heart   he professes   devastation - like</small>

2. For their heart studies destruction, and their lips talk of mischief.

בְּחָכְמָה יִבָּנֶה בָּיִת וּבִתְבוּנָה יִתְכּוֹנָן:
<small>he established   and in understanding   house   he built   in wisdom</small>

3. By wisdom a house is built; and by understanding it is established;

וּבְדַעַת חֲדָרִים יִמָּלְאוּ כָּל־הוֹן יָקָר וְנָעִים:
<small>and pleasant   precious   wealth - all   they filled   rooms   and in knowledge</small>

4. And by knowledge shall the chambers be filled with all precious and pleasant riches.

גֶּבֶר־חָכָם בַּעוֹז וְאִישׁ־דַּעַת מְאַמֶּץ־כֹּחַ:
<small>vigor – resolute   knowledge   and man   in strength   wise - gentlemen</small>

5. A wise man is strong; and a man of knowledge increases strength.

כִּי בְתַחְבֻּלוֹת תַּעֲשֶׂה־לְּךָ מִלְחָמָה וּתְשׁוּעָה בְּרֹב יוֹעֵץ:
<small>counselor   in many   and safety   war   to you – you make   in strategies   like</small>

6. For by wise counsel you shall make your war; and in a multitude of counsellors there is victory.

רָאמוֹת לֶאֱוִיל חָכְמוֹת בַּשַּׁעַר לֹא יִפְתַּח־פִּיהוּ:
<small>his mouth – he opens   not   in gate   wisdom   to fool   high place</small>

7. Wisdom is too high for a fool; he opens not his mouth in the gate.

מְחַשֵּׁב לְהָרֵעַ לוֹ בַּעַל־מְזִמּוֹת יִקְרָאוּ:
<small>they will be called   schemes – master   to him   to the evil   plans</small>

8. He who plans to do evil shall be called a mischief maker.

זִמַּת אִוֶּלֶת חַטָּאת וְתוֹעֲבַת לְאָדָם לֵץ:
<small>mocking   to Adam   and abomination   sin   folly   scheme</small>

9. The planning of folly is sin; and the scorner is an abomination to men.

הִתְרַפִּיתָ בְּיוֹם צָרָה צַר כֹּחֶכָה:
<small>your vigor   constricted   trouble   in day   you falter</small>

10. If you faint in the day of adversity, your strength is small.

הַצֵּל לְקֻחִים לַמָּוֶת וּמָטִים לַהֶרֶג אִם־תַּחְשׂוֹךְ:
<small>you hold back – with   to the killing   and slipping ones   to death   to taken ones   rescue</small>

11. If you forbear to rescue those who are drawn to death, and those who are ready to be slain,

כִּי־תֹאמַר הֵן לֹא־יָדַעְנוּ זֶה הֲלֹא־תֹכֵן לִבּוֹת הוּא־יָבִין

he understands - he hearts establisher – the not this we knew – not thus you say - like

וְנֹצֵר נַפְשְׁךָ הוּא יֵדָע וְהֵשִׁיב לְאָדָם כְּפָעֳלוֹ:

like his deeds to Adam and the repay knows he your soul and keeps

12. If you say, Behold, we knew it not; does not he who ponders the heart consider it? And he who keeps your soul, does not he know it? And shall he not render to every man according to his deeds?

אֱכָל־בְּנִי דְבַשׁ כִּי־טוֹב וְנֹפֶת מָתוֹק עַל־חִכֶּךָ:

your palate – upon sweet and honeycomb good – like honey my son - eat

13. My son, eat honey, because it is good; and the honeycomb, which is sweet to your taste;

כֵּן דְּעֵה חָכְמָה לְנַפְשֶׁךָ אִם־מָצָאתָ וְיֵשׁ אַחֲרִית

afterwards and there is you find - if to your soul wisdom know thus

וְתִקְוָתְךָ לֹא תִכָּרֵת:

it be cut off not and your hope

14. Know that wisdom is such to your soul; when you have found it, then there shall be a reward, and your expectation shall not be cut off.

אַל־תֶּאֱרֹב רָשָׁע לִנְוֵה צַדִּיק אַל־תְּשַׁדֵּד רִבְצוֹ:

his reclining place you devastate – don't righteous to house grounds wicked you ambush – don't

15. Lie not in wait, O wicked man, against the dwelling of the righteous; do not plunder his resting place;

כִּי שֶׁבַע יִפּוֹל צַדִּיק וָקָם וּרְשָׁעִים יִכָּשְׁלוּ בְרָעָה:

in evil they stumble and wicked ones and rise righteous he falls seven like

16. For a just man falls seven times, and yet rises up again; but the wicked stumble into calamity.

בִּנְפֹל אוֹיִבְךָ [אוֹיַבְךָ] אַל־תִּשְׂמָח וּבִכָּשְׁלוֹ אַל־יָגֵל לִבֶּךָ:

your heart exulting – don't and in his stumble you happy – don't your enemy in fall

17. (K) Rejoice not when your enemy falls, and let not your heart be glad when he stumbles;

פֶּן־יִרְאֶה יְהוָה וְרַע בְּעֵינָיו וְהֵשִׁיב מֵעָלָיו אַפּוֹ:

his anger from upon him and cause turn in his eyes and bad ihvh he see - lest

18. Lest the Lord see it, and be displeased, and he turn away his wrath from him.

אַל־תִּתְחַר בַּמְּרֵעִים אַל־תְּקַנֵּא בָּרְשָׁעִים:

in wicked ones you jealous – don't in from evil doers you fret – don't

19. Do not fret because of evil men, nor should you be envious of the wicked;

כִּי לֹא־תִהְיֶה אַחֲרִית לָרָע נֵר רְשָׁעִים יִדְעָךְ:

extinguished wicked ones candle to evil afterwards it be – not like

20. For there shall be no reward to the evil man; the candle of the wicked shall be put out.

Proverbs - Chapter 24

יְרָא אֶת־יְהוָֹה בְּנִי וָמֶלֶךְ עִם־שׁוֹנִים אַל־תִּתְעָרָב:
you fad – don't   hater ones – with   and king   my son   ihvh – that   fear

21. My son, fear the Lord and the king; and meddle not with those who are given to change;

כִּי־פִתְאֹם יָקוּם אֵידָם וּפִיד שְׁנֵיהֶם מִי יוֹדֵעַ:
knows   who   two them   and ruin   their calamity   he rise   suddenly - like

22. For their calamity shall rise suddenly; and who knows the ruin of them both?

גַּם־אֵלֶּה לַחֲכָמִים הַכֵּר־פָּנִים בְּמִשְׁפָּט בַּל־טוֹב:
good – without   in judgment   faces – recognize   to wise ones   these - also

23. These things also belong to the wise. It is not good to have respect of persons in judgment.

אֹמֵר לְרָשָׁע צַדִּיק אָתָּה יִקְּבֻהוּ עַמִּים יִזְעָמוּהוּ לְאֻמִּים:
to multitudes   they loathe him   peoples   they curse him   you   righteous   to wicked   says

24. He who says to the wicked, You are righteous; him shall the people curse, nations shall loathe him;

וְלַמּוֹכִיחִים יִנְעָם וַעֲלֵיהֶם תָּבוֹא בִרְכַּת־טוֹב:
good – blessing   it come   and upon them   he pleasant   and to rebuking ones

25. But those who rebuke him shall have delight, and a good blessing shall come on them.

שְׂפָתַיִם יִשָּׁק מֵשִׁיב דְּבָרִים נְכֹחִים:
right ones   speaking ones   responding   he kisses   lips

26. He who gives a right answer kisses the lips.

הָכֵן בַּחוּץ מְלַאכְתֶּךָ וְעַתְּדָהּ בַּשָּׂדֶה לָךְ אַחַר וּבָנִיתָ בֵיתֶךָ:
your house   and you build   after   to you   in field   and you equip   your work   in outside   prepare

27. Prepare your work outside, and make it fit for yourself in the field; and afterwards build your house.

אַל־תְּהִי עֵד־חִנָּם בְּרֵעֶךָ וַהֲפִתִּיתָ בִּשְׂפָתֶיךָ:
in your lips   and you entice   in your neighbor   without cause – witness   you be – don't

28. Be not a witness against your neighbor without cause; and deceive not with your lips.

אַל־תֹּאמַר כַּאֲשֶׁר עָשָׂה־לִי
to me – did   when   you say – don't

כֵּן אֶעֱשֶׂה־לּוֹ אָשִׁיב לָאִישׁ כְּפָעֳלוֹ:
like his works   to man   I recompense   to him – I do   thus

29. Say not, I will do so to him as he has done to me; I will render to the man according to what he has done.

עַל־שְׂדֵה אִישׁ־עָצֵל עָבַרְתִּי וְעַל־כֶּרֶם אָדָם חֲסַר־לֵב:
heart – lacking   Adam   vineyards – and upon   I passed   sluggard – man   field - upon

30. I went by the field of a lazy man, and by the vineyard of a man void of understanding;

וְהִנֵּה עָלָה כֻלּוֹ קִמְּשֹׂנִים כָּסּוּ פָנָיו חֲרֻלִּים
      nettles   his face they covered thorns all him upon and here

וְגֶדֶר אֲבָנָיו נֶהֱרָסָה׃
  it pulled down his stones and wall

31. And, behold, it was all grown over with thorns, and nettles had covered it over, and its stone wall was broken down.

וָאֶחֱזֶה אָנֹכִי אָשִׁית לִבִּי רָאִיתִי לָקַחְתִּי מוּסָר׃
 instruction to me taking I saw my heart I set I am and I observed

32. Then I saw, and considered it well; I looked upon it, and received instruction.

מְעַט שֵׁנוֹת מְעַט תְּנוּמוֹת מְעַט חִבֻּק יָדַיִם לִשְׁכָּב׃
 to lie down hands folding little slumbers little sleep little

33. A little sleep, a little slumber, a little folding of the hands to sleep;

וּבָא־מִתְהַלֵּךְ רֵישֶׁךָ וּמַחְסֹרֶיךָ כְּאִישׁ מָגֵן׃
 shield like man and your scarcities your destruction strolling – and comes

34. And poverty will come upon you like a marauder; and want like an armed man.

Chapter 25

ספר משלי פרק כה

גַּם־אֵלֶּה מִשְׁלֵי שְׁלֹמֹה
_{Solomon proverbs these - also}

אֲשֶׁר הֶעְתִּיקוּ אַנְשֵׁי חִזְקִיָּה מֶלֶךְ־יְהוּדָה:
_{Judah – king Hezekiah men they copied which}

1. These are also proverbs of Solomon, which the men of Hezekiah king of Judah copied out.

כְּבֹד אֱלֹהִים הַסְתֵּר דָּבָר וּכְבֹד מְלָכִים חֲקֹר דָּבָר:
_{matter search kings and honor matter the conceal Elohim honor}

2. It is the glory of God to conceal a thing; but the honor of kings is to search out a matter.

שָׁמַיִם לָרוּם וָאָרֶץ לָעֹמֶק וְלֵב מְלָכִים אֵין חֵקֶר:
_{searchable isn't kings and heart to depths. and earth to heights heaven}

3. The sky for height, and the earth for depth, and the heart of kings is unsearchable.

הָגוֹ סִיגִים מִכָּסֶף וַיֵּצֵא לַצֹּרֵף כֶּלִי:
_{vessel to silversmith and he come out from silver drosses remove}

4. Take away the dross from the silver, and a vessel emerges for the refiner.

הָגוֹ רָשָׁע לִפְנֵי־מֶלֶךְ וְיִכּוֹן בַּצֶּדֶק כִּסְאוֹ:
_{his chair in righteous and he establish king – before wicked remove}

5. Take away the wicked from the presence of the king, and his throne shall be established in righteousness.

אַל־תִּתְהַדַּר לִפְנֵי־מֶלֶךְ וּבִמְקוֹם גְּדֹלִים אַל־תַּעֲמֹד:
_{you stand – don't great ones and in place king – before honor yourself – don't}

6. Do not put yourself forward in the presence of the king, and do not stand in the place of great men;

כִּי טוֹב אֲמָר־לְךָ עֲלֵה הֵנָּה מֵהַשְׁפִּילְךָ
_{from your humility here ascend to you – say good like}

לִפְנֵי נָדִיב אֲשֶׁר רָאוּ עֵינֶיךָ:
_{your eyes they see which noble man before}

7. For better it is that it be said to you, Come up here; than that you should be put lower in the presence of the prince whom your eyes have seen.

אַל־תֵּצֵא לָרִב מַהֵר
_{quickly to quarrel you go out – don't}

פֶּן מַה־תַּעֲשֶׂה בְּאַחֲרִיתָהּ בְּהַכְלִים אֹתְךָ רֵעֶךָ:
_{your neighbor to you in shame ones in afterwards you do – what lest}

8. Do not proceed hastily to litigation, lest you know not what to do the end of it, when your neighbor has put you to shame.

רִיבְךָ רִיב אֶת־רֵעֶךָ וְסוֹד אַחֵר אַל־תְּגָל׃

9. Debate your cause with your neighbor; and do not reveal the secret of another;

פֶּן־יְחַסֶּדְךָ שֹׁמֵעַ וְדִבָּתְךָ לֹא תָשׁוּב׃

10. Lest he who hears you bring shame upon you, and your calumny be carried back.

תַּפּוּחֵי זָהָב בְּמַשְׂכִּיּוֹת כָּסֶף דָּבָר דָּבֻר עַל־אָפְנָיו׃

11. A word fitly spoken is like apples of gold in a setting of silver.

נֶזֶם זָהָב וַחֲלִי־כָתֶם מוֹכִיחַ חָכָם עַל־אֹזֶן שֹׁמָעַת׃

12. As an earring of gold, and an ornament of fine gold, so is a wise reprover to a listening ear.

כְּצִנַּת־שֶׁלֶג בְּיוֹם קָצִיר צִיר נֶאֱמָן לְשֹׁלְחָיו וְנֶפֶשׁ אֲדֹנָיו יָשִׁיב׃

13. As the cold of snow in the time of harvest, so is a faithful messenger to those who send him; for he refreshes the soul of his master.

נְשִׂיאִים וְרוּחַ וְגֶשֶׁם אָיִן אִישׁ מִתְהַלֵּל בְּמַתַּת־שָׁקֶר׃

14. Whoever boasts of a gift which he did not give is like clouds and wind without rain.

בְּאֹרֶךְ אַפַּיִם יְפֻתֶּה קָצִין וְלָשׁוֹן רַכָּה תִּשְׁבָּר־גָּרֶם׃

15. By long forbearing is a prince persuaded, and a soft tongue breaks the bone.

דְּבַשׁ מָצָאתָ אֱכֹל דַּיֶּךָּ פֶּן־תִּשְׂבָּעֶנּוּ וַהֲקֵאתוֹ׃

16. Have you found honey? Eat so much as is sufficient for you, lest you be filled with it, and vomit it.

הֹקַר רַגְלְךָ מִבֵּית רֵעֶךָ פֶּן־יִשְׂבָּעֲךָ וּשְׂנֵאֶךָ׃

17. Let your foot be seldom in your neighbor's house; lest he become weary of you, and hate you.

מֵפִיץ וְחֶרֶב וְחֵץ שָׁנוּן אִישׁ־עֹנֶה בְרֵעֵהוּ עֵד שָׁקֶר׃

18. A man who bears false witness against his neighbor is like a maul, and a sword, and a sharp arrow.

שֵׁן רֹעָה וְרֶגֶל מוּעָדֶת מִבְטָח בּוֹגֵד בְּיוֹם צָרָה׃

19. Confidence in an unfaithful man in time of trouble is like a broken tooth, and a foot out of joint.

מַעֲדֶה־בֶּגֶד בְּיוֹם קָרָה חֹמֶץ עַל־נָתֶר
soda – upon   vinegar   cold   in day   garment – taking off

וְשָׁר בַּשִּׁרִים עַל לֶב־רָע׃
bad – heart   upon   in songs   and sing

20. As one who takes off a garment in cold weather, and as acid on nitre, so is he who sings songs to a heavy heart.

אִם־רָעֵב שֹׂנַאֲךָ הַאֲכִלֵהוּ לָחֶם וְאִם־צָמֵא הַשְׁקֵהוּ מָיִם׃
water   the drink him   thirsty – and with   bread   the eat him   your hating one   hungry – with

21. If your enemy be hungry, give him bread to eat; and if he is thirsty, give him water to drink;

כִּי גֶחָלִים אַתָּה חֹתֶה עַל־רֹאשׁוֹ וַיהוָה יְשַׁלֶּם־לָךְ׃
to you – he will pay   and ihvh   his head – upon   heaping   you   hot coals   like

22. For you shall heap coals of fire upon his head, and the Lord shall reward you.

רוּחַ צָפוֹן תְּחוֹלֵל גָּשֶׁם וּפָנִים נִזְעָמִים לְשׁוֹן סָתֶר׃
concealed   tongue   menacing ones   and faces   rain   it travails   north   wind

23. The north wind brings rain; and a backbiting tongue angry looks.

טוֹב שֶׁבֶת עַל־פִּנַּת־גָּג מֵאֵשֶׁת מִדּוֹנִים [מִדְיָנִים] וּבֵית חָבֶר׃
charm   and house   quarrels   from woman   roof – corners – upon   dwell   good

24. (K) It is better to dwell in the corner of the housetop, than with a brawling woman in a roomy house.

מַיִם קָרִים עַל־נֶפֶשׁ עֲיֵפָה וּשְׁמוּעָה טוֹבָה מֵאֶרֶץ מֶרְחָק׃
distance   from land   better   and news   tired   soul – upon   cold ones   waters

25. As cold waters to a thirsty soul, so are good news from a far country.

מַעְיָן נִרְפָּשׂ וּמָקוֹר מָשְׁחָת צַדִּיק מָט לִפְנֵי־רָשָׁע׃
wicked – before   slipping   righteous   corrupted   and fountain   muddied   spring

26. A righteous man who falls down before the wicked is like a muddied fountain, and a polluted spring.

אָכֹל דְּבַשׁ הַרְבּוֹת לֹא־טוֹב וְחֵקֶר כְּבֹדָם כָּבוֹד׃
honor   honor of them   and search   good – not   the many   honey   eat

27. It is not good to eat much honey; so glory is for men who search glory.

עִיר פְּרוּצָה אֵין חוֹמָה אִישׁ אֲשֶׁר אֵין מַעְצָר לְרוּחוֹ׃
to his spirit   restraint   isn't   which   man   wall   isn't   broken down   city

28. He who has no rule over his own spirit is like a city that is broken down, and without walls.

Chapter 26

ספר משלי פרק כו

כְּשֶׁלֶג בַּקַּיִץ וְכַמָּטָר בַּקָּצִיר כֵּן לֹא־נָאוֶה לִכְסִיל כָּבוֹד:
honor / to fool / fitting – not / thus / in harvest / and like rain / in summer / like snow

1. As snow in the summer, and as rain in the harvest, so is honor not fitting for a fool.

כַּצִּפּוֹר לָנוּד כַּדְּרוֹר לָעוּף כֵּן קִלְלַת חִנָּם לֹא [לוֹ] תָבֹא:
will come / [to him] / not / causeless / curse / thus / to fly / like swallow / to flutter / like bird

2. (K) Like a wandering sparrow, like a flying swallow, a curse that is causeless shall not come.

שׁוֹט לַסּוּס מֶתֶג לַחֲמוֹר וְשֵׁבֶט לְגֵו כְּסִילִים:
fool ones / to body / and rod / to donkey / bridle / to horse / whip

3. A whip for the horse, a bridle for the ass, and a rod for the fool's back.

אַל־תַּעַן כְּסִיל כְּאִוַּלְתּוֹ פֶּן־תִּשְׁוֶה־לּוֹ גַם־אָתָּה:
you – also / to him – you equal – lest / like his folly / fool / you answer – don't

4. Do not answer a fool according to his folly, lest you become like him.

עֲנֵה כְסִיל כְּאִוַּלְתּוֹ פֶּן־יִהְיֶה חָכָם בְּעֵינָיו:
in his eyes / wise / he will be – lest / like his folly / fool / answer

5. Answer a fool according to his folly, lest he be wise in his own eyes.

מְקַצֶּה רַגְלַיִם חָמָס שֹׁתֶה שֹׁלֵחַ דְּבָרִים בְּיַד־כְּסִיל:
fool – in hand / matters / sending / drinks / violence / feet / cutting off

6. He who sends a message by the hand of a fool cuts off his own feet, and drinks violence.

דַּלְיוּ שֹׁקַיִם מִפִּסֵּחַ וּמָשָׁל בְּפִי כְסִילִים:
fool ones / in mouth / and proverb / lame one / legs / impoverished

7. As the legs of a lame which hang useless, so is a parable in the mouth of fools.

כִּצְרוֹר אֶבֶן בְּמַרְגֵּמָה כֵּן־נוֹתֵן לִכְסִיל כָּבוֹד:
honor / to fool / gives – lest / in sling / stone / like to tie up

8. As one who binds a stone in a sling, so is he who gives honor to a fool.

חוֹחַ עָלָה בְיַד־שִׁכּוֹר וּמָשָׁל בְּפִי כְסִילִים:
fool ones / in mouth / and proverb / drunk – in hand / rises / thorn

9. As a thorn that goes into the hand of a drunkard, so is a parable in the mouth of fools.

רַב מְחוֹלֵל־כֹּל וְשֹׂכֵר כְּסִיל וְשֹׂכֵר עֹבְרִים:
passing ones / and hires / fool / and hires / all – travails / many

10. A master craftsman performs everything; but he who hires a fool is as he who hires the passers by.

כְּכֶלֶב שָׁב עַל־קֵאוֹ כְּסִיל שׁוֹנֶה בְאִוַּלְתּוֹ:
in his folly / repeating / fool / his vomit – upon / returns / like dog

11. As a dog returns to his vomit, so a fool returns to his folly.

רָאִיתָ אִישׁ חָכָם בְּעֵינָיו תִּקְוָה לִכְסִיל מִמֶּנּוּ׃

from him   to fool   hope   in his eyes   wise   man   you see

12. Do you see a man who is wise in his own eyes? There is more hope for a fool than for him.

אָמַר עָצֵל שַׁחַל בַּדָּרֶךְ אֲרִי בֵּין הָרְחֹבוֹת׃

the streets   between   lion   in way   black lion   lazy   says

13. The lazy man says, There is a lion in the way; a lion is in the streets.

הַדֶּלֶת תִּסּוֹב עַל־צִירָהּ וְעָצֵל עַל־מִטָּתוֹ׃

his bed – upon   and lazy   hinge – upon   it revolves   the door

14. As the door turns on its hinges, so does the lazy man turn on his bed.

טָמַן עָצֵל יָדוֹ בַּצַּלָּחַת נִלְאָה לַהֲשִׁיבָהּ אֶל־פִּיו׃

his mouth – unto   to the return it   too tired   in dish   his hand   lazy   he buries

15. The lazy man hides his hand in the dish; and will not even bring it back to his mouth.

חָכָם עָצֵל בְּעֵינָיו מִשִּׁבְעָה מְשִׁיבֵי טָעַם׃

discretion   from replying   from seven   in his eyes   lazy one   wise

16. The sluggard is wiser in his own eyes than seven men that can give sensible answers.

מַחֲזִיק בְּאָזְנֵי־כָלֶב עֹבֵר מִתְעַבֵּר עַל־רִיב לֹא־לוֹ׃

to him – not   quarrel – upon   meddling   passer by   dog – in ears   seizing

17. He who passes by, and meddles in a quarrel not his own, is like one who takes a dog by the ears.

כְּמִתְלַהְלֵהַּ הַיֹּרֶה זִקִּים חִצִּים וָמָוֶת׃

and death   arrows   firebrands   the shooting   like frantic

18. As a mad man who throws firebrands, arrows, and death,

כֵּן־אִישׁ רִמָּה אֶת־רֵעֵהוּ וְאָמַר הֲלֹא־מְשַׂחֵק אָנִי׃

I   joking – the not   and says   his neighbor – that   deceives   man – thus

19. So is the man who deceives his neighbor, and says, I was only joking!

בְּאֶפֶס עֵצִים תִּכְבֶּה־אֵשׁ וּבְאֵין נִרְגָּן יִשְׁתֹּק מָדוֹן׃

quarrel   he calms   gossiping   and in isn't   fire – it goes out   woods   in limit

20. Where no wood is, there the fire goes out; so where there is no talebearer, the quarrel ceases.

פֶּחָם לְגֶחָלִים וְעֵצִים לְאֵשׁ

to fire   and woods   to embers   charcoal

וְאִישׁ מִדְיָנִים [מִדּוֹנִים] לְחַרְחַר־רִיב׃

strife – to kindle   quarrels   and man

21. (K) As coals are for burning coals, and wood is for fire; so is a quarrelsome man for kindling a quarrel.

דִּבְרֵי נִרְגָּן כְּמִתְלַהֲמִים וְהֵם יָרְדוּ חַדְרֵי־בָטֶן:

22. The words of a talebearer are like delicacies, and they go down into the innermost parts of the body.

כֶּסֶף סִיגִים מְצֻפֶּה עַל־חָרֶשׂ שְׂפָתַיִם דֹּלְקִים וְלֶב־רָע:

23. Burning lips and a wicked heart are like a earthenware dish covered with silver dross.

בִּשְׂפָתָו [בִּשְׂפָתָיו] יִנָּכֵר שׂוֹנֵא וּבְקִרְבּוֹ יָשִׁית מִרְמָה:

24. He who hates dissembles with his lips, and harbors deceit in his heart;

כִּי־יְחַנֵּן קוֹלוֹ אַל־תַּאֲמֶן־בּוֹ כִּי שֶׁבַע תּוֹעֵבוֹת בְּלִבּוֹ:

25. When he speaks graciously, believe him not; for there are seven abominations in his heart.

תִּכַּסֶּה שִׂנְאָה בְּמַשָּׁאוֹן תִּגָּלֶה רָעָתוֹ בְקָהָל:

26. Thought his hatred is covered by deceit, his wickedness will be exposed before the whole congregation.

כֹּרֶה שַּׁחַת בָּהּ יִפֹּל וְגֹלֵל אֶבֶן אֵלָיו תָּשׁוּב:

27. Whoever digs a pit shall fall in it; and whoever rolls a stone, it will return upon him.

לְשׁוֹן־שֶׁקֶר יִשְׂנָא דַכָּיו וּפֶה חָלָק יַעֲשֶׂה מִדְחֶה:

28. A lying tongue hates its victims; and a flattering mouth works ruin.

Chapter 27

ספר משלי פרק כז

אַל־תִּתְהַלֵּל בְּיוֹם מָחָר כִּי לֹא־תֵדַע מַה־יֵּלֶד יוֹם׃

1. Boast not yourself of tomorrow; for you know not what today may bring forth.

יְהַלֶּלְךָ זָר וְלֹא־פִיךָ נָכְרִי וְאַל־שְׂפָתֶיךָ׃

2. Let another man praise you, and not your own mouth; a stranger, and not your own lips.

כֹּבֶד אֶבֶן וְנֵטֶל הַחוֹל וְכַעַס אֱוִיל כָּבֵד מִשְּׁנֵיהֶם׃

3. A stone is heavy, and the sand weighty; but a fool's wrath is heavier than both of them.

אַכְזְרִיּוּת חֵמָה וְשֶׁטֶף אָף וּמִי יַעֲמֹד לִפְנֵי קִנְאָה׃

4. Wrath is cruel, and anger is overwhelming; but who is able to stand before envy?

טוֹבָה תּוֹכַחַת מְגֻלָּה מֵאַהֲבָה מְסֻתָּרֶת׃

5. Open rebuke is better than secret love.

נֶאֱמָנִים פִּצְעֵי אוֹהֵב וְנַעְתָּרוֹת נְשִׁיקוֹת שׂוֹנֵא׃

6. Faithful are the wounds of a friend; but the kisses of an enemy are profuse.

נֶפֶשׁ שְׂבֵעָה תָּבוּס נֹפֶת וְנֶפֶשׁ רְעֵבָה כָּל־מַר מָתוֹק׃

7. The soul who is sated loathes a honeycomb; but to the hungry soul every bitter thing is sweet.

כְּצִפּוֹר נוֹדֶדֶת מִן־קִנָּהּ כֵּן אִישׁ נוֹדֵד מִמְּקוֹמוֹ׃

8. As a bird that wanders from its nest, so is a man who wanders from his place.

שֶׁמֶן וּקְטֹרֶת יְשַׂמַּח־לֵב וּמֶתֶק רֵעֵהוּ מֵעֲצַת־נָפֶשׁ׃

9. Ointment and perfume rejoice the heart; so does the sweetness of a man's friend by hearty counsel.

רֵעֲךָ וְרֵעֶה [וְרֵעַ] אָבִיךָ אַל־תַּעֲזֹב וּבֵית אָחִיךָ

אַל־תָּבוֹא בְּיוֹם אֵידֶךָ

טוֹב שָׁכֵן קָרוֹב מֵאָח רָחוֹק:

10. (K) Do not forsake your own friend, nor your father's friend; nor go into your brother's house in the day of your calamity; for better is a neighbor who is near than a brother who is far away.

חֲכַם בְּנִי וְשַׂמַּח לִבִּי וְאָשִׁיבָה חֹרְפִי דָבָר:

11. My son, be wise, and make my heart glad, that I may answer him who reproaches me.

עָרוּם רָאָה רָעָה נִסְתָּר פְּתָאיִם עָבְרוּ נֶעֱנָשׁוּ:

12. A prudent man sees the evil, and hides himself; but the simpletons pass on, and are punished.

קַח־בִּגְדוֹ כִּי־עָרַב זָר וּבְעַד נָכְרִיָּה חַבְלֵהוּ:

13. Take his garment when he has given surety for a stranger, and take his pledge on behalf of an alien woman.

מְבָרֵךְ רֵעֵהוּ בְּקוֹל גָּדוֹל בַּבֹּקֶר הַשְׁכֵּים קְלָלָה תֵּחָשֶׁב לוֹ:

14. He who blesses his friend with a loud voice, rising early in the morning, it shall be counted a curse to him.

דֶּלֶף טוֹרֵד בְּיוֹם סַגְרִיר וְאֵשֶׁת מִדְוָנִים [מִדְיָנִים] נִשְׁתָּוָה:

15. (K) A continual dripping in a very rainy day and a quarrelsome woman are alike.

צֹפְנֶיהָ צָפַן־רוּחַ וְשֶׁמֶן יְמִינוֹ יִקְרָא:

16. Whoever hides her hides the wind, like the ointment of his right hand, which betrays itself.

בַּרְזֶל בְּבַרְזֶל יָחַד וְאִישׁ יַחַד פְּנֵי־רֵעֵהוּ:

17. Iron sharpens iron; so a man sharpens another.

נֹצֵר תְּאֵנָה יֹאכַל פִּרְיָהּ וְשֹׁמֵר אֲדֹנָיו יְכֻבָּד:

18. Whoever guards the fig tree shall eat its fruit; so he who waits on his master shall be honored.

כַּמַּיִם הַפָּנִים לַפָּנִים כֵּן לֵב־הָאָדָם לָאָדָם:

19. As in water face answers face, so does the heart of man to man.

שְׁאוֹל וַאֲבַדֹּה [וַאֲבַדּוֹ] לֹא תִשְׂבַּעְנָה

Proverbs - Chapter 27

וְעֵינֵי הָאָדָם לֹא תִשְׂבַּעְנָה׃
<small>it be full them   not   the Adam   and eye</small>

20. Sheol and Avaddon are never full; and the eyes of man are never satisfied.

מַצְרֵף לַכֶּסֶף וְכוּר לַזָּהָב וְאִישׁ לְפִי מַהֲלָלוֹ׃
<small>his praise   to mouth   and man   to gold   and crucible   to silver   refinery</small>

21. The refining pot is for silver, and the furnace for gold; and a man is judged according to his praise.

אִם־תִּכְתּוֹשׁ אֶת־הָאֱוִיל בַּמַּכְתֵּשׁ בְּתוֹךְ הָרִיפוֹת בַּעֱלִי
<small>in pestle   the grains   among   in mortar   the fool – that   you grind - with</small>

לֹא־תָסוּר מֵעָלָיו אִוַּלְתּוֹ׃
<small>his folly   from upon him   it depart - not</small>

22. Though you should grind a fool with a pestle in a mortar among wheat, his folly would not depart from him.

יָדֹעַ תֵּדַע פְּנֵי צֹאנֶךָ שִׁית לִבְּךָ לַעֲדָרִים׃
<small>to herd ones   your heart   attend   your flock   face   you know   know</small>

23. Be diligent to know the state of your flocks, and look well to your herds.

כִּי לֹא לְעוֹלָם חֹסֶן וְאִם־נֵזֶר לְדוֹר דּוֹר [וָדוֹר]׃
<small>and generation   to generation   crown - and with   safeguards   to forever   not   like</small>

24. (K)For riches are not for ever; and does a crown endure to all generations?

גָּלָה חָצִיר וְנִרְאָה־דֶשֶׁא וְנֶאֶסְפוּ עִשְּׂבוֹת הָרִים׃
<small>mountains   herbs   and they gathered   vegetation – and it appears   grass   rolled</small>

25. When the grass sprouts forth, and the young grass appears, and herbs are gathered on the mountains,

כְּבָשִׂים לִלְבוּשֶׁךָ וּמְחִיר שָׂדֶה עַתּוּדִים׃
<small>goats   field   and price   to your clothes   like lambs</small>

26. Lambs shall provide your clothing, and goats the price of a field,

וְדֵי חֲלֵב עִזִּים לְלַחְמְךָ לְלֶחֶם בֵּיתֶךָ וְחַיִּים לְנַעֲרוֹתֶיךָ׃
<small>to your maiden girls   and life   your house   to bread   to your bread   goats   milk   and enough</small>

27. And you shall have goats' milk enough for your food, for the food of your household, and for the maintenance of your maidens.

Chapter 28

ספר משלי פרק כח

נָסוּ וְאֵין־רֹדֵף רָשָׁע וְצַדִּיקִים כִּכְפִיר יִבְטָח:

1. The wicked flee when no man pursues; but the righteous are bold as a lion.

בְּפֶשַׁע אֶרֶץ רַבִּים שָׂרֶיהָ וּבְאָדָם מֵבִין יֹדֵעַ כֵּן יַאֲרִיךְ:

2. When a land transgresses its princes are many; but when there is a man of understanding and knowledge, he shall endure.

גֶּבֶר רָשׁ וְעֹשֵׁק דַּלִּים מָטָר סֹחֵף וְאֵין לָחֶם:

3. A poor man who oppresses the poor is like a sweeping rain which leaves no food.

עֹזְבֵי תוֹרָה יְהַלְלוּ רָשָׁע וְשֹׁמְרֵי תוֹרָה יִתְגָּרוּ בָם:

4. Those who forsake the Torah praise the wicked; but those who keep the Torah strive with them.

אַנְשֵׁי־רָע לֹא־יָבִינוּ מִשְׁפָּט וּמְבַקְשֵׁי יְהֹוָה יָבִינוּ כֹל:

5. Evil men do not understand justice; but those who seek the Lord understand all things.

טוֹב־רָשׁ הוֹלֵךְ בְּתֻמּוֹ מֵעִקֵּשׁ דְּרָכַיִם וְהוּא עָשִׁיר:

6. Better is the poor who walks in his uprightness, than a rich man who is perverse in his ways.

נוֹצֵר תּוֹרָה בֵּן מֵבִין וְרֹעֶה זוֹלְלִים יַכְלִים אָבִיו:

7. Whoever keeps the Torah is a wise son; but he who is a companion of riotous men shames his father.

מַרְבֶּה הוֹנוֹ בְּנֶשֶׁךְ וּבְתַרְבִּית [וְתַרְבִּית] לְחוֹנֵן דַּלִּים יִקְבְּצֶנּוּ:

8. (K) He who by usury and unjust gain increases his wealth, gathers it for him who graciously regards the poor.

מֵסִיר אָזְנוֹ מִשְּׁמֹעַ תּוֹרָה גַּם־תְּפִלָּתוֹ תּוֹעֵבָה:

9. He who turns away his ear from hearing the Torah, even his prayer shall be abomination.

Proverbs - Chapter 28

מַשְׁגֶּה יְשָׁרִים בְּדֶרֶךְ רָע בִּשְׁחוּתוֹ הוּא־יִפּוֹל
וּתְמִימִים יִנְחֲלוּ־טוֹב׃

10. Whoever causes the righteous to go astray in an evil way, he shall fall himself into his own pit; but the upright shall have a goodly inheritance.

חָכָם בְּעֵינָיו אִישׁ עָשִׁיר וְדַל מֵבִין יַחְקְרֶנּוּ׃

11. The rich man is wise in his own eyes; but the poor who has understanding searches him out.

בַּעֲלֹץ צַדִּיקִים רַבָּה תִפְאָרֶת וּבְקוּם רְשָׁעִים יְחֻפַּשׂ אָדָם׃

12. When righteous men rejoice, there is great glory; but when the wicked rise, men hide themselves.

מְכַסֶּה פְשָׁעָיו לֹא יַצְלִיחַ וּמוֹדֶה וְעֹזֵב יְרֻחָם׃

13. He who covers his sins shall not prosper; but whoever confesses and forsakes them shall have mercy.

אַשְׁרֵי אָדָם מְפַחֵד תָּמִיד וּמַקְשֶׁה לִבּוֹ יִפּוֹל בְּרָעָה׃

14. Happy is the man who fears always; but he who hardens his heart shall fall into mischief.

אֲרִי־נֹהֵם וְדֹב שׁוֹקֵק מֹשֵׁל רָשָׁע עַל עַם־דָּל׃

15. As a roaring lion, and a charging bear, so is a wicked ruler over the poor people.

נָגִיד חֲסַר תְּבוּנוֹת וְרַב מַעֲשַׁקּוֹת שֹׂנְאֵי [שֹׂנֵא] בֶצַע יַאֲרִיךְ יָמִים׃

16. (K) The prince who lacks understanding is also a great oppressor; but he who hates covetousness shall prolong his days.

אָדָם עָשֻׁק בְּדַם־נָפֶשׁ עַד־בּוֹר יָנוּס אַל־יִתְמְכוּ־בוֹ׃

17. If a man burdened with the blood of another flees to the pit, let no man help him.

הוֹלֵךְ תָּמִים יִוָּשֵׁעַ וְנֶעְקַשׁ דְּרָכַיִם יִפּוֹל בְּאֶחָת׃

18. Whoever walks uprightly shall be saved; but he who is perverse in his ways shall fall at once.

עֹבֵד אַדְמָתוֹ יִשְׂבַּֽע־לָחֶם וּמְרַדֵּף רֵקִים יִֽשְׂבַּע־רִֽישׁ׃
poverty – he be full   empty ones   and pursuing   bread – he full   his soil   server

19. He who tills his land shall have plenty of bread; but he who follows after vain persons shall have poverty enough.

אִישׁ אֱמוּנוֹת רַב־בְּרָכוֹת וְאָץ לְהַעֲשִׁיר לֹא יִנָּקֶֽה׃
he innocent   not   to the rich   and rushing   his blessings – many   faithfulness   man

20. A faithful man shall abound with blessings; but he who makes haste to be rich shall not go unpunished.

הַכֵּר־פָּנִים לֹא־טוֹב וְעַל־פַּת־לֶחֶם יִפְשַׁע־גָּֽבֶר׃
gentlemen – he transgress   bread – piece – and upon   good – not   faces – respect

21. To have respect for persons is not good; for a piece of bread a man will transgress.

נִבֳהָל לַהוֹן אִישׁ רַע עָיִן וְלֹֽא־יֵדַע כִּי־חֶסֶר יְבֹאֶֽנּוּ׃
he comes to him   lack – like   he know – and not   eye   bad   man   to wealth   hastens

22. He who hastens to be rich has an evil eye, and considers not that want shall come upon him.

מוֹכִיחַ אָדָם אַחֲרַי חֵן יִמְצָא מִֽמַּחֲלִיק לָשֽׁוֹן׃
tongue   from flattering   he find   grace   afterwards   Adam   corrector

23. He who rebukes a man afterwards shall find more favor than he who flatters with the tongue.

גּוֹזֵל אָבִיו וְאִמּוֹ וְאֹמֵר אֵֽין־פָּשַׁע
transgression – isn't   and says   and mother   his father   pillager

חָבֵר הוּא לְאִישׁ מַשְׁחִֽית׃
destroyer   to man   he   young man

24. He who robs his father or his mother, and says, This is no transgression; he is the companion of a destroyer.

רְחַב־נֶפֶשׁ יְגָרֶה מָדוֹן וּבוֹטֵחַ עַל־יְהוָה יְדֻשָּֽׁן׃
he enriched   ihvh – upon   and truster   quarrel   he stirs up   soul – greedy

25. He, whose heart is greedy, stirs up quarrel; but he who puts his trust in the Lord shall be enriched.

בּוֹטֵחַ בְּלִבּוֹ הוּא כְסִיל וְהוֹלֵךְ בְּחָכְמָה הוּא יִמָּלֵֽט׃
he escapes   he   in wisdom   and walker   fool   he   in his heart   trust

26. He who trusts in his own heart is a fool; but he who walks wisely, shall be saved.

נוֹתֵן לָרָשׁ אֵין מַחְסוֹר וּמַעְלִים עֵינָיו רַב־מְאֵרֽוֹת׃
curses – many   his eyes   and obscuring ones   lacking one   isn't   to poor   giver

27. He who gives to the poor shall not lack; but he who hides his eyes shall have many a curse.

בְּקוּם רְשָׁעִים יִסָּתֵר אָדָם וּבְאָבְדָם יִרְבּוּ צַדִּיקִֽים׃
righteous ones   they increase   and in their perishing   Adam   he hides   wicked ones   in rising

28. When the wicked rise, men hide themselves; but when they perish, the righteous increase.

Chapter 29

ספר משלי פרק כט

אִישׁ תּוֹכָחוֹת מַקְשֶׁה־עֹרֶף פֶּתַע יִשָּׁבֵר וְאֵין מַרְפֵּא:

1. He, who being often rebuked hardens his neck, shall suddenly be destroyed, beyond remedy.

בִּרְבוֹת צַדִּיקִים יִשְׂמַח הָעָם

וּבִמְשֹׁל רָשָׁע יֵאָנַח עָם:

2. When the righteous are in authority, the people rejoice; but when the wicked rule, the people mourn.

אִישׁ־אֹהֵב חָכְמָה יְשַׂמַּח אָבִיו וְרֹעֶה זוֹנוֹת יְאַבֶּד־הוֹן:

3. He who loves wisdom makes his father glad; but he who keeps company with harlots wastes his capital.

מֶלֶךְ בְּמִשְׁפָּט יַעֲמִיד אָרֶץ וְאִישׁ תְּרוּמוֹת יֶהֶרְסֶנָּה:

4. The king by justice establishes the land; but he who exacts gifts overthrows it.

גֶּבֶר מַחֲלִיק עַל־רֵעֵהוּ רֶשֶׁת פּוֹרֵשׂ עַל־פְּעָמָיו:

5. A man who flatters his neighbor spreads a net for his feet.

בְּפֶשַׁע אִישׁ רָע מוֹקֵשׁ וְצַדִּיק יָרוּן וְשָׂמֵחַ:

6. In the transgression of an evil man there is a trap; but the righteous sings and rejoices.

יֹדֵעַ צַדִּיק דִּין דַּלִּים רָשָׁע לֹא־יָבִין דָּעַת:

7. The righteous man knows the rights of the poor; but the wicked does not have that knowledge.

אַנְשֵׁי לָצוֹן יָפִיחוּ קִרְיָה וַחֲכָמִים יָשִׁיבוּ אָף:

8. Scornful men stir up a city into quarrel; but wise men turn away wrath.

אִישׁ־חָכָם נִשְׁפָּט אֶת־אִישׁ אֱוִיל וְרָגַז וְשָׂחַק וְאֵין נָחַת:

9. If a wise man disputes with a foolish man, whether he rage or laugh, there is no rest.

אַנְשֵׁי דָמִים יִשְׂנְאוּ־תָם וִישָׁרִים יְבַקְשׁוּ נַפְשׁוֹ:
his soul   they seek   and upright ones   perfect one – they hate   bloods   men

10. The bloodthirsty hate the upright; but the just seek his soul.

כָּל־רוּחוֹ יוֹצִיא כְסִיל וְחָכָם בְּאָחוֹר יְשַׁבְּחֶנָּה:
he triumphs   in afterwards   and wise   fool   comes out   his spirit – all

11. A fool vents all his anger; but a wise man quietly holds it back.

מֹשֵׁל מַקְשִׁיב עַל־דְּבַר־שָׁקֶר כָּל־מְשָׁרְתָיו רְשָׁעִים:
wicked ones   his officials – all   lie – speaking – upon   listening   ruler

12. If a ruler listens to lies, all his servants are wicked.

רָשׁ וְאִישׁ תְּכָכִים נִפְגָּשׁוּ מֵאִיר־עֵינֵי שְׁנֵיהֶם יְהֹוָה:
ihvh   both them   eyes – from light   they meet   deceitful ones   and man   poor

13. The poor and the deceitful man meet together; the Lord gives light to the eyes of both.

מֶלֶךְ שׁוֹפֵט בֶּאֱמֶת דַּלִּים כִּסְאוֹ לָעַד יִכּוֹן:
he established   to time   his throne   poor ones   in truth   judger   king

14. The king who faithfully judges the poor, his throne shall be established for ever.

שֵׁבֶט וְתוֹכַחַת יִתֵּן חָכְמָה וְנַעַר מְשֻׁלָּח מֵבִישׁ אִמּוֹ:
his mother   disgraces   let go   and child   wisdom   he gives   and correction   rod

15. The rod and reproof give wisdom; but a child left to himself brings shame to his mother.

בִּרְבוֹת רְשָׁעִים יִרְבֶּה־פָּשַׁע וְצַדִּיקִים בְּמַפַּלְתָּם יִרְאוּ:
they will see   in downfall them   and righteous ones   transgression – he increases   wicked ones   in increases

16. When the wicked are multiplied, transgression increases; but the righteous shall witness their fall.

יַסֵּר בִּנְךָ וִינִיחֶךָ וְיִתֵּן מַעֲדַנִּים לְנַפְשֶׁךָ:
and your soul   delight ones   and he gives   and he be your rest   your son   discipline

17. Correct your son, and he shall give you rest; he shall give delight to your soul.

בְּאֵין חָזוֹן יִפָּרַע עָם וְשֹׁמֵר תּוֹרָה אַשְׁרֵהוּ:
happiest him   Torah   and heeder   people   he unbridled   vision   in isn't

18. Where there is no vision, the people cast off restraint; but he who keeps the Torah is happy.

בִּדְבָרִים לֹא־יִוָּסֶר עָבֶד כִּי־יָבִין וְאֵין מַעֲנֶה:
response   and isn't   he understands – like   servant   he disciplined – not   in speakings

19. A servant will not be corrected by words; for though he understands he will not answer.

חָזִיתָ אִישׁ אָץ בִּדְבָרָיו תִּקְוָה לִכְסִיל מִמֶּנּוּ:
from himself   to fool   hope   in his speakings   rushing   man   you perceive

20. Do you see a man who is hasty in his words? There is more hope for a fool than for him.

מְפַנֵּק מִנֹּעַר עַבְדּוֹ וְאַחֲרִיתוֹ יִהְיֶה מָנוֹן׃
propagator   he be   and his afterwards   his servant   from youth   pampered

21. He who pampers his servant from childhood shall have him become his master at last.

אִישׁ־אַף יְגָרֶה מָדוֹן וּבַעַל חֵמָה רַב־פָּשַׁע׃
transgression – much   hot   and master   dissension   stirs up   anger - man

22. An angry man stirs up quarrel, and a furious man abounds in transgression.

גַּאֲוַת אָדָם תַּשְׁפִּילֶנּוּ וּשְׁפַל־רוּחַ יִתְמֹךְ כָּבוֹד׃
honor   he attains   spirit – and humble   it brings him low   Adam   pride

23. A man's pride shall bring him low; but the humble in spirit shall attain honor.

חוֹלֵק עִם־גַּנָּב שׂוֹנֵא נַפְשׁוֹ אָלָה יִשְׁמַע וְלֹא יַגִּיד׃
he tells   and not   he hears   oath   his soul   hater   thief – with   partner

24. Whoever is partner with a thief hates his own soul; he hears the curse, but discloses nothing.

חֶרְדַּת אָדָם יִתֵּן מוֹקֵשׁ וּבוֹטֵחַ בַּיהוָה יְשֻׂגָּב׃
he impregnable   in ihvh   and truster   trap   he gives   Adam   trembling

25. The fear of man lays a trap; but whoever puts his trust in the Lord shall be safe.

רַבִּים מְבַקְשִׁים פְּנֵי־מוֹשֵׁל וּמֵיְהוָה מִשְׁפַּט־אִישׁ׃
man – judgment   and from ihvh   ruler – face   seeking ones   many ones

26. Many seek the ruler's favor; but a man's justice comes from the Lord.

תּוֹעֲבַת צַדִּיקִים אִישׁ עָוֶל וְתוֹעֲבַת רָשָׁע יְשַׁר־דָּרֶךְ׃
way – upright   wicked and abomination   iniquity   man   righteous ones   abomination

27. An unjust man is an abomination to the just; and he who is upright in the way is an abomination to the wicked.

Chapter 30

ספר משלי פרק ל

דִּבְרֵי ׀ אָגוּר בִּן־יָקֶה הַמַּשָּׂא נְאֻם הַגֶּבֶר
the gentleman   declaration   the load   Jakeh – son   Agur   speakings

לְאִיתִיאֵל לְאִיתִיאֵל וְאֻכָל׃
and Ucal   to Ithiel   to Ithiel

1. The words of Agur the son of Jakeh, the burden. Thus says the man: I am weary, O God, I am weary, O God, and I am consumed.

כִּי בַעַר אָנֹכִי מֵאִישׁ וְלֹא־בִינַת אָדָם לִי׃
to me   Adam   understandings – and not   from man   I am   brutish   like

2. Surely I am more stupid than any man, and do not have the understanding of a man.

וְלֹא־לָמַדְתִּי חָכְמָה וְדַעַת קְדֹשִׁים אֵדָע׃
I acknowledge   holy ones   and knowledge   wisdom   my learning – and not

3. I did not learn wisdom, nor do I have knowledge of the holy.

מִי עָלָה־שָׁמַיִם ׀ וַיֵּרַד מִי אָסַף־רוּחַ ׀ בְּחָפְנָיו
in his cupped hands   soul – gathered   who   and descended   heavens – ascended   who

מִי צָרַר־מַיִם ׀ בַּשִּׂמְלָה
in [a] dress   waters – wrapped   who

מִי הֵקִים כָּל־אַפְסֵי־אָרֶץ מַה־שְּׁמוֹ וּמַה־שֶּׁם־בְּנוֹ כִּי תֵדָע׃
you know   like   his son – name – and what   his name – what   earth – limits – all   established   who

4. Who has ascended to heaven and come down? Who has gathered the wind in his fists? Who has bound the waters in a garment? Who has established all the ends of the earth? What is his name, and what is his son's name, if you can tell?

כָּל־אִמְרַת אֱלוֹהַּ צְרוּפָה מָגֵן הוּא לַחֹסִים בּוֹ׃
in him   to taking refuge ones   he   shield   refined   Elohim   words – all

5. Every word of God is proven; he is a shield to those who put their trust in him.

אַל־תּוֹסְףְּ עַל־דְּבָרָיו פֶּן־יוֹכִיחַ בְּךָ וְנִכְזָבְתָּ׃
and you prove liar   in you   he rebuke – lest   his speech – upon   you add – don't

6. Do not add to his words, lest he reprove you, and you be found a liar.

שְׁתַּיִם שָׁאַלְתִּי מֵאִתָּךְ אַל־תִּמְנַע מִמֶּנִּי בְּטֶרֶם אָמוּת׃
I die   in before   from me   you refuse – don't   from you   I ask   twice

7. Two things have I asked of you; do not deny them before I die;

שָׁוְא ׀ וּדְבַר־כָּזָב הַרְחֵק מִמֶּנִּי
from me   the far   lie – and speech   vanity

רֵאשׁ וָעֹשֶׁר אַל־תִּתֶּן־לִי הַטְרִיפֵנִי לֶחֶם חֻקִּי׃
my portion   bread   the feed me   to me – give – don't   and riches   poverty

8. Remove far from me falsehood and lies; do not give me poverty nor riches; feed me

with the food that is needful for me;

פֶּן אֶשְׂבַּע וְכִחַשְׁתִּי וְאָמַרְתִּי מִי יְהוָה וּפֶן־אִוָּרֵשׁ
I be poor – and lest   ihvh   who   and I say   and I deny   I be full   lest

וְגָנַבְתִּי וְתָפַשְׂתִּי שֵׁם אֱלֹהָי׃
my Elohim   name   and I denigrate   and I steal

9. Lest I be full, and deny you, and say, Who is the Lord? or lest I be poor, and steal, and profane the name of my God.

אַל־תַּלְשֵׁן עֶבֶד אֶל־אֲדֹנָו [אֲדֹנָיו] פֶּן־יְקַלֶּלְךָ וְאָשָׁמְתָּ׃
and you be guilty   he curse you – lest   his master   - unto   servant   you slander – don't

10. Do not accuse a servant to his master, lest he curse you, and you be found guilty.

דּוֹר אָבִיו יְקַלֵּל וְאֶת־אִמּוֹ לֹא יְבָרֵךְ׃
he blesses   not   his mother – and that   he curses   his father   generation

11. There is a generation that curses their father, and does not bless their mother.

דּוֹר טָהוֹר בְּעֵינָיו וּמִצֹּאָתוֹ לֹא רֻחָץ׃
washed   not   and his filth   in his eyes   pure   generation

12. There is a generation who are pure in their own eyes, and yet are not washed from their filthiness.

דּוֹר מָה־רָמוּ עֵינָיו וְעַפְעַפָּיו יִנָּשֵׂאוּ׃
they lifted up   and his eyelids   his eyes   lofty – what   generation

13. There is a generation, O how lofty are their eyes! and their eyelids are lifted up.

דּוֹר חֲרָבוֹת שִׁנָּיו וּמַאֲכָלוֹת מְתַלְּעֹתָיו לֶאֱכֹל
to eat   his jaws   and knives   his teeth   swords   generation

עֲנִיִּים מֵאֶרֶץ וְאֶבְיוֹנִים מֵאָדָם׃
from Adam   and needy ones   from earth   poor ones

14. There is a generation, whose teeth are like swords, and their jaw teeth like knives, to devour the poor from off the earth, and the needy from among men.

לַעֲלוּקָה שְׁתֵּי בָנוֹת הַב הַב שָׁלוֹשׁ
three   grant   grant   daughters   two   to leech

הֵנָּה לֹא תִשְׂבַּעְנָה אַרְבַּע לֹא־אָמְרוּ הוֹן׃
enough   they say – not   four   satisfied   not   here

15. The leech has two daughters, crying, Give, give. There are three things that are never satisfied, four things that never say, It is enough:

שְׁאוֹל וְעֹצֶר רָחַם אֶרֶץ לֹא־שָׂבְעָה מַּיִם וְאֵשׁ לֹא־אָמְרָה הוֹן׃
enough   says – not   and fire   waters   it full – not   earth   womb and restrained   Shoel

16. Sheol; and the barren womb; the earth that is not filled with water; and the fire that never says, It is enough.

עַיִן תִּלְעַג לְאָב וְתָבוּז לִיקֲּהַת־אֵם יִקְּרוּהָ עֹרְבֵי־נַחַל
river – ravens   they peck her   her mother – to obey   and she despises   to father   she mocks   eye

וְיֹאכְל֥וּהָ בְנֵי־נָֽשֶׁר׃

vultures – sons   and they eat her

17. The eye that mocks at his father, and scorns to obey his mother, will be picked out by the ravens of the valley, and the young vultures shall eat it.

שְׁלֹשָׁ֣ה הֵ֭מָּה נִפְלְא֣וּ מִמֶּ֑נִּי וְאַרְבָּע [וְאַרְבָּעָ֣ה] לֹ֣א יְדַעְתִּֽים׃

I knowing ones not and four from me they wonderful they are three

18. There are three things which are too wonderful for me, indeed, four which I know not;

דֶּ֤רֶךְ הַנֶּ֨שֶׁר ׀ בַּשָּׁמַיִם֮ דֶּ֥רֶךְ נָחָ֗שׁ עֲלֵ֫י צ֥וּר

rock   upon   serpent   way   in heavens   the vulture   way

דֶּֽרֶךְ־אֳנִיָּ֥ה בְלֶב־יָ֑ם וְדֶ֖רֶךְ גֶּ֣בֶר בְּעַלְמָֽה׃

in young woman gentlemen and way   sea – in heart   ship – way

19. The way of a vulture in the sky; the way of a serpent on a rock; the way of a ship in the midst of the sea; and the way of a man with a young woman.

כֵּ֤ן ׀ דֶּ֥רֶךְ אִשָּׁ֗ה מְנָ֫אָ֥פֶת אָ֭כְלָה וּמָ֣חֲתָה פִ֑יהָ

her mouth   and she wipes   she eats   adulteress   woman   way   thus

וְ֝אָמְרָ֗ה לֹֽא־פָעַ֥לְתִּי אָֽוֶן׃

inequity   my works – not   and she says

20. This is the way of an adulterous woman; she eats, and wipes her mouth, and says, I have done nothing wrong.

תַּ֣חַת שָׁ֭לוֹשׁ רָ֣גְזָה אֶ֑רֶץ וְתַ֥חַת אַ֝רְבַּ֗ע לֹא־תוּכַ֥ל שְׂאֵֽת׃

bear she able – not   four   and under   earth she disturbed   three   under

21. For three things the earth is disquieted, and for four it cannot bear;

תַּֽחַת־עֶ֭בֶד כִּ֣י יִמְל֑וֹךְ וְ֝נָבָ֗ל כִּ֣י יִֽשְׂבַּֽע־לָֽחֶם׃

bread – he full   like   and decadent   he reign   like   servant   under

22. For a slave when he becomes king; and a fool when he is filled with bread;

תַּ֣חַת שְׂ֭נוּאָה כִּ֣י תִבָּעֵ֑ל וְ֝שִׁפְחָ֗ה כִּֽי־תִירַ֥שׁ גְּבִרְתָּֽהּ׃

her lady   she heir – like   and maid   married   like   hated woman   under

23. For an unloved woman when she is married; and a maidservant who is heir to her mistress.

אַרְבָּ֣עָה הֵ֭ם קְטַנֵּי־אָ֑רֶץ וְ֝הֵ֗מָּה חֲכָמִ֥ים מְחֻכָּמִֽים׃

from wise ones   wise ones   and they are   are earth – small   them   four

24. There are four things on earth which are small, but they are exceedingly wise;

הַ֭נְּמָלִים עַ֣ם לֹא־עָ֑ז וַיָּכִ֖ינוּ בַקַּ֣יִץ לַחְמָֽם׃

their bread   in summer   and they prepare   strong – not   people   the ants

25. The ants are not a strong people, yet they prepare their bread in the summer;

שְׁ֭פַנִּים עַ֣ם לֹא־עָצ֑וּם וַיָּשִׂ֖ימוּ בַסֶּ֣לַע בֵּיתָֽם׃

their houses   in crag   and they make themselves   powerful – not   people   badgers

26. The badgers are a feeble folk, yet they make their houses in the rocks;

Proverbs - Chapter 30

מֶלֶךְ אֵין לָאַרְבֶּה וַיֵּצֵא חֹצֵץ כֻּלּוֹ׃
_{king   isn't   to locust and he goes out divisions his all}

27. The locusts have no king, yet they go forth all of them by bands;

שְׂמָמִית בְּיָדַיִם תְּתַפֵּשׂ וְהִיא בְּהֵיכְלֵי מֶלֶךְ׃
_{lizard   in their hands you grasp and she in palace king}

28. The lizard climbs up with her hands, and she is in kings' palaces.

שְׁלֹשָׁה הֵמָּה מֵיטִיבֵי צָעַד וְאַרְבָּעָה מֵיטִבֵי לָכֶת׃
_{three   they are   stately   step   and four   stately   stride}

29. There are three things stately in their tread; four are handsome in their stride:

לַיִשׁ גִּבּוֹר בַּבְּהֵמָה וְלֹא־יָשׁוּב מִפְּנֵי־כֹל׃
_{long maimed lion mighty in beasts he turns - and not all – from face}

30. A lion which is strongest among beasts, and turns not away for anyone;

זַרְזִיר מָתְנַיִם אוֹ־תָיִשׁ וּמֶלֶךְ אַלְקוּם עִמּוֹ׃
_{girded waists male goat – or and king irresistible with him}

31. A greyhound; a male goat also; and a king, against whom there is no rising up.

אִם־נָבַלְתָּ בְהִתְנַשֵּׂא וְאִם־זַמּוֹתָ יָד לְפֶה׃
_{if and – you disgraced in causing exalt and if – you schemed hand to mouth}

32. If you have done foolishly in lifting up yourself, or if you have thought evil, lay your hand on your mouth.

כִּי מִיץ חָלָב יוֹצִיא חֶמְאָה וּמִיץ־אַף יוֹצִיא דָם
_{like juice milk comes out butter juice and – nose comes out blood}

וּמִיץ אַפַּיִם יוֹצִיא רִיב׃
_{and juice angers comes out strife}

33. Surely the wringing of milk brings forth butter, and the wringing of the nose brings forth blood; so the forcing of wrath brings forth quarrel.

Chapter 31

ספר משלי פרק לא

דִּבְרֵי לְמוּאֵל מֶלֶךְ מַשָּׂא אֲשֶׁר־יִסְּרַתּוּ אִמּוֹ׃

1. The words of king Lemuel, the prophecy that his mother taught him.

מַה־בְּרִי וּמַה־בַּר־בִּטְנִי וּמֶה בַּר־נְדָרָי׃

2. What, my son? and what, the son of my womb? and what, son of my vows?

אַל־תִּתֵּן לַנָּשִׁים חֵילֶךָ וּדְרָכֶיךָ לַמְחוֹת מְלָכִין׃

3. Give not your strength to women, nor your ways to those who destroy kings.

אַל לַמְלָכִים לְמוֹאֵל אַל לַמְלָכִים שְׁתוֹ־יָיִן

וּלְרוֹזְנִים אוֹ [אֵי] שֵׁכָר׃

4. (K) It is not for kings, O Lemuel, it is not for kings to drink wine; nor for princes to say, Where is strong drink;

פֶּן־יִשְׁתֶּה וְיִשְׁכַּח מְחֻקָּק וִישַׁנֶּה דִּין כָּל־בְּנֵי־עֹנִי׃

5. Lest he drink, and forget the decree, and pervert the judgment of any of the afflicted.

תְּנוּ־שֵׁכָר לְאוֹבֵד וְיַיִן לְמָרֵי נָפֶשׁ׃

6. Give strong drink to him who is ready to perish, and wine to those whose hearts are heavy.

יִשְׁתֶּה וְיִשְׁכַּח רִישׁוֹ וַעֲמָלוֹ לֹא יִזְכָּר־עוֹד׃

7. Let him drink, and forget his poverty, and remember his misery no more.

פְּתַח־פִּיךָ לְאִלֵּם אֶל־דִּין כָּל־בְּנֵי חֲלוֹף׃

8. Open your mouth for the dumb, for the cause of all who are appointed to destruction.

פְּתַח־פִּיךָ שְׁפָט־צֶדֶק וְדִין עָנִי וְאֶבְיוֹן׃

9. Open your mouth, judge righteously, and plead the cause of the poor and the needy.

אֵשֶׁת־חַיִל מִי יִמְצָא וְרָחֹק מִפְּנִינִים מִכְרָהּ׃

10. A worthy woman who can find? For her price is far above rubies.

Proverbs - Chapter 31

בָּטַח בָּהּ לֵב בַּעְלָהּ וְשָׁלָל לֹא יֶחְסָר׃
he will lack   not   and loot   her husband   heart   in her   trusts

11. The heart of her husband safely trusts in her, and he shall have no lack of gain.

גְּמָלַתְהוּ טוֹב וְלֹא־רָע כֹּל יְמֵי חַיֶּיהָ׃
her life   days   all   bad – and not   good   she favors him

12. She will do him good and not evil all the days of her life.

דָּרְשָׁה צֶמֶר וּפִשְׁתִּים וַתַּעַשׂ בְּחֵפֶץ כַּפֶּיהָ׃
her palms   in eagerness   and she does   and flaxes   wool   she selects

13. She seeks wool, and flax, and works willingly with her hands.

הָיְתָה כָּאֳנִיּוֹת סוֹחֵר מִמֶּרְחָק תָּבִיא לַחְמָהּ׃
her food   she brings   from far away   merchant   like ships   she is

14. She is like the ships of the merchant; she brings her food from far away.

וַתָּקָם בְּעוֹד לַיְלָה וַתִּתֵּן טֶרֶף לְבֵיתָהּ וְחֹק לְנַעֲרֹתֶיהָ׃
to her young girls   and portion   to her house   meal   and gives   night   in still   and she gets up

15. She rises also while it is yet night, and gives food to her household, and a portion to her maidens.

זָמְמָה שָׂדֶה וַתִּקָּחֵהוּ מִפְּרִי כַפֶּיהָ נָטַע [נָטְעָה] כָּרֶם׃
vineyard   she plants   her palms   from fruits   and she takes it   field   she plans out

16. She considers a field, and buys it; with the fruit of her hands she plants a vineyard.

חָגְרָה בְעוֹז מָתְנֶיהָ וַתְּאַמֵּץ זְרוֹעֹתֶיהָ׃
her arms   and she resolutes   her loins   in vigor   she girds

17. She girds her loins with strength, and makes her arms strong.

טָעֲמָה כִּי־טוֹב סַחְרָהּ לֹא־יִכְבֶּה בַלַּיִל [בַלַּיְלָה] נֵרָהּ׃
her candle   in night   it ceases - not   her trading   good – like   she perceives

18. She perceives that her merchandise is good; her candle does not go out by night.

יָדֶיהָ שִׁלְּחָה בַכִּישׁוֹר וְכַפֶּיהָ תָּמְכוּ פָלֶךְ׃
spindle   grasp   and her palms   in distaff   she extends   her hands

19. She puts her hands to the distaff, and her hands hold the spindle.

כַּפָּהּ פָּרְשָׂה לֶעָנִי וְיָדֶיהָ שִׁלְּחָה לָאֶבְיוֹן׃
to needy   she extends   and her hands   to poor   she stretches   her palm

20. She stretches out her hand to the poor; she reaches forth her hands to the needy.

לֹא־תִירָא לְבֵיתָהּ מִשָּׁלֶג כִּי כָל־בֵּיתָהּ לָבֻשׁ שָׁנִים׃
scarlet ones   clothed   her house – all   like   from snow   to her house   she fears - not

21. She is not afraid of the snow for her household; for all her household are clothed with scarlet.

מַרְבַדִּים עָשְׂתָה־לָּהּ שֵׁשׁ וְאַרְגָּמָן לְבוּשָׁהּ׃
her clothing   and purple   fine linen   to her – she does   coverings

22. She makes herself coverlets; her clothing is fine linen and purple.

נוֹדָע בַּשְּׁעָרִים בַּעְלָהּ בְּשִׁבְתּוֹ עִם־זִקְנֵי־אָרֶץ:

land – elders – with   in his sitting   her husband   in gates   known

23. Her husband is known in the gates, when he sits among the elders of the land.

סָדִין עָשְׂתָה וַתִּמְכֹּר וַחֲגוֹר נָתְנָה לַכְּנַעֲנִי:

to Canaanite   she delivers   and girdle   and sells   she makes   lengthy shirt

24. She makes linen garments, and sells them; and delivers girdles to the merchant.

עֹז־וְהָדָר לְבוּשָׁהּ וַתִּשְׂחַק לְיוֹם אַחֲרוֹן:

future   to day   and she laughs   her clothing   and honor - strength

25. Strength and dignity are her clothing; and she shall rejoice at the time to come.

פִּיהָ פָּתְחָה בְחָכְמָה וְתוֹרַת־חֶסֶד עַל־לְשׁוֹנָהּ:

her tongue – upon   kindness – and Torah   in wisdom   she opens   her mouth

26. She opens her mouth with wisdom; and in her tongue is the Torah of loving kindness.

צוֹפִיָּה הֲילִכוֹת [הֲלִיכוֹת] בֵּיתָהּ וְלֶחֶם עַצְלוּת לֹא תֹאכֵל:

she eats   not   laziness   and bread   her house   the goings   watcher over

27. (K) She looks well to the ways of her household, and does not eat the bread of idleness.

קָמוּ בָנֶיהָ וַיְאַשְּׁרוּהָ בַּעְלָהּ וַיְהַלְלָהּ:

and he praises her   her husband   and they make happy her   her sons   they arise

28. Her children rise up, and call her blessed; her husband also, and he praises her.

רַבּוֹת בָּנוֹת עָשׂוּ חָיִל וְאַתְּ עָלִית עַל־כֻּלָּנָה:

all them – upon   excel   and you   able   they do   daughters   many

29. Many daughters have done virtuously, but you excel them all.

שֶׁקֶר הַחֵן וְהֶבֶל הַיֹּפִי אִשָּׁה יִרְאַת־יְהוָה הִיא תִתְהַלָּל:

she be praised   she   ihvh – fear   woman   the beauty   and vanity   the grace   lie

30. Charm is deceitful, and beauty is vain; but a woman who fears the Lord shall be praised.

תְּנוּ־לָהּ מִפְּרִי יָדֶיהָ וִיהַלְלוּהָ בַשְּׁעָרִים מַעֲשֶׂיהָ:

her deeds   in gates   and they praise her   her hands   from fruit   to her - you give

31. Give her of the fruit of her hands; and let her own deeds praise her in the gates.

Song of Songs

Chapter 1

מגילת שיר השירים פרק א

שִׁיר הַשִּׁירִים אֲשֶׁר לִשְׁלֹמֹה׃
to Solomon   which   the songs   song

1. The song of songs, which is Solomon's.

יִשָּׁקֵנִי מִנְּשִׁיקוֹת פִּיהוּ כִּי־טוֹבִים דֹּדֶיךָ מִיָּיִן׃
from wine   your close love   good ones – like   his mouth   from kisses   he kisses me

2. Let him kiss me with the kisses of his mouth; for your love is better than wine.

לְרֵיחַ שְׁמָנֶיךָ טוֹבִים שֶׁמֶן תּוּרַק שְׁמֶךָ
your name   emptied out   oils   good ones   your oils   to fragrance

עַל־כֵּן עֲלָמוֹת אֲהֵבוּךָ׃
they love you   maidens   thus – upon

3. Your anointing oils are fragrant, your name is oil poured out, therefore the maidens love you.

מָשְׁכֵנִי אַחֲרֶיךָ נָּרוּצָה הֱבִיאַנִי הַמֶּלֶךְ חֲדָרָיו
his room   the king   brought me   we will run   after you   draw me

נָגִילָה וְנִשְׂמְחָה בָּךְ נַזְכִּירָה דֹדֶיךָ מִיַּיִן מֵישָׁרִים אֲהֵבוּךָ׃
they love you   fairness's   from wine   your close love   we recall   in you   and we happy   we rejoice

4. Draw me after you, we will run; the king has brought me into his chambers; we will be glad and rejoice in you, we will praise your love more than wine; rightly they love you.

שְׁחוֹרָה אֲנִי וְנָאוָה בְּנוֹת יְרוּשָׁלִָם
Jerusalem   daughters   and attractive   I   black

כְּאָהֳלֵי קֵדָר כִּירִיעוֹת שְׁלֹמֹה׃
Solomon   like curtains   Kedar   like tents

5. I am black, but comely, O daughters of Jerusalem, like the tents of Kedar, like the curtains of Solomon.

אַל־תִּרְאוּנִי שֶׁאֲנִי שְׁחַרְחֹרֶת שֶׁשְּׁזָפַתְנִי הַשָּׁמֶשׁ
the sun   that catches sight me   darkened   that I   you look at me - don't

בְּנֵי אִמִּי נִחֲרוּ־בִי שָׂמֻנִי נֹטֵרָה אֶת־הַכְּרָמִים
the vineyards - that   maintainer   put me   in me - they burned   my mother   sons

כַּרְמִי שֶׁלִּי לֹא נָטָרְתִּי׃
I maintained   not   of mine   my vineyard

6. Gaze not upon me, for I am dark, because the sun has scorched me. My mother's children were angry with me; they made me the keeper of the vineyards; but my own vineyard I have not kept.

הַגִּידָה לִּי שֶׁאָהֲבָה נַפְשִׁי
my soul   that she loves   to me   the explain

אֵיכָה תִרְעֶה אֵיכָה תַּרְבִּיץ בַּצָּהֳרָיִם
in noon   rest   where   graze   where

שַׁלָּמָה אֶהְיֶה כְּעֹטְיָה עַל עֶדְרֵי חֲבֵרֶיךָ:
your friends   flock   upon   veils   I be   that why

7. Tell me, O you whom my soul loves, where do you pasture your flock, where do you make it rest at noon; for why should I be like one who veils himself by the flocks of your companions?

אִם־לֹא תֵדְעִי לָךְ הַיָּפָה בַּנָּשִׁים צְאִי־לָךְ בְּעִקְבֵי הַצֹּאן
the flock   in footsteps   to you - go out   in women   the beautiful her   to you   you know   not - if

וּרְעִי אֶת־גְּדִיֹּתַיִךְ עַל מִשְׁכְּנוֹת הָרֹעִים:
the shepherds   tent dwellings   upon   your female goat – that   and graze

8. If you know not, O most beautiful among women, go your way forth by the footsteps of the flock, and pasture your kids beside the shepherds' tents.

לְסֻסָתִי בְּרִכְבֵי פַרְעֹה דִּמִּיתִיךְ רַעְיָתִי:
my girl friend   your resemblance   Pharaoh   in chariots   to my female horse

9. I compare you, O my love, to a mare of the chariots of Pharaoh.

נָאווּ לְחָיַיִךְ בַּתֹּרִים צַוָּארֵךְ בַּחֲרוּזִים:
in chains   neck   in beads   to your cheeks   they fair

10. Your cheeks are comely with rows of jewels, your neck with strings of beads.

תּוֹרֵי זָהָב נַעֲשֶׂה־לָּךְ עִם נְקֻדּוֹת הַכָּסֶף:
the silver   accent dots   with   to you - we make   gold   bead rows

11. We will make you ornaments of gold studded with silver.

עַד־שֶׁהַמֶּלֶךְ בִּמְסִבּוֹ נִרְדִּי נָתַן רֵיחוֹ:
its fragrance   it gives   my spikenard   in his divan   that the king - till

12. While the king was reclining at his table, my nard sent forth its fragrance.

צְרוֹר הַמֹּר דּוֹדִי לִי בֵּין שָׁדַי יָלִין:
he spends night   my breasts   between   to me   my close friend   the myrrh   bundle

13. My beloved is to me a bundle of myrrh, that lies between my breasts.

אֶשְׁכֹּל הַכֹּפֶר דּוֹדִי לִי בְּכַרְמֵי עֵין גֶּדִי:
Gedi   Ein   in vineyards   to me   my close love   the henna   cluster

14. My beloved is to me a cluster of henna in the vineyards of Ein-Gedi.

הִנָּךְ יָפָה רַעְיָתִי הִנָּךְ יָפָה עֵינַיִךְ יוֹנִים:
doves   your eyes   beautiful   here you   my girl friend   beautiful   here you

15. Behold, you are beautiful, my love; behold, you are beautiful; your eyes are doves.

הִנְּךָ יָפֶה דוֹדִי אַף נָעִים אַף־עַרְשֵׂנוּ רַעֲנָנָה:
flourishing vegetation   our couch - then   pleasant   then   my close friend   beautiful   here you

16. Behold, you are beautiful, my beloved, truly lovely; our couch is green.

קֹרוֹת בָּתֵּינוּ אֲרָזִים רַחִיטֵנוּ [רַהִיטֵנוּ] בְּרוֹתִים׃
    in cypresses   our ceiling boards   cedar   our house   beams

17. (K) The beams of our house are cedar, and our rafters are of cypress.

Chapter 2

מגילת שיר השירים פרק ב

אֲנִי חֲבַצֶּלֶת הַשָּׁרוֹן שׁוֹשַׁנַּת הָעֲמָקִים:
<small>I   rose   the Sharon   lily   the valleys</small>

1. I am the rose of Sharon, a lily of the valleys.

כְּשׁוֹשַׁנָּה בֵּין הַחוֹחִים כֵּן רַעְיָתִי בֵּין הַבָּנוֹת:
<small>like lily   between   the thorns   thus   my girl friend   between   the daughters</small>

2. Like a lily among thorns, so is my love among the maidens.

כְּתַפּוּחַ בַּעֲצֵי הַיַּעַר כֵּן דּוֹדִי בֵּין הַבָּנִים
<small>like apple   in trees   the forest   thus   my lover   between   the sons</small>

בְּצִלּוֹ חִמַּדְתִּי וְיָשַׁבְתִּי וּפִרְיוֹ מָתוֹק לְחִכִּי:
<small>in his shade   my great desire   and I sat   and his fruit   sweet   to my taste</small>

3. Like the apple tree among the trees of the wood, so is my beloved among young men. I sat down under his shadow with great delight, and his fruit was sweet to my taste.

הֱבִיאַנִי אֶל־בֵּית הַיָּיִן וְדִגְלוֹ עָלַי אַהֲבָה:
<small>brought to me   house – unto   the wine   and his banner   upon me   love</small>

4. He brought me to the banqueting house, and his banner over me was love.

סַמְּכוּנִי בָּאֲשִׁישׁוֹת רַפְּדוּנִי בַּתַּפּוּחִים כִּי־חוֹלַת אַהֲבָה אָנִי:
<small>prop me up   in raisin cakes   spread me out   in apples   sick one – like   love   I</small>

5. Sustain me with raisins, comfort me with apples; for I am sick with love.

שְׂמֹאלוֹ תַּחַת לְרֹאשִׁי וִימִינוֹ תְּחַבְּקֵנִי:
<small>his left   under   to my head   and his right hand   embraces me</small>

6. His left hand is under my head, and his right hand embraces me.

הִשְׁבַּעְתִּי אֶתְכֶם בְּנוֹת יְרוּשָׁלַם בִּצְבָאוֹת אוֹ בְּאַיְלוֹת הַשָּׂדֶה
<small>I sware   to you   daughters   Jerusalem   in female gazelles   or   in female deers   the field</small>

אִם־תָּעִירוּ וְאִם־תְּעוֹרְרוּ אֶת־הָאַהֲבָה עַד שֶׁתֶּחְפָּץ:
<small>if – rouse you   and if - awake you   that – the love   till   that you please</small>

7. I adjure you, O daughters of Jerusalem, by the gazelles or by the hinds of the field, that you stir not up, nor awake my love, until it please.

קוֹל דּוֹדִי הִנֵּה־זֶה
<small>voice   my lover   this – here</small>

בָּא מְדַלֵּג עַל־הֶהָרִים מְקַפֵּץ עַל־הַגְּבָעוֹת:
<small>comes   leaping   the mountains - upon   from drawing close   the hills - upon</small>

8. The voice of my beloved! Behold, he comes leaping upon the mountains, skipping upon the hills.

דּוֹמֶה דוֹדִי לִצְבִי אוֹ לְעֹפֶר הָאַיָּלִים
<small>resembles   my close friend   to gazelle   or   to fawn   the deers</small>

Song of Songs - Chapter 2

הִנֵּה־זֶה עוֹמֵד אַחַר כָּתְלֵנוּ
our wall behind he stands this - here

מַשְׁגִּיחַ מִן־הַחֲלֹּנוֹת מֵצִיץ מִן־הַחֲרַכִּים׃
the lattice – from sparkling gaze the windows – from staring

9. My beloved is like a gazelle or a young hart; Behold, he stands behind our wall, gazing in at the windows, looking through the lattice.

עָנָה דוֹדִי וְאָמַר לִי קוּמִי לָךְ רַעְיָתִי יָפָתִי וּלְכִי־לָךְ׃
to you (f) - and go my beautiful my girl friend to you (f) arise to me and says my close friend he answers

10. My beloved speaks and says to me, Arise, my love, my beautiful one, and come away.

כִּי־הִנֵּה הַסְּתָו [הַסְּתָיו] עָבָר הַגֶּשֶׁם חָלַף הָלַךְ לוֹ׃
to it gone pass through the rain past his winter here - like

11. For, behold, the winter is past, the rain is over and gone;

הַנִּצָּנִים נִרְאוּ בָאָרֶץ עֵת הַזָּמִיר הִגִּיעַ
arrived the song season in earth they appeared the blossoms

וְקוֹל הַתּוֹר נִשְׁמַע בְּאַרְצֵנוּ׃
in our land we hear the turtle dove and voice

12. The flowers appear on the earth; the time of the singing bird has come, and the voice of the turtledove is heard in our land;

הַתְּאֵנָה חָנְטָה פַגֶּיהָ וְהַגְּפָנִים סְמָדַר נָתְנוּ רֵיחַ
scent they give it blossoms and the grape vines unripe figs ripens the fig tree

קוּמִי לָכִי [לָךְ] רַעְיָתִי יָפָתִי וּלְכִי־לָךְ׃
to you - and go my beautiful my girl friend go arise

13. (K) The fig tree puts forth her green figs, and the vines in blossom give forth their scent. Arise, my love, my beautiful one, and come away.

יוֹנָתִי בְּחַגְוֵי הַסֶּלַע בְּסֵתֶר הַמַּדְרֵגָה
the inaccessible in hidden place the rocks in cleft my dove

הַרְאִינִי אֶת־מַרְאַיִךְ הַשְׁמִיעִינִי אֶת־קוֹלֵךְ
your(f) voice – that the my hearing your appearance – that the my seeing

כִּי־קוֹלֵךְ עָרֵב וּמַרְאֵיךְ נָאוֶה׃
pleasant and your appearance congenial your voice - like

14. O my dove, in the clefts of the rock, in the secret places of the cliff, let me see your countenance, let me hear your voice, for your voice is sweet, and your countenance is comely.

אֶחֱזוּ־לָנוּ שׁוּעָלִים שֻׁעָלִים קְטַנִּים מְחַבְּלִים כְּרָמִים
vineyards destroying ones little ones foxes foxes to us - catch it

וּכְרָמֵינוּ סְמָדַר׃
blossom and our vineyards

15. Catch us the foxes, the little foxes, that spoil the vineyards; for our vineyards are in

blossom.

דּוֹדִי לִי וַאֲנִי לוֹ הָרֹעֶה בַּשּׁוֹשַׁנִּים:
in lilies · the shepherd · to him · and I · to me · my close friend

16. My beloved is mine, and I am his; he pastures his flock among the lilies.

עַד שֶׁיָּפוּחַ הַיּוֹם וְנָסוּ הַצְּלָלִים סֹב דְּמֵה־לְךָ דוֹדִי
my close friend · to you(m) - resemble · surround · the shadows · and travel · the day · that breeze · until

לִצְבִי אוֹ לְעֹפֶר הָאַיָּלִים עַל־הָרֵי בָתֶר:
Bether · mountains – upon · the deers · to fawn · or · to gazelle

17. Until the day cools, and the shadows flee away, turn, my beloved, and be like a gazelle or a young hart upon the mountains of Bether.

Chapter 3

מגילת שיר השירים פרק ג

עַל־מִשְׁכָּבִי֙ בַּלֵּיל֔וֹת בִּקַּ֕שְׁתִּי אֵ֥ת שֶׁאָהֲבָ֖ה נַפְשִׁ֑י בִּקַּשְׁתִּ֖יו
in my searching him   my soul   that I love   that   in my searching   in nights   my bed – upon

וְלֹ֥א מְצָאתִֽיו׃
found him   and not

1. By night on my bed I sought him whom my soul loves; I sought him, but I found him not.

אָק֨וּמָה נָּ֜א וַאֲסוֹבְבָ֣ה בָעִ֗יר בַּשְּׁוָקִים֙ וּבָ֣רְחֹב֔וֹת
and in streets   in market areas   in city   and go around   now   I will rise

אֲבַקְשָׁ֕ה אֵ֥ת שֶׁאָהֲבָ֖ה נַפְשִׁ֑י בִּקַּשְׁתִּ֖יו וְלֹ֥א מְצָאתִֽיו׃
I found him   and not   in my search him   my soul   that I love   that   I seek

2. I will rise now, and go around in the city; in the markets and in the broad streets will I seek him whom my soul loves; I sought him, but I found him not.

מְצָא֙וּנִי֙ הַשֹּׁ֣מְרִ֔ים הַסֹּבְבִ֖ים בָּעִ֑יר אֵ֧ת שֶׁאָהֲבָ֛ה נַפְשִׁ֖י רְאִיתֶֽם׃
they saw   my soul   that I love   that   in city   the around ones   the heeder ones   they found me

3. The watchmen that go around in the city found me; Have you seen him whom my soul loves?

כִּמְעַט֙ שֶׁעָבַ֣רְתִּי מֵהֶ֔ם עַ֣ד שֶֽׁמָּצָ֔אתִי אֵ֥ת שֶׁאָהֲבָ֖ה נַפְשִׁ֑י
my soul   that loves   that   that I found   till   from them   that I passed over   like little

אֲחַזְתִּיו֙ וְלֹ֣א אַרְפֶּ֔נּוּ עַד־שֶׁ֤הֲבֵיאתִיו֙ אֶל־בֵּ֣ית אִמִּ֔י
my mother   house – unto   that the his house – till   I let relax   and not   I seized him

וְאֶל־חֶ֖דֶר הוֹרָתִֽי׃
my conceiving   room - and unto

4. I had just passed them when I found him whom my soul loves; I held him, and would not let him go, until I had brought him into my mother's house, and into the chamber of her that conceived me.

הִשְׁבַּ֨עְתִּי אֶתְכֶ֜ם בְּנ֤וֹת יְרוּשָׁלִַ֙ם֙ בִּצְבָא֔וֹת א֖וֹ בְּאַיְל֣וֹת הַשָּׂדֶ֑ה
the field   in female deers   or   in gazelles   Jerusalem   daughters   to you   my swearing

אִם־תָּעִ֧ירוּ ׀ וְֽאִם־תְּעֽוֹרְר֛וּ אֶת־הָאַהֲבָ֖ה עַ֥ד שֶׁתֶּחְפָּֽץ׃
that it please   till   the love – that   you awake – and if   you open eyes – if

5. I adjure you, O daughters of Jerusalem, by the gazelles, or by the hinds of the field, that you stir not up, nor awake my love, until it please.

מִ֣י זֹ֗את עֹלָה֙ מִן־הַמִּדְבָּ֔ר כְּתִֽימֲר֖וֹת עָשָׁ֑ן
smoke   like columns   the desert – from   ascends   this   who

מְקֻטֶּ֤רֶת מוֹר֙ וּלְבוֹנָ֔ה מִכֹּ֖ל אַבְקַ֥ת רוֹכֵֽל׃
merchant   powders   from all   and frankincense   myrrh   from burning incense

6. Who is this who comes from the wilderness like columns of smoke, perfumed with myrrh and frankincense, with all powders of the merchant?

הִנֵּה מִטָּתוֹ שֶׁל שְׁלֹמֹה
      Solomon of my his bed here

שִׁשִּׁים גִּבֹּרִים סָבִיב לָהּ מִגִּבֹּרֵי יִשְׂרָאֵל׃
Israel from mighty men her around mighty ones sixty

7. Behold, it is the litter of Solomon; sixty mighty men are around it, of the mighty men of Israel.

כֻּלָּם אֲחֻזֵי חֶרֶב מְלֻמְּדֵי מִלְחָמָה אִישׁ
man war trained sword seize all them

חַרְבּוֹ עַל־יְרֵכוֹ מִפַּחַד בַּלֵּילוֹת׃
in nights from dread his thigh – upon his sword

8. All girt with swords and expert in war; every man has his sword at his thigh because of the fear in the nights.

אַפִּרְיוֹן עָשָׂה לוֹ הַמֶּלֶךְ שְׁלֹמֹה מֵעֲצֵי הַלְּבָנוֹן׃
the Lebanon from wood Solomon the king to him made palanquin

9. King Solomon made himself a palanquin from the wood of Lebanon.

עַמּוּדָיו עָשָׂה כֶסֶף רְפִידָתוֹ זָהָב מֶרְכָּבוֹ אַרְגָּמָן
purple his chariot gold his support silver done his pillar

תּוֹכוֹ רָצוּף אַהֲבָה מִבְּנוֹת יְרוּשָׁלָ͏ִם׃
Jerusalem from daughters love patterned its midst

10. He made its pillars of silver, its back of gold, its seat of purple, its interior inlaid with love by the daughters of Jerusalem.

צְאֶינָה וּרְאֶינָה בְּנוֹת צִיּוֹן בַּמֶּלֶךְ שְׁלֹמֹה
Solomon in king Zion daughters and see now go out now

בָּעֲטָרָה שֶׁעִטְּרָה־לּוֹ אִמּוֹ בְּיוֹם חֲתֻנָּתוֹ וּבְיוֹם שִׂמְחַת לִבּוֹ׃
his heart happiness and in day his canopy in day his mother to him - that crowned in crown

11. Go forth, O daughters of Zion, and behold King Solomon with the crown with which his mother crowned him on the day of his wedding, and on the day of the gladness of his heart.

Chapter 4

מגילת שיר השירים פרק ד

הִנָּךְ יָפָה רַעְיָתִי הִנָּךְ יָפָה
beautiful here you my girl friend beautiful here you

עֵינַיִךְ יוֹנִים מִבַּעַד לְצַמָּתֵךְ שַׂעְרֵךְ
your black to your hair from in side doves your eyes

כְּעֵדֶר הָעִזִּים שֶׁגָּלְשׁוּ מֵהַר גִּלְעָד:
Gilead from mount that they appear the goats like flock

1. Behold, you are beautiful, my love; behold, you are beautiful; your eyes are doves behind your veil; your hair is like a flock of goats, sliding down from Mount Gilead.

שִׁנַּיִךְ כְּעֵדֶר הַקְּצוּבוֹת שֶׁעָלוּ מִן־הָרַחְצָה
the washing – from that they ascend the shorn ones like flock your (f) teeth

שֶׁכֻּלָּם מַתְאִימוֹת וְשַׁכֻּלָה אֵין בָּהֶם:
in them isn't and barren from paired ones that all them

2. Your teeth are like a flock of shorn ewes, that have come up from the washing; all of which bear twins, and none among them is bereft.

כְּחוּט הַשָּׁנִי שִׂפְתוֹתַיִךְ וּמִדְבָּרֵיךְ נָאוֶה
pleasant and from your (f) speaking your (f) lips scarlet like cord

הָרִמּוֹן רַקָּתֵךְ מִבַּעַד לְצַמָּתֵךְ:
to your (f) hair from beside your (f) cheeks the pomegranate

3. Your lips are like a thread of scarlet, and your mouth is comely; your cheeks are like a piece of a pomegranate behind your veil.

כְּמִגְדַּל דָּוִיד צַוָּארֵךְ בָּנוּי לְתַלְפִּיּוֹת אֶלֶף
thousand to armories built your (f) neck David like tower

הַמָּגֵן תָּלוּי עָלָיו כֹּל שִׁלְטֵי הַגִּבּוֹרִים:
the mighty ones shields all above him hung the shield

4. Your neck is like the tower of David built with turrets, on which hang one thousand bucklers, all of them shields of mighty men.

שְׁנֵי שָׁדַיִךְ כִּשְׁנֵי עֳפָרִים תְּאוֹמֵי צְבִיָּה הָרוֹעִים בַּשּׁוֹשַׁנִּים:
in lilies the grazing ones twins female gazelle fawn ones like two your (f) breasts two

5. Your two breasts are like two fawns, twins of a gazelle, that feed among the lilies.

עַד שֶׁיָּפוּחַ הַיּוֹם וְנָסוּ הַצְּלָלִים
the shadows it flees the day that breeze till

אֵלֶךְ לִי אֶל־הַר הַמּוֹר וְאֶל־גִּבְעַת הַלְּבוֹנָה:
frankincense little hill - and unto the myrrh mount – unto to me I will go

6. Until the day cools, and the shadows flee away, I will get me to the mountain of myrrh, and to the hill of frankincense.

כֻּלָּךְ יָפָה רַעְיָתִי וּמוּם אֵין בָּךְ:
all you (f) beautiful my girl friend and blemish isn't in you (f)

7. You are all beautiful, my love; there is no blemish in you.

אִתִּי מִלְּבָנוֹן כַּלָּה אִתִּי מִלְּבָנוֹן תָּבוֹאִי תָּשׁוּרִי מֵרֹאשׁ אֲמָנָה
with you Amana from top bride from Lebanon to you it I come you observe me from top Lebanon from bride you observe me

מֵרֹאשׁ שְׂנִיר וְחֶרְמוֹן מִמְּעֹנוֹת אֲרָיוֹת מֵהַרְרֵי נְמֵרִים:
from top Senir and Hermon from dens lions from mountains leopards

8. Come with me from Lebanon, my bride, come with me from Lebanon; look from the peak of Amana, from the peak of Senir and Hermon, from the lions' dens, from the mountains of the leopards.

לִבַּבְתִּנִי אֲחֹתִי כַלָּה לִבַּבְתִּינִי
you heartened me my sister bride you heartened me

בְּאַחַד [בְּאַחַת] מֵעֵינַיִךְ בְּאַחַד עֲנָק מִצַּוְּרֹנָיִךְ:
in one from your (f) eyes in one necklace from your neck

9. (K) You have ravished my heart, my sister, my bride; you have ravished my heart with one of your eyes, with one link of your necklace.

מַה־יָּפוּ דֹדַיִךְ אֲחֹתִי כַלָּה מַה־טֹּבוּ דֹדַיִךְ מִיָּיִן
what - they beautiful your (f) lovingness my sister bride what - they good your lovingness from wine

וְרֵיחַ שְׁמָנַיִךְ מִכָּל־בְּשָׂמִים:
and odor your (f) oils from all - spices

10. How beautiful is your love, my sister, my bride! how much better is your love than wine! and the aroma of your anointing oils than all spices!

נֹפֶת תִּטֹּפְנָה שִׂפְתוֹתַיִךְ כַּלָּה דְּבַשׁ וְחָלָב תַּחַת לְשׁוֹנֵךְ
honeycomb drips your lips bride honey and milk under your tongue

וְרֵיחַ שַׂלְמֹתַיִךְ כְּרֵיחַ לְבָנוֹן:
and odor your(f) dress like odor Lebanon

11. Your lips, O my bride, distil like the honeycomb; honey and milk are under your tongue; and the scent of your garments is like the scent of Lebanon.

גַּן נָעוּל אֲחֹתִי כַלָּה גַּל נָעוּל מַעְיָן חָתוּם:
garden locked my sister bride spring locked fountain sealed up

12. A locked garden is my sister, my bride; a locked spring, a sealed fountain.

שְׁלָחַיִךְ פַּרְדֵּס רִמּוֹנִים עִם פְּרִי מְגָדִים כְּפָרִים עִם־נְרָדִים:
your shoots (f) orchards pomegranates with fruit fine ones like hennas with - spikenards

13. Your shoots are an orchard of pomegranates, with pleasant fruits, henna, and nard.

נֵרְדְּ וְכַרְכֹּם קָנֶה וְקִנָּמוֹן עִם כָּל־עֲצֵי לְבוֹנָה
spikenard and saffron calamus and cinnamon with all - trees frankincense

מֹר וַאֲהָלוֹת עִם כָּל־רָאשֵׁי בְשָׂמִים:
myrrh and aloes with all - top spices

14. Nard and saffron; calamus and cinnamon, with all trees of frankincense; myrrh and aloes, with all the chief spices;

מַעְיַ֣ן גַּנִּ֔ים בְּאֵ֖ר מַ֣יִם חַיִּ֑ים וְנֹזְלִ֖ים מִן־לְבָנֽוֹן׃
fountains from   gardens   well   water   life   and flows   Lebanon – from

15. A fountain of gardens, a well of living waters, and streams from Lebanon.

ע֤וּרִי צָפוֹן֙ וּב֣וֹאִי תֵימָ֔ן הָפִ֥יחִי גַנִּ֖י
rouse   north wind   and come   south   breeze   my garden

יִזְּל֣וּ בְשָׂמָ֑יו יָבֹ֤א דוֹדִי֙ לְגַנּ֔וֹ וְיֹאכַ֖ל פְּרִ֥י מְגָדָֽיו׃
they flow   his spices   he comes   my close friend   to his garden   and he eats   fruit   his fine ones

16. Awake, O north wind; and come, O south wind! blow upon my garden, let its spices flow out. Let my beloved come into his garden, and eat its pleasant fruits.

Chapter 5

מגילת שיר השירים פרק ה

בָּאתִי לְגַנִּי אֲחֹתִי כַלָּה אָרִיתִי מוֹרִי עִם־בְּשָׂמִי
my spice - with / my myrrh / I gathered / bride / my sister / to my garden / I come

אָכַלְתִּי יַעְרִי עִם־דִּבְשִׁי שָׁתִיתִי יֵינִי עִם־חֲלָבִי
my milk – with / my wine / I drank / my honey – with / my honeycomb / I have eaten

אִכְלוּ רֵעִים שְׁתוּ וְשִׁכְרוּ דּוֹדִים:
close friend ones / and be intoxicated / you drink up / neighbor ones / you eat

1. I have come into my garden, my sister, my bride; I have gathered my myrrh with my spice; I have eaten my honeycomb with my honey; I have drunk my wine with my milk. Eat, O friends; drink, drink deeply, O loved ones.

אֲנִי יְשֵׁנָה וְלִבִּי עֵר קוֹל דּוֹדִי
my close friend / voice / awakes / and my heart / sleep (f) / I

דוֹפֵק פִּתְחִי־לִי אֲחֹתִי רַעְיָתִי יוֹנָתִי תַמָּתִי
my perfect one / my dove / my girl friend / my sister / to me – open / knocking

שֶׁרֹּאשִׁי נִמְלָא־טָל קְוֻצּוֹתַי רְסִיסֵי לָיְלָה:
night / dripping / my flock / dew – has filled / that my head

2. I sleep, but my heart is awake. Knocking; it is the voice of my beloved; Open to me, my sister, my love, my dove, my perfect one; for my head is filled with dew, and my locks with the drops of the night.

פָּשַׁטְתִּי אֶת־כֻּתָּנְתִּי אֵיכָכָה אֶלְבָּשֶׁנָּה
I dress(f) / how / my robe – that / I stripped off

רָחַצְתִּי אֶת־רַגְלַי אֵיכָכָה אֲטַנְּפֵם:
I dirty them / how / my feet – that / I washed

3. I have taken off my robe; how could I put it on? I have bathed my feet; how could I soil them?

דּוֹדִי שָׁלַח יָדוֹ מִן־הַחוֹר וּמֵעַי הָמוּ עָלָיו:
upon him / they clamored / and my internal / the hole – from / his hand / put / my close friend

4. My beloved put his hand through the hole of the door, and my insides were thrilled by him.

קַמְתִּי אֲנִי לִפְתֹּחַ לְדוֹדִי וְיָדַי נָטְפוּ־מוֹר
myrrh – they dripped / and my hands / to my close friend / to open / I / I arose

וְאֶצְבְּעֹתַי מוֹר עֹבֵר עַל כַּפּוֹת הַמַּנְעוּל:
the lock bolt / palms / upon / cover / myrrh / and dripped

5. I arose to open to my beloved; and my hands dripped with myrrh, and my fingers with flowing myrrh, upon the handles of the lock.

Song of Songs - Chapter 5

פָּתַחְתִּי אֲנִי לְדוֹדִי וְדוֹדִי חָמַק עָבָר
cover withdrawn and my close friend to my close friend I I opened

נַפְשִׁי יָצְאָה בְדַבְּרוֹ בִּקַּשְׁתִּיהוּ
I sought him in his speaking it gone out my soul

וְלֹא מְצָאתִיהוּ קְרָאתִיו וְלֹא עָנָנִי׃
my answer and not I called him I found him and not

6. I opened to my beloved; but my beloved had turned away, and was gone. My soul failed when he spoke; I sought him, but I could not find him; I called him, but he gave me no answer.

מְצָאֻנִי הַשֹּׁמְרִים הַסֹּבְבִים בָּעִיר
in city the patroler ones the heeder ones they found me

הִכּוּנִי פְצָעוּנִי נָשְׂאוּ אֶת־רְדִידִי מֵעָלַי שֹׁמְרֵי הַחֹמוֹת׃
the walls heeders from upon me my large wrap – that they lifted they bruised me they struck me

7. The watchmen that went around in the city found me, they struck me, they wounded me; the keepers of the walls took away my veil from me.

הִשְׁבַּעְתִּי אֶתְכֶם בְּנוֹת יְרוּשָׁלִָם
Jerusalem daughters that you I swear

אִם־תִּמְצְאוּ אֶת־דּוֹדִי מַה־תַּגִּידוּ לוֹ שֶׁחוֹלַת אַהֲבָה אָנִי׃
I love that sick to him you declare – what my close friend - that you find him - if

8. I adjure you, O daughters of Jerusalem, if you find my beloved, that you tell him, that I am sick with love.

מַה־דּוֹדֵךְ מִדּוֹד הַיָּפָה בַּנָּשִׁים
in women the beautiful from close friend your (f) close friend - what

מַה־דּוֹדֵךְ מִדּוֹד שֶׁכָּכָה הִשְׁבַּעְתָּנוּ׃
cause us to be sworn that thus from close friend your(f) close friend – what

9. Why is your beloved more than another beloved, O you most beautiful among women? why is your beloved more than another beloved, that you thus adjure us?

דּוֹדִי צַח וְאָדוֹם דָּגוּל מֵרְבָבָה׃
from multitudes distinguished and red bright my close friend

10. My beloved is white and ruddy, distinguished among ten thousand.

רֹאשׁוֹ כֶּתֶם פָּז קְוֻצּוֹתָיו תַּלְתַּלִּים שְׁחֹרוֹת כָּעוֹרֵב׃
like raven blackened wavy ones his locks pure gold fine gold his head

11. His head is like the finest gold, his locks are wavy, and black like a raven.

עֵינָיו כְּיוֹנִים עַל־אֲפִיקֵי מָיִם
water courses – upon like doves his eyes

רֹחֲצוֹת בֶּחָלָב יֹשְׁבוֹת עַל־מִלֵּאת׃
full ones – upon settings in milk washings

12. His eyes are like doves by the water courses, washed with milk, and fitly set.

לְחָיָו כַּעֲרוּגַת הַבֹּשֶׂם מִגְדְּלוֹת מֶרְקָחִים
    aromatic   from towers   the spices   like bed   his cheek

שִׂפְתוֹתָיו שׁוֹשַׁנִּים נֹטְפוֹת מוֹר עֹבֵר:
    cover   myrrh   drips   lilies   his lips

13. His cheeks are like a bed of spices, like fragrant flowers; his lips like lilies, distilling liquid myrrh.

יָדָיו גְּלִילֵי זָהָב מְמֻלָּאִים בַּתַּרְשִׁישׁ
    in topaz   from set ones   gold   weighty   his hands

מֵעָיו עֶשֶׁת שֵׁן מְעֻלֶּפֶת סַפִּירִים:
    sapphires   overlaid   tooth   polished fabrication   his torso

14. His hands are like circlets of gold set with emeralds; his belly is like polished ivory overlaid with sapphires.

שׁוֹקָיו עַמּוּדֵי שֵׁשׁ מְיֻסָּדִים עַל־אַדְנֵי־פָז
    pure gold - sockets - upon   from foundations   marble   column   his calves

מַרְאֵהוּ כַּלְּבָנוֹן בָּחוּר כָּאֲרָזִים:
    like cedars   choice   like Lebanon   his appearance

15. His legs are like pillars of marble, set upon sockets of fine gold; his countenance is like Lebanon, excellent like the cedars.

חִכּוֹ מַמְתַקִּים וְכֻלּוֹ מַחֲמַדִּים
    sweet ones   and his all   from sweet ones   his inside mouth

זֶה דוֹדִי וְזֶה רֵעִי בְּנוֹת יְרוּשָׁלָםִ:
    Jerusalem   daughters   my friend   and this   my lover   this

16. His mouth is most sweet; and he is altogether lovely. This is my beloved, and this is my friend, O daughters of Jerusalem.

Chapter 6

מגילת שיר השירים פרק ו

אָנָה הָלַךְ דּוֹדֵךְ הַיָּפָה בַּנָּשִׁים
where / has gone / your (f) lover / the beautiful / in women

אָנָה פָּנָה דּוֹדֵךְ וּנְבַקְשֶׁנּוּ עִמָּךְ:
where / face / your close friend / and we seek / with you

1. Where has your beloved gone, O you most beautiful among women? where has your beloved turned? that we may seek him with you.

דּוֹדִי יָרַד לְגַנּוֹ לַעֲרוּגוֹת הַבֹּשֶׂם
my close friend / descended / to his garden / to beds / the spices

לִרְעוֹת בַּגַּנִּים וְלִלְקֹט שׁוֹשַׁנִּים:
to grazings / in gardens / and to pick / lilies

2. My beloved has gone down to his garden, to the beds of spices, to pasture his flock in the gardens, and to gather lilies.

אֲנִי לְדוֹדִי וְדוֹדִי לִי הָרֹעֶה בַּשּׁוֹשַׁנִּים:
I / to my close friend / and my close friend / to me / the shepherd / in lilies

3. I am my beloved's, and my beloved is mine; he pastures his flock among the lilies.

יָפָה אַתְּ רַעְיָתִי כְּתִרְצָה נָאוָה כִּירוּשָׁלָיִם אֲיֻמָּה כַּנִּדְגָּלוֹת:
beautiful / you (f) / girl friend / like Tirzah / pleasant / like Jerusalem / dreadful / like army with banners

4. You are beautiful, O my love, as Tirzah, comely as Jerusalem, awesome as an army with banners.

הָסֵבִּי עֵינַיִךְ מִנֶּגְדִּי שֶׁהֵם הִרְהִיבֻנִי
the revolve / your eyes (f) / from opposite / that them / urge severely

שַׂעְרֵךְ כְּעֵדֶר הָעִזִּים שֶׁגָּלְשׁוּ מִן־הַגִּלְעָד:
your hair / like flock / the goats / that they slide down / from – the Gilead

5. Turn away your eyes from me, for they have overcome me; your hair is like a flock of goats sliding down from Gilead.

שִׁנַּיִךְ כְּעֵדֶר הָרְחֵלִים שֶׁעָלוּ מִן־הָרַחְצָה
your (f) teeth / like flock / the female sheeps / that they ascend / from – the washing

שֶׁכֻּלָּם מַתְאִימוֹת וְשַׁכֻּלָה אֵין בָּהֶם:
that all of them / from paired / and barren / isn't / in them

6. Your teeth are like a flock of sheep which have come up from the washing, all of them bear twins, and there is not one bereaved among them.

כְּפֶלַח הָרִמּוֹן רַקָּתֵךְ מִבַּעַד לְצַמָּתֵךְ:
like slice / the pomegranate / your (f) cheeks / from side / to your veil

7. Like a piece of a pomegranate are your cheeks behind our veil.

שִׁשִּׁים הֵמָּה מְלָכוֹת וּשְׁמֹנִים פִּילַגְשִׁים וַעֲלָמוֹת אֵין מִסְפָּר:

8. There are sixty queens, and eighty concubines, and maidens without number.

אַחַת הִיא יוֹנָתִי תַמָּתִי אַחַת
הִיא לְאִמָּהּ בָּרָה הִיא לְיוֹלַדְתָּהּ
רָאוּהָ בָנוֹת וַיְאַשְּׁרוּהָ מְלָכוֹת וּפִילַגְשִׁים וַיְהַלְלוּהָ:

9. My dove, my perfect one, is only one; she is the only one of her mother, she is the choice one of her that bore her. The maidens saw her, and called her happy; the queens and the concubines praised her.

מִי־זֹאת הַנִּשְׁקָפָה כְּמוֹ־שָׁחַר יָפָה כַלְּבָנָה בָּרָה
כַּחַמָּה אֲיֻמָּה כַּנִּדְגָּלוֹת:

10. Who is she that looks forth like the dawn, beautiful like the moon, bright like the sun, and awesome like an army with banners?

אֶל־גִּנַּת אֱגוֹז יָרַדְתִּי לִרְאוֹת בְּאִבֵּי הַנָּחַל
לִרְאוֹת הֲפָרְחָה הַגֶּפֶן הֵנֵצוּ הָרִמֹּנִים:

11. I went down into the garden of nuts to see the fruits of the valley, and to see if the vine had blossomed, to see if the pomegranates were in bloom.

לֹא יָדַעְתִּי נַפְשִׁי שָׂמַתְנִי מַרְכְּבוֹת עַמִּי־נָדִיב:

12. Without my knowing it, my soul set me among the chariots of a princely people.

Chapter 7

מגילת שיר השירים פרק ז

שׁוּבִי שׁוּבִי הַשּׁוּלַמִּית שׁוּבִי שׁוּבִי
return return the Shulamite return return

וְנֶחֱזֶה־בָּךְ מַה־תֶּחֱזוּ בַּשּׁוּלַמִּית כִּמְחֹלַת הַמַּחֲנָיִם:
the Mahanaim like dances in Shulamite will you perceive – what in you (f) - and we perceive

1. Return, return, O Shulamite; return, return, that we may look upon you. What will you see in the Shulamite? as it were the dance of Mahanaim.

מַה־יָּפוּ פְעָמַיִךְ בַּנְּעָלִים בַּת־נָדִיב
prince – daughter in sandals your twice they beautiful - How

חַמּוּקֵי יְרֵכַיִךְ כְּמוֹ חֲלָאִים מַעֲשֵׂה יְדֵי אָמָּן:
artisan hands work jewels like as your loins curves

2. How beautiful are your feet in sandals, O prince's daughter! your rounded thighs are like jewels, the work of the hands of an artist.

שָׁרְרֵךְ אַגַּן הַסַּהַר אַל־יֶחְסַר הַמָּזֶג
the blended wine it lacks – don't the round bowl your(f) navel

בִּטְנֵךְ עֲרֵמַת חִטִּים סוּגָה בַּשּׁוֹשַׁנִּים:
in lilies hedged wheat mound your(f) belly

3. Your navel is like a round goblet, that never lacks blended wine; your belly is like a heap of wheat set about with lilies.

שְׁנֵי שָׁדַיִךְ כִּשְׁנֵי עֳפָרִים תָּאֳמֵי צְבִיָּה:
female gazelle twin fawns like two your breasts two

4. Your two breasts are like two fawns, twins of a gazelle.

צַוָּארֵךְ כְּמִגְדַּל הַשֵּׁן
ivory like tower your(f) neck

עֵינַיִךְ בְּרֵכוֹת בְּחֶשְׁבּוֹן עַל־שַׁעַר בַּת־רַבִּים
Rabbim – Bath gate – upon in Heshbon pools your(f) eyes

אַפֵּךְ כְּמִגְדַּל הַלְּבָנוֹן צוֹפֶה פְּנֵי דַמָּשֶׂק:
Damascus face looks out the Lebanon like tower your(f) nose

5. Your neck is like a tower of ivory; your eyes like the pools in Heshbon, by the gate of Bath-Rabbim; your nose is like the tower of Lebanon which looks toward Damascus.

רֹאשֵׁךְ עָלַיִךְ כַּכַּרְמֶל
like Karmel upon you your(f) head

וְדַלַּת רֹאשֵׁךְ כָּאַרְגָּמָן מֶלֶךְ אָסוּר בָּרְהָטִים:
in tresses captive king like purple your(f) head and long hair

6. Your head upon you is like Carmel, and the hair of your head like purple; a king is caught in its tresses.

מַה־יָּפִית וּמַה־נָּעַמְתְּ אַהֲבָה בַּתַּעֲנוּגִים׃

7. How beautiful and how lovely are you, O love, for delights!

זֹאת קוֹמָתֵךְ דָּמְתָה לְתָמָר וְשָׁדַיִךְ לְאַשְׁכֹּלוֹת׃

8. This your stature is like a palm tree, and your breasts are like clusters of grapes.

אָמַרְתִּי אֶעֱלֶה בְתָמָר אֹחֲזָה בְּסַנְסִנָּיו

וְיִהְיוּ־נָא שָׁדַיִךְ כְּאֶשְׁכְּלוֹת הַגֶּפֶן וְרֵיחַ אַפֵּךְ כַּתַּפּוּחִים׃

9. I said, I will go up to the palm tree, I will take hold of its boughs; may your breasts be like clusters of the vine, and the scent of your breath like apples;

וְחִכֵּךְ כְּיֵין הַטּוֹב הוֹלֵךְ לְדוֹדִי לְמֵישָׁרִים

דּוֹבֵב שִׂפְתֵי יְשֵׁנִים׃

10. And the roof of your mouth like the best wine for my beloved, that goes down sweetly, causing the sleepers' lips to murmur.

אֲנִי לְדוֹדִי וְעָלַי תְּשׁוּקָתוֹ׃

11. I am my beloved's, and his desire is for me.

לְכָה דוֹדִי נֵצֵא הַשָּׂדֶה נָלִינָה בַּכְּפָרִים׃

12. Come, my beloved, let us go forth into the field; let us lodge in the villages.

נַשְׁכִּימָה לַכְּרָמִים נִרְאֶה אִם פָּרְחָה הַגֶּפֶן

פִּתַּח הַסְּמָדַר הֵנֵצוּ הָרִמּוֹנִים שָׁם אֶתֵּן אֶת־דֹּדַי לָךְ׃

13. Let us go early to the vineyards; let us see if the vine has flowered, if the grape blossoms have opened, if the pomegranates are in bloom; there will I give you my loves.

הַדּוּדָאִים נָתְנוּ־רֵיחַ וְעַל־פְּתָחֵינוּ כָּל־מְגָדִים חֲדָשִׁים

גַּם־יְשָׁנִים דּוֹדִי צָפַנְתִּי לָךְ׃

14. The mandrakes give forth fragrance, and at our gates are all kinds of choice fruits, new and old, which I have laid up for you, O my beloved.

Chapter 8

מגילת שיר השירים פרק ח

מִי יִתֶּנְךָ כְּאָח לִי יוֹנֵק שְׁדֵי אִמִּי
who / he give you / like brother / to me / he sucked / breasts / my mother

אֶמְצָאֲךָ בַחוּץ אֶשָּׁקְךָ גַּם לֹא־יָבֻזוּ לִי:
I find you / in outside / I kiss you / also / not – they despised / to me

1. O that you were like a brother to me, that nursed at my mother breasts! If I should find you outside, I would kiss you; and none would despise me.

אֶנְהָגֲךָ אֲבִיאֲךָ אֶל־בֵּית אִמִּי תְּלַמְּדֵנִי
I drive you (m) / I bring you / unto – house / my mother / she teaches me

אַשְׁקְךָ מִיַּיִן הָרֶקַח מֵעֲסִיס רִמֹּנִי:
I give you drink / from wine / the spiced / from juices / my pomegranate

2. I would lead you, and bring you into the house of my mother, who teaches me; I would give you to drink of spiced wine of the juice of my pomegranate.

שְׂמֹאלוֹ תַּחַת רֹאשִׁי וִימִינוֹ תְּחַבְּקֵנִי:
his left hand / under / my head / and his right hand / it embraces me

3. His left hand should be under my head, and his right hand should embrace me.

הִשְׁבַּעְתִּי אֶתְכֶם בְּנוֹת יְרוּשָׁלָ͏ִם מַה־תָּעִירוּ וּמַה־תְּעֹרְרוּ
caused my swearing / that them / daughters / Jerusalem / what – you stir it / and what - you arouse

אֶת־הָאַהֲבָה עַד שֶׁתֶּחְפָּץ:
that – the love / till / that it please

4. I adjure you, O daughters of Jerusalem, that you stir not up, nor awake my love, until it please.

מִי זֹאת עֹלָה מִן־הַמִּדְבָּר מִתְרַפֶּקֶת עַל־דּוֹדָהּ
who / this / ascends / from – the desert / from her leaning / upon – close friend

תַּחַת הַתַּפּוּחַ עוֹרַרְתִּיךָ
under / the apple / I aroused you

שָׁמָּה חִבְּלַתְךָ אִמֶּךָ שָׁמָּה חִבְּלָה יְלָדַתְךָ:
there / caused labor you / your mother / there / cramped / your begetting

5. Who is this that comes up from the wilderness, leaning upon her beloved? I awakened you up under the apple tree; there your mother was in labor with you; there she who bore you was in labor.

שִׂימֵנִי כַחוֹתָם עַל־לִבֶּךָ כַּחוֹתָם עַל־זְרוֹעֶךָ
put me / like seal / upon – your heart(m) / like seal / upon – your arm

כִּי־עַזָּה כַמָּוֶת אַהֲבָה קָשָׁה כִשְׁאוֹל קִנְאָה
like - strong / like death / love / hard / like Sheol / jealousy

רְשָׁפֶ֕יהָ רִשְׁפֵּ֖י אֵ֥שׁ שַׁלְהֶֽבֶתְיָֽה:
Ya   flame   fire   coals   its coals

6. Set me as a seal upon your heart, as a seal upon your arm; for love is strong as death; jealousy is cruel as Sheol; its coals are coals of fire, which has a most vehement flame.

מַ֣יִם רַבִּ֗ים לֹ֤א יֽוּכְלוּ֙ לְכַבּ֣וֹת אֶת־הָֽאַהֲבָ֔ה
the love – that   to quench   they can   not   many   water

וּנְהָר֖וֹת לֹ֣א יִשְׁטְפ֑וּהָ
overflow it   not   and floods

אִם־יִתֵּ֨ן אִ֜ישׁ אֶת־כָּל־ה֤וֹן בֵּיתוֹ֙ בָּאַ֣הֲבָ֔ה
in love   his house   wealth - all - that   man   he gives - if

בּ֖וֹז יָב֥וּזוּ לֽוֹ:
to him   it be disrespected   disrespect

7. Many waters cannot quench love, neither can floods drown it; if a man would give all the wealth of his house for love, it would be utterly scorned.

אָח֥וֹת לָ֨נוּ֙ קְטַנָּ֔ה וְשָׁדַ֖יִם אֵ֣ין לָ֑הּ
to her   isn't   and breasts   small   to us   sister

מַֽה־נַּעֲשֶׂה֙ לַאֲחֹתֵ֔נוּ בַּיּ֖וֹם שֶׁיְּדֻבַּר־בָּֽהּ:
in her - that will be spoken for   in day   to our sister   we will do - what

8. We have a little sister, and she has no breasts; what shall we do for our sister on the day when she shall be spoken for?

אִם־חוֹמָ֣ה הִ֔יא נִבְנֶ֥ה עָלֶ֖יהָ טִ֣ירַת כָּ֑סֶף
money   fortress   upon her   we will build   she   wall - if

וְאִם־דֶּ֣לֶת הִ֔יא נָצ֥וּר עָלֶ֖יהָ ל֥וּחַ אָֽרֶז:
cedar   boards   upon her   we will confine   she   door - and if

9. If she be a wall, we will build upon her a battlement of silver; and if she be a door, we will enclose her with boards of cedar.

אֲנִ֣י חוֹמָ֔ה וְשָׁדַ֖י כַּמִּגְדָּל֑וֹת
like towers   and my breasts   wall   I

אָ֣ז הָיִ֧יתִי בְעֵינָ֖יו כְּמוֹצְאֵ֥ת שָׁלֽוֹם:
peace   like find   in his eyes   it was   then

10. I was a wall, and my breasts were like towers; then was I in his eyes as one that finds peace.

כֶּ֣רֶם הָיָ֤ה לִשְׁלֹמֹה֙ בְּבַ֣עַל הָמ֔וֹן נָתַ֥ן אֶת־הַכֶּ֖רֶם לַנֹּטְרִ֑ים
to guarding ones   the vineyard - that   gave   - in Baal-Hamon -   to Solomon   was   vineyard

אִ֛ישׁ יָבִ֥א בְּפִרְי֖וֹ אֶ֥לֶף כָּֽסֶף:
money   thousand   in his fruit   he brings   man

11. Solomon had a vineyard at Baal-Hamon; he let out the vineyard to keepers; every one for his fruit was to bring one thousand pieces of silver.

Song of Songs - Chapter 8

כַּרְמִי שֶׁלִּי לְפָנָי הָאֶלֶף לְךָ שְׁלֹמֹה
Solomon   to you   the thousand   before   of mine   my vineyard

וּמָאתַיִם לְנֹטְרִים אֶת־פִּרְיוֹ:
his fruit – that   to guard ones   and two hundred

12. My vineyard, which is mine, is before me; you, O Solomon, must have one thousand, and those that keep its fruit two hundred.

הַיּוֹשֶׁבֶת בַּגַּנִּים חֲבֵרִים מַקְשִׁיבִים לְקוֹלֵךְ הַשְׁמִיעִינִי:
the hear me it   to your voice(f)   attentions   companions   in gardens   the dwellers

13. O you who dwell in the gardens, the companions listen to your voice; let me hear it.

בְּרַח דּוֹדִי וּדְמֵה־לְךָ לִצְבִי
to gazelle   to you - and resemble   my close friend   flee away

אוֹ לְעֹפֶר הָאַיָּלִים עַל הָרֵי בְשָׂמִים:
spices   mount   upon   the deers   to fawn   or

14. Make haste, my beloved, and be like a gazelle or like a young hart upon the mountains of spices.

About the Author

Daniel A. Elias, J.D., is an author, lecturer, who is known around the world as an expert in tzeruf meditation. He is interested in meditations of other culture and has traveled to many nations since he was in grade school.

Throughout his life he has been interested on what effects sound has on the mind. He became interested in sounds in grade school when he bought a silent dog whistle to call the family dog. At eighteen he studied for several months under the famous Maharish Mehesh Yogi, the Beatle's guru. He has chanted for hours mantras like "ohm" and "ohm ma ni padre hom," only to find the results were a sore throat and the feeling of having wasted a lot of time. He has tried many different silent mantras. He has studied under a college professor who had practiced zen meditation all his life. He has experienced many well being programs such as Gestalt therapy, primal screaming, fasting detox, smell therapy, subliminal sound therapy, sleep therapy, alkaline detox, hug therapy, Reiki, chiropractic, etc., etc.

He became interested in sounds affecting the subconscious mind. He is a subliminal expert who has helped others by using custom made subliminals. He has participated in a successful therapy of stopping bed wetting using subliminals. He has participated in a controlled study of subliminal influences on a high school class. He has experimented with subliminal phrases played backwards, white sound, etc.

He has experimented with string piano tuning harmonics inputting the sound to a computer showing the various results as graphics. He has experimented with sound frequencies to effect advanced dream states.

He became fascinated with the fact that the shem hamephorish was not to be pronounced out loud and about its true pronunciation only being known to the high priest of Jerusalem who could pronounce it only once a year on the holiest day of the year. This lead him to discover tzeruf meditation where the Hebrew letters of the shem hamephorish are pronounced within the building blocks of creation, the Hebrew alphabet. He was lured also because of the stated effects resulting from this vocalization meditation, leading one into penetrating the rakia of higher dream states.

Today Daniel spends his time spreading the knowledge of tzeruf meditation.

www.ingramcontent.com/pod-product-compliance
Lightning Source LLC
Chambersburg PA
CBHW071455040426
42444CB00008B/1353